Basic Food & Beverage Service : Skill and Techniques

Basic Food & Beverage Service : Skill and Techniques

Jagmohan Negi
&
Gaurav Manoher

Himalaya Publishing House

MUMBAI • NEW DELHI • NAGPUR • BENGALURU • HYDERABAD • CHENNAI • PUNE
LUCKNOW • AHMEDABAD • ERNAKULAM • BHUBANESWAR • INDORE • KOLKATA • GUWAHATI

First Edition : 2014

Published by : Mrs. Meena Pandey for **Himalaya Publishing House Pvt. Ltd.,**
"Ramdoot", Dr. Bhalerao Marg, Girgaon, **Mumbai - 400 004.**
Phone: 022-23860170/23863863, Fax: 022-23877178
E-mail: himpub@vsnl.com; Website: www.himpub.com

Branch Offices :

New Delhi : "Pooja Apartments", 4-B, Murari Lal Street, Ansari Road, Darya Ganj, New Delhi - 110 002. Phone: 011-23270392, 23278631; Fax: 011-23256286

Nagpur : Kundanlal Chandak Industrial Estate, Ghat Road, Nagpur - 440 018. Phone: 0712-2738731, 3296733; Telefax: 0712-2721215

Bengaluru : No. 16/1 (Old 12/1), 1st Floor, Next to Hotel Highlands, Madhava Nagar, Race Course Road, Bengaluru - 560 001. Phone: 080-32919385; Telefax: 080-22286611

Hyderabad : No. 3-4-184, Lingampally, Besides Raghavendra Swamy Matham, Kachiguda, Hyderabad - 500 027. Phone: 040-27560041, 27550139; Mobile: 09390905282

Chennai : No. 8/2, Modley 2nd Street, Ground Floor, T. Nagar, Chennai - 600 017. Phone: 044-28144004/28144005; Mobile: 09345345051

Pune : First Floor, "Laksha" Apartment, No. 527, Mehunpura, Shaniwarpeth (Near Prabhat Theatre), Pune - 411 030. Phone: 020-24496323/24496333; Mobile: 09370579333

Lucknow : House No. 731, Sehkhupura Colony, Near B.D. Convent School, Lucknow -226024. Mobile : 09307501549

Ahmedabad : 114, "SHAIL", 1st Floor, Opp. Madhu Sudan House, C.G. Road, Navrang Pura, Ahmedabad - 380 009. Phone: 079-26560126; Mobile: 09377088847

Ernakulam : 39/176 (New No: 60/251) 1st Floor, Karikkamuri Road, Ernakulam, Kochi – 682011. Phone: 0484-2378012, 2378016; Mobile: 09387122121

Bhubaneswar : 5 Station Square, Bhubaneswar - 751 001 (Odisha). Phone: 0674-2532129, Mobile: 09338746007

Indore : Kesardeep Avenue Extension, 73, Narayan Bagh, Flat No. 302, IIIrd Floor, Near Humpty Dumpty School, Indore - 452 007 (M.P.). Mobile: 09301386468

Kolkata : 108/4, Beliaghata Main Road, Near ID Hospital, Opp. SBI Bank, Kolkata - 700 010, Phone: 033-32449649, Mobile: 09910440956

Guwahati : House No. 15, Behind Pragjyotish College, Near Sharma Printing Press, P.O. Bharalumukh, Guwahati - 781009, (Assam). Mobile: 09883055590, 09883055536

Typeset at : Elite-Art, Daryaganj, New Delhi-110002

Printed at : Jaico Printers, Daryaganj, New Delhi-110002

Preface

Hospitality industry offers several services. Food and Beverage is one of the basic services, provided by the hospitality industry. Quality of food (diet), nutritional quantity, vitamin contents and proper cooking methods are some of the vital elements, the management has to keep in mind, while providing food and beverage services to its customers.

In this age of globalization competition in providing food and beverage services is on increase. Many reputed MNCs have entered the arena and they are delivering better quality foods and beverages services. In fact, it is a big challenge for Indian Hotel Industry, to cope with the transforming global environment. At present except in star category hotels and premium restaurants food services are not comparable to the global standards. In this consumer age, consumers are well aware of all aspects and very cautious about what they are getting. Better service is the one of the basic requirement of the customers.

This book is timely, authoritative, and practical in all its aspects. It is an incomparable guide for the students and trainees who aim to be "different" and for restaurateurs to keep customers and patrons coming back. When it comes to customers' satisfaction, good food served in a timely and attractive manner is only a part of the story. The book takes the readers beyond those basics to offer a comprehensive guide to important skills and techniques and amenities that customers feel comfortable and turn a meal in a restaurant a memorable event and experience.

This incomparable book enlists all basic guidelines that must feature and be reflected in a food and beverage establishment. In very easy and simple language the book provides step- by -step guidance on extraordinary table and guest service- from meeting, greeting, and seating, order taking, serving, and handling of check to settlement of bill, taking reservations, and handling customers' complaints. It is comprehensive guide to help in buying, storing, displaying, preparing, and serving beverages and many more.

This is an essential guide to acquire service skills and techniques that guarantee success. The preferences for cuisine may vary, but the demand for great service - the keystone of any restaurant's success - never fades. This concise yet comprehensive guide helps restaurants managers and staff in all types of dinning establishments to provide first-class food and beverage service to every customer and create an excellent dinning experience.

This book is a comprehensive training guide to modern food and beverage service. It explains the technical and inter-personal skills required in all types of establishment from sandwich bars to formal dining rooms. Throughout the book the emphasis is placed on the importance of all aspects of good service, product knowledge, and communication, personal organization and technical skills.

The book is user-friendly with a straightforward writing style providing all the essential information. Outstanding glossary for quick reference explaining technical terms, culinary words, French phrases and other cooking traditions.

The book takes a practical approach to service training. It discusses different types of service, including French, American, English, Russian, family-style, banquet, and more. With clear, step- by - step instructions, it successfully demonstrates the technical skills associated with various food and beverage service. It provides step-by-step instructions on how to greet and seat guests, take orders, answer questions, serve food, time a meal, and handle the check. It also features a chapter devoted exclusively to wine and bar service techniques. It also includes helpful guidelines on safety, sanitation, risk management, and emergency procedures. It shows restaurant professionals, students and trainees the proper ways to :

- Greet the guests
- Seat guests
- Take orders
- Answer questions
- Time the food and beverages (meal)
- Serve food and beverages,
- Present the checks ,and
- Accept the payments.
- Respond to emergency situations
- Use the computer system to support service
- Serving of alcoholic beverages

The book is highly illustrative with photographs and line drawings. Supplemented with helpful photographs, drawings charts, diagrams the book illustrates every thing from napkin folding, equipment design to laying tables to order taking. The knowledge acquired from the book gives a trainee server the knowledge and skills he/she need to satisfy customers, increase gratuities, ad develop a faithful clientele that keeps coming back for more.

Broadly the contents of the book are:

Food and beverages - *mise en place*

Food and Beverage s Service Techniques Service of Breakfast and Afternoon Tea Display Cooking or Guerdon Service

Functions Banquets Conferences: Conventions and Exhibitions

These contents concentrate on some of the most important technical skills, such as

1. Hospitality and the food and beverage service employees
2. The menu
3. Food service equipment

4. Food service preparation
5. Food service procedure
6. Taking orders and correcting the covers
7. Styles of service: plate service
8. Silver service
9. Clearing the table
10. Other forms of service
11. Other food service procedures
12. The use of the Guerdon
13. Beverage equipment and service knowledge
14. Beverage product knowledge
15. Beverage service procedures
16. End-of-service procedures
17. Function operations.

The book is very helpful to the restaurant managers and their staffs for quickly up and running with the essentials of providing excellent service and enhancing the dining experience.No matter how superb the cuisine or attractive the decor, nothing alienates customers quicker than poor service. That is why service is one of the major assessment criteria found in virtually every popular book to food and beverage service.

Written for a market of 10,00,000 restaurant managers and their waiting staffs and more than 1,00,000 students, this valuable book guides the readers in the basics of providing good food and beverage service and assisting in the creation of an excellent dining experience. In a concise style, the book acquaints readers with the different service categories—including French, American, English, Russian, Family-Style, and Banquet.

It is an essential guide to service skills and techniques that guarantee success. Preferences in cuisine may vary, but the demand for great service-the keystone of any restaurant's success-never fades. This concise yet comprehensive guide helps restaurant managers and staffs in all types of dining establishments provide first-rate food and beverage service to every customer and create an excellent dining experience.

We profoundly thank all well wishers of hotels, restaurants, airlines, railway catering, banquet halls, clubs, bars and pubs for their generous assistance in providing the necessary information and reference material. Our special thanks to Shri Yogender Singh Negi and Shri Sudhir Joshi, Managing Partner Director, Shri Neeraj Pandey and the dedicated staff of Himalaya Publishing House, for their valued cooperation in bringing out this book in the present form.

Jagmohan Negi
&
Gaurav M.J.

Contents

List of Tables

List of Figures

1 Food and Beverage Service : Mise En Place

After learning this lesson, you should be able :

1. *Understand the menage routines required for an effective service;*
2. *Explain the term 'mise-en-place';*
3. *Draw a suitable duty roaster;*
4. *Equip the sideboard with required items;*
5. *Prepare the dispense bar;*
6. *Prepare tables, clothing of tables, 'mise en place' for table napkin folding:*
7. *Lay the cover as per the menu;*
8. *Explain the various service styles; and*
9. *Understand the technical skills in holding the service spoon, service fork, carrying plates, using service salver, changing of glasses, carrying clean cutlery and flatware, carrying coffee service, using a service plate, clearing carrying trays, and carrying trays.*

Apart from service at table, the waiter also has other duties everyday, which are affected by the nature of the operation, its degree of luxury, its style of appointments and furnishings. Preparation of the restaurant, cleanliness of furniture and equipment (including ancillary sections) is commonly referred to as doing the menage, means the housework. Menage or housework is part of being ready for service. In hotel terminology, equipment or food prepared in readiness for service is described as *'mise en place'* (put in place) or as being in place. The following are mange routines for an effective food and beverage service :

1. Morning duties
2. Evening duties
3. Duty allocation
4. Menage tasks and methods
5. Sweeping and vacuuming
6. Dusting
7. Table cleaning

8. Service tables and side tables
9. Chair cleaning
10. Furniture glass
11. Pastry and sandwich cases
12. Flowers.

MISE EN PLACE FOR A RESTAURANT

In the preparation of any restaurant for the service of a meal there will be an established pattern of work and a recognized list of items that must be done before any customer can be admitted to the room. The French term 'mise en place' is used for this preparatory work that must be completed before service can commence. In small restaurant this work is done together by the staff whereas in a big sized restaurant it is necessary to put up a roaster of duties for the waiters, waitresses and commie waiters. Thus, the sequence of the preparation will vary from restaurant to restaurant, but the following most important items need consideration :

1. ***Ventilation*** :
   (a) Open the windows to ventilate the room and remove the stale smell of food and tobacco fumes.
   (b) Proper room temperature needs to be adjusted.
2. ***Linen*** :
   (a) Collect all the dirty table clothes, table napkins, waiters cloth and other items of linen. Tie them in bundle of ten.
   (b) Get issue clean linen from the linen room.
3. ***Cleaning*** :
   (*a*) Remove all tables, chairs, etc.
   (b) Vacuum cleaning of the carpets.
   (c) Regular sweeping and polishing, clean all equipment on regular basis.
   (d) All silver plated items, table works need cleaning.
   (e) Apart from items of silverware or stainless steel which will be used in the service, all items of crockery and glassware needed for special service such as flambe (chaffing lamps and pans) must be cleaned, checked for service, polished and place on the tables or sideboards.
   (f) Cruet sets be cleaned or polished and filled.
4. ***Reserve Equipment*** :
   (a) Prepare the sideboards or 'dumb waiters' with reserve equipment necessary for day's menu.
   (b) All necessary plates and cutlery and reserve linen be reserved.
   (c) The tables are laid with clean clothes and their cutlery, glasses, plates and either paper or linen napkins.
   (d) Bring flowers and place at appropriate places.
   (e) The wine waiter will check all his equipment and glasses and prepare his wine collars, wine cradles and jugs of iced water.
   (f) Wine list must be up to date and any changes in the vintages of new stock of wine are noted.

5. *Inspection* : By restaurant manager/headwaiter.

6. *Final Stage* : (a) Placing of butter, toast Melba and rolls on the table.
   (b) Placing of sauces on the sideboards and bring into room the trolley from the kitchen containing hors d'oeuvre, sweets and perhaps cheeses.
   (c) If necessary, heated trolley is brought in containing some joints of meats to be carved in front of the customer during the course of the service.

7. *Instructions* : (a) The restaurant manager/headwaiter instructs the staff on any new dishes on the menu, the method of service and accompaniments that must be served with the dishes.
   (b) He will also advice the staff on the requirement of a particular customer so that they will know exactly what is expected of them.
   (c) Once he has finally inspected the staff to satisfy himself they are clean and have clean uniforms, he will open the restaurant for service.

Menu Knowledge

Familiarity with the menu helps the waiter to improve customer relations to improve customer relations and build the image of the restaurant. Knowing the menu helps to suggest additional side orders. With knowledge of food ingredients suggestions could be made to clienting guests and knowledge of the prices helps to make suggestions to budget conscious guests.

The food in a menu is grouped into categories related to foods according to custom and performance of management. Appetizer category includes juices and fruits, soup may be placed in a separate category grouped with appetizer or included with table d'hote entrees. Entree categories vary extensively. The dessert listing includes ice cream, sundaes and specialization of the area/region. Beverages include coffee, tea, milk and other drinks. Cocktails and wine may also be listed on the food menu. A special of the day may be attached to the menu. A seasonal special is also attached to the menu. Then an abundant supply of a particular food is available at low price. A chef's special is a dish that the chef prepares exceptionally well.

Guest often asks how foods on the menu are prepared, therefore, know some the common methods of food preparation such as :

1. *Baked* : Cooked by dry continuous heating in oven.
2. *Boiled* : Cooked in liquid.
3. *Braised* : Browned in small amount of fat and then cooked s slowly in a little liquid in a covered pan.
4. *Broiled* : Cooked by direct heat, either under the source of heat as in a broiler or over the source of heat, as on grill.
5. *Fried* : Cooked in a hot. Pan fried and sauteed mean cooked in a small amount of fat. Deep fat fried means cooked while immersed in a large amount of fat.

6. ***Grilled*** : Cooked over direct heat, usually hot coals.
7. ***Pan-broiled*** : Cooked in heavy frying pan over direct heat, using little or no fat.
8. ***Poached*** : Simmered in enough liquid to cover the food.
9. ***Roasted*** : Cooked uncovered without water added, usually in an oven.
10. ***Sauteed*** : Browned and cooked in a small amount of hot fat.
11. ***Simmered*** : Cooked gently in a liquid over low heat just below the boiling point.
12. ***Steamed*** : Cooked in steam with or without pressure.
13. ***Stewed*** : Simmered slowly in enough liquid to cover the food.

Meal Accompaniments

Condiments, decorative garnishes and foods that complement the entree are known as accompaniments. Condiments are to be brought to the table to complete the order and garnishes and complementary food to an entree prepared by the chef need to be added. Garnishes should look attractive and condiment containers must be clean. Some accompaniments may be kept at the side stand for convenience. Some of the meal accompaniments are :

1. Apple sauce with potato pancakes.
2. Butter with bread and rolls
3. Catsup and pickles with hamburger
4. Crackers with soup
5. Clarified butter with lobster
6. Cream and sugar with coffee
7. Dressing with salads
8. Lemon and sugar with tea
9. Lemon wedge with fish
10. Mustard with hot-dogs
11. Parsley to add colour to an entree
12. Steak sauce with steak
13. Syrup with pancakes
14. Tarter sauce with fish.

Condiments

Condiments include those things, which are used to give relish to food, and include items such as cruets,, bowls, bottles or other containers or holders of condiments and table commodities should be kept clean. Salt and pepper containers should be refilled and wiped daily and emptied and washed weekly.

Commodities include seasonings, bottled sauces, sugars and preserves such as :

1. Salt
2. Vinegar

3. Proprietary sauces
4. Pepper
5. Sugar
6. Mustard
7. Preserves (jams; marmalade)
8. Oil

Preparation Time

The time required to cook and dish up a food item on the menu is known as preparation time. This time will depend on many factors such as kitchen equipment, the efficiency of the chef and number of orders directly placed by other waiter/res. Some of the more common food preparation times are given in Table 1.1.

TABLE 1.1
Preparation Time for Some Food Items

S. No.	*Food Items*	*Preparation Time*
1	Eggs	10 minutes
2	Fish - fried or broiled	10–15 minutes
3	Liver	15 minutes
4	Chateaubriau	30 minutes
5	Steak, 1-inch thick	
	— rare	10 minutes
	— medium	15 minutes
	— well done	20 minutes
6	Lamb Chops	20 minutes
7	Pork Chops	15–20 minutes
8	Game	30–40 minutes
9	Fried Chicken	10–20 minutes
10	Souffle	35 minutes

Equipment

The total washing and maintenance of silver plates is normally the responsibility of the restaurant manager or headwaiter. Cutlery and other special silver are often the responsibility of the waiting staff. Usually, the care of the following equipment and activities is required :

1. Trolley, rechaud lamps and other special silver
2. Trays
3. Cutlery
4. Glassware
5. Chinaware
6. Provision of ice
7. Pantry and other duties.

On arrival in the morning, waiting staff should open the windows, clear cigar and other meals and switch on the air conditioners. Thereafter staff members shall attend their duties as assigned to them. These duties include :

1. Vacuuming the carpet or sweeping the floor. In case of some restaurant this work is performed by housekeeping staff
2. Dusting furniture
3. Polishing of glass: mirrors, glass, shelves, show pieces, etc.
4. Cleaning of silver
5. Change the linen
6. Restock sideboards and dummy waiters
7. Prepare the cold buffet table
8. Sharpen knives
9. Set the table for breakfast/lunch etc.

Before the start of service, close all the windows. Thereafter, the waiters must go to their dressing room to wash, tidy and clean their uniform. For lunch service the waiting staff should have an early lunch and return to the restaurant shortly before service. They should give final touches to their station attend to trolleys and place cold dishes on the buffet.

After the final meal service of the day, the duties of a waiter include :

1. Cleaning the restaurant
2. Plan the condiments on a table near the service doors
3. Empty mustards and wash linen
4. Remove floors to the floor room, cool place
5. Fold clean tables clothes and piles them neatly on the tables
6. Adjust/place chairs
7. Check before leaving.

The restaurant needs to be properly managed and all the routine duties need to be properly allocated

1. Vacuuming and cleaning
2. Linen
3. Cutlery layout
4. Glasses
5. Wine and sideboards
6. Cruet and accompaniments
7. Pantry and hot plates.

Preparation for Food and Beverage Service (Mise en place)

When the restaurant is clean and en place, a number of duties need to be carried out before the service commence. The term *'mise en place'* (preparation for service) is the term used for all the duties that have to be carried out to have the room ready for service. A duty rota showing the tasks and duties to be completed before service and which member of the staff is responsible needs to be drawn up. Figure 1.1 is an example of a duty rota for preservice duties in table service and shows how they may be allocated to a team of staff. The exact nature of the duty rota varies with every establishment — duties to be performed, the number of staff, time off and whether a split/straight shift is worked, etc.

Specimen Duty Rota for Preservice Duties

Waiter	*1.10.2009*	*2*	*3*	*4*	*5*	*6*	*7*	*8*	*9*	*10*	*11*	*12*	*13*	*14.10.2009*	*Task Number*
Anil	1	11	10	9	8	7		6	5	4	3	2	1		1. Menus
Beenu	2	1	11	10	9	8		7	6	5	4	3	2		2. Restaurant Cleaning
Chander	3	2	1	11	10	9		8	7	6	5	4	3		3. Linen
Dchu	4	3	2	1	11	10	D	9	8	7	6	5	4	D	4. Hot Plate
E-aglc	5	4	3	2	1	11	E	10	9	8	7	6	5	E	5. Silver
Faleh	6	5	4	3	2	1	S	11	1`0	9	8	7	6	S	6. Accompaniments
Gollu	7	6	5	4	3	2	O	1	11	10	9	8	7	O	7. Sideboard
Hemant	8	7	6	5	4	3	L	2	1	11	10	9	8	L	8. Dispense Bar
Indei	9	8	7	6	5	4	C	3	2	1	11	10	9	C	9. Stillroom
John	10	9	8	7	6	5		4	3	2	1	11	10		10. Mliscellaneous
Kundan	11	10	9	8	7	6		5	4	3	2	1	11		11. Day off

FIG. 1.1. Specimen of a Daily Duty Rota

Supervisor's Duties

1. Check the booking dairy for reservations.
2. Make out the seating plan for the day and allocate customers accordingly.
3. Make out a plan of the various stations and show where the staff will be working.
4. Go over the menu with staff immediately before service due to commence.
5. Check that all the duties of the rota are covered and that a full team of staff is present.

Housekeeping Duties

1. Everyday vacuums the carpet and brush surroundings.
2. Clean and polish door and glass.
3. Empty waste bins and ashtrays.
4. Performance of one of the task, as appropriate

(a) Brush and dust tables and chairs — Monday.
(b) Polish all sideboards, window edges and cash desk — Tuesday.
(c) Polish all brasses — Wednesday.
(d) Clean and polish the reception — Thursday.
Commence again on Monday.

5. Each day, on completion of duties, lineup tables and chairs for laying up.

Linen/Paper

Responsibilities for linen before or after as well as during service include :

1. Changing Linen
2. Linen book
3. Handling linen
4. Service cloth
5. Napkin handling.

This applies to table, buffet and slip clothes, glass and water clothes, paper slip clothes, napkins plus dish paper and doilies. Main duties are :

1. Collecting the cleaning linen from the housekeeping department, checking items against
2. Collect the list, distributing them to various service points, laying table clothes and folding serviettes. Spare linen should be folded neatly into the linen basket.
3. Ensure that stocks are sufficient to meet the needs.
4. Ensure that glass clothes and waiter's clothes are available.
5. Provide dish paper and doilies as required.
6. The preparation of linen basket for return to the linen rooms.

Hot Plate

1. Switch on the switchboard.
2. Ensure all doors are closed.
3. Placed the items in the hot plate, as per the menu offered, *e.g.*
   (a) Soup plates
   (b) Sweet plates
   (c) Fish plates
   (d) Coffee cups
   (e) Joint plates.
4. Set out the required kitchen silver on top of the hot plate, including cloches.
5. Stock up after each service with clean and polished china in readiness for next meal service.

Silver

Obtain silver from the plate room (silver pantry). Every piece must be clean. These must be sorted out into knives, forks, spoons, etc. and placed properly in the respective compartments or the drawers of the side table. It is convenient to keep the handle towards the outer part of the drawer, the prongs of forks and spoons facing sideways.

1. Collection of cutlery and tableware from the silver room.
2. Polishing and sorting into trays the following items as agreed by the supervisor :
   - (a) Service spoon
   - (b) Fish knives
   - (c) Joint/service forks
   - (d) Fish forks
   - (e) Dessert spoons
   - (f) Side knives
   - (g) Soup spoons
   - (h) Special services as required for the menu.
   - (i) Tea/coffee spoons
   - (j) Stocking of sideboards
   - (k) Dessert forks.
3. Daily cleaning :
   - (a) Spirit and electric heaters
   - (b) Flare lamps, spirit and gas
   - (c) Ashtrays
   - (d) Carving trolleys.
4. Additional cleaning of cutlery, flatware and hollowware as per the daily rota.

Crockery

1. The checking and polishing of side plates ready for lay up.
2. The checking and polishing of crockery for hot plate according to menu and service requirements.
3. Preparation of service plates/flats for sideboards.
4. Preparation of stocks of crockery for sideboards, *e.g.*,
   - (a) Fish plates
   - (b) Side plates
   - (c) Coffee saucers.

Cruets, Ashtrays, Table Numbers and Butter Dishes

1. The collection of cruets, ashtrays, table numbers and butter dishes from silver room.

2. Checking, filling and polish cruets.
3. The laying of table of cruets, ashtrays, table numbers and butter dishes with knives, according to headwaiters instructions.
4. Restoring following service.

Still Room

1. The ordering of store requirements (check with bar and accompaniments).
2. The preparation of :

   (a) Coffee service and beverage service items.

   (b) Melba toasts.

   (c) Other toasts, butter and bread for special dishes.
3. The clearing of still room area following service.
4. Polishing and refilling oil and vinegar stands, sugar basins and dredges, paper mills and cayenne, pepper pots.
5. Preparing all accompaniments: tomato ketchup, French and English mustard, ground ginger, horseradish sauce, mint sauce, Worcester sauce, Parmesan cheese.
6. Distributing the cruets to the table and the accompaniments to the sideboards.

The waiters/ress are assigned the tables at which their guest will eat. Immediately thereafter they would attend to side work, i.e. all duties to be per-formed other than those directly related to serving the guests. Side works then includes such as preparing the dinning room and studying the menu, as well as leaving the work area in proper order upon completion of the shift.

A station is a section of the dinning room assigned as a work area to a waiter/ress. Each station has seating for about 12 or more guests at tables, booths or counters. The dinning room is divided into stations that are equal to one another in all aspects such as number of guests they seat, distance from sideboards and kitchen and desirably seat to the guests. Tables are often numbered, and stations are assigned by giving the numbers of the tables to a waiter/ress. The servers use their respective number on their orders and guest checks to identify the party of guests being served.

The main duties of a waiter before the arrival of guest may be grouped as follows :

1. *Dinning room preparation* — Preparing tables;
   Preparing the side stand.
2. *Studying the menu* — Methods of food preparation;
   Preparation time;
   Meal accompaniments.
3. *Closing the dinning room.*

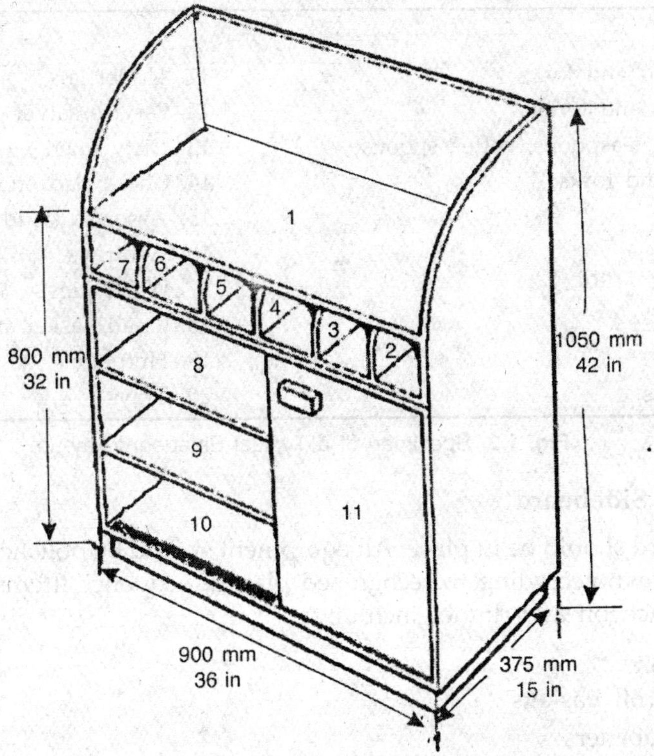

FIG. 1.2. A Typical Sideboard for a Restaurant

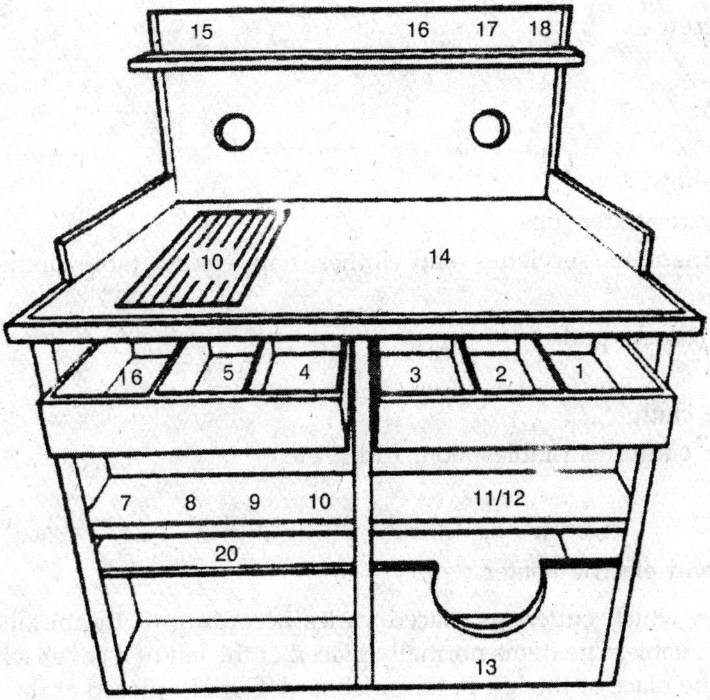

KEY

1. Service spoons and forks
2. Sweet spoons and forks
3. Soup spoons, teaspoons, coffee spoons
4. Fish knives and forks
5. Joint knives
6. Side knives
7. Fish plates
8. Sweet plates
9. Side plates
10. Coffee saucers
11. Underflats
12. Service salver
13. Dirty linen
14. Check pad on service plate
15. Assorted condiments
16. Ashtrays
17. Water jugs
18. Bread basket and butter
19. Hotplate
20. Trays

Fig. 1.3. Specimen of a Typical Sideboard Lay-up

Service Station Sideboard

The sideboard should be in place. All equipment should be polished and clothed up and should be laid down according to recognized plan or sequence. Items to be placed on the sideboard for luncheon and dinner include :

1. Ashtrays
2. Bread/roll baskets
3. Bottle openers
4. Butter dishes
5. Condiments (sauces, pickles, chutney, etc.)
6. Corkscrew
7. Cruet
8. Cutlery
9. Doilies
10. Finger-bowls
11. Glassware Water jugs
12. Linen (napkins/serviettes, slip clothes, nappersons, table clothes)
13. Matches
14. Order (check) pad
15. Pencil
16. Service cloth
17. Service equipment-tablespoon, forks, etc.
18. Trays
19. Menus
20. Spirit and electric heater.

The order in which cutlery is placed varies according to the number of sideboard's compartments available. The items normally placed at the left of a cover when setting a table should similarly be place to the left in the sideboard. Cutlery placed at the right of the cover should similarly be placed to the right in the sideboard.

Miscellaneous Items

Ice bowls, rolls of bread, butter, crater, and doilies, should also be obtained from the appropriate room and placed in readin‹ ›s on the sideboard. Butter should be kept fresh and cool on ice or in ice or water.

DISPENSE BAR

Mise en Place

A 'dispense bar' is situated within a food and beverageservice are that dispenses wine or other alcoholic drinks which are to be served to a customer consuning a meal or using a lounge area. However, in many establishments, because of the plaming and layout, wine and other alcoholic drinks for consumption with a meal are sametime disk used from bars situated outside the food and beverage service are itself — in other words from one of the public bars. All drinks dispensed must be checked for and controlle in same way. All alcoholic drinks are usually served by the member of the sence team often known as a sommelier or wine butler, unless it is the custom for the food service waiters to serve their own customers with the wine and drinks they require.

Equipment

In order to carry out efficiently the service of all forms of wine and drink requested, the bar should have available all the necessary equipment for making cocktails, decanting wine, serving wine correctly, making fruit cups and so on. The equipment should include the following items.

Main items

1. *Cocktail shaker.* The ideal utensil for mixing ingredients that will not normally blend together well by stirring. A three-part utensil.
2. *Boston shaker.* Consists of two cones, one of which overlaps the other to seal in the 'mix' Made of stainless steel, glass or plated silver. The mix is strained using a Hawthorn strainer.
3. *Mixing glass :* Like a glass jug without a handle, but has a lip. Used for mixing clear drinks which do not contain juices or cream.
4. *Strainer :* There are many types, the most popular being the Hawthorn. This is a flat spoon-shaped utensil with a spring coiled round its edge. It is used in conjunction with the cocktail shaker and mixing glass to hold back the ice after the drink is prepared. A special design is available for use with liquidisers and blenders.
5. *Bar spoon:* For use with the mixing glass when stirring cocktails. The flat 'muddler' end is used for crushing sugar and mint in certain drinks.
6. *Bar liquidiser or blender :* Used for making drinks that require pureed fruit
7. *Drink mixer :* Used for drinks that do not need liquidising, especially those containing cream or ice cream. If ice is required, use only crushed ice.

Other items

1. assorted glasses
2. ice buckets and stands
3. wine baskets
4. water jugs
5. assorted bitters : peach, orange, Angostura
6. cutting board and knife
7. coasters
8. refrigerator
9. cork extractor
10. ice pick
11. ice making machine
12. drinking stras
13. cocktail sticks
14. carafes
15. wine and coktails lists
16. glass cloths, napkins and service cloths
17. small ice buckets and tongs
18. soda syphons
19. coloured sugars
20. sink unit
21. glass washing machine
22. optics/spirit measures
23. wine measures
24. cooling trays
25. bottle opener
26. ice crushing machine
27. muslin and funnel
28. lemon squeezing machine
29. swizzle sticks
30. strainer and funnel
31. service salvers
32. wine knife and cigar cutter
33. bin
34. hot beverage maker.

Food items

1. olives
2. Worcestershire sauce
3. salt and pepper

4. nutmeg
5. Angostura bitters
6. caster sugar
7. Maraschino cherries
8. Tabasco sauce
9. cinnamon
10. cloves
11. cube sugar
12. Demerara sugar
13. eggs
14. mint
15. organge
16. coconut cream
17. cream
18. cucumber
19. lemon
20. lime.

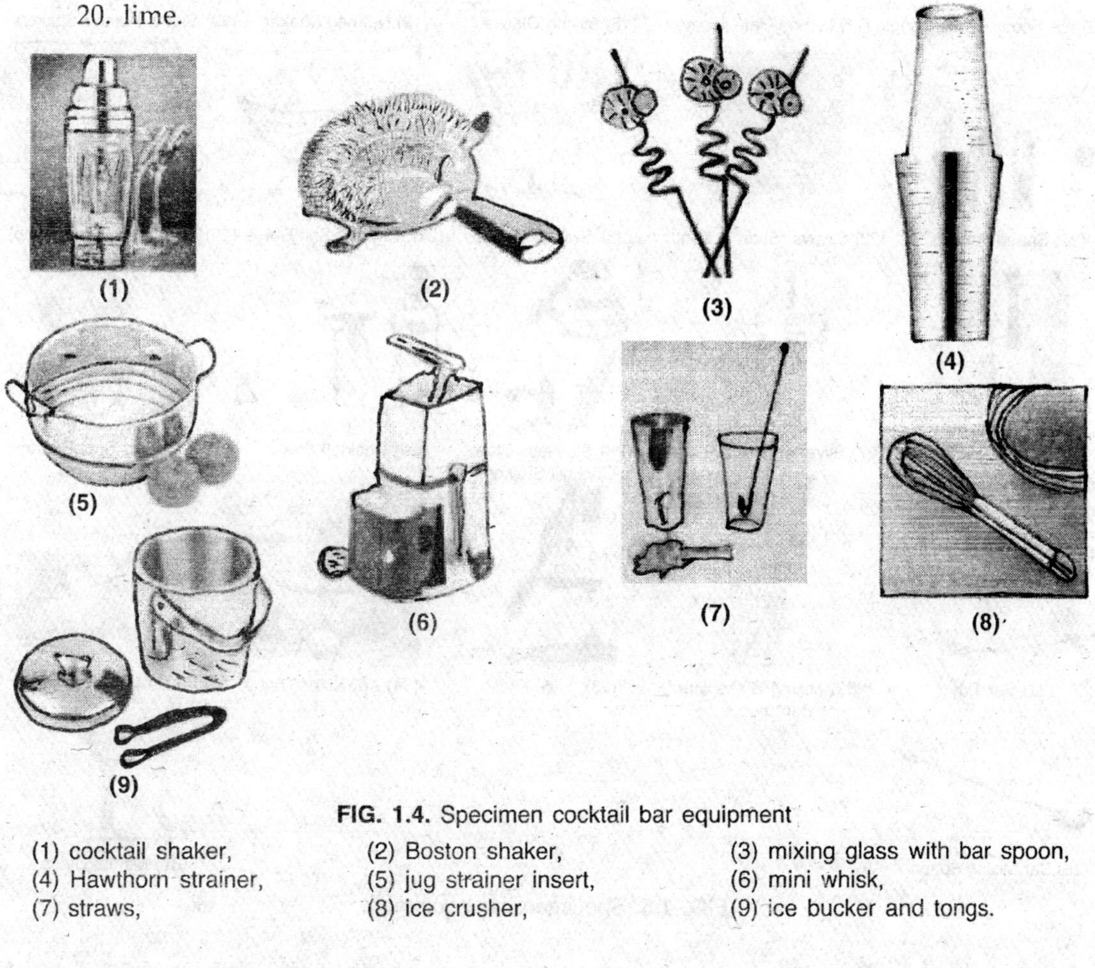

FIG. 1.4. Specimen cocktail bar equipment

(1) cocktail shaker, (2) Boston shaker, (3) mixing glass with bar spoon, (4) Hawthorn strainer, (5) jug strainer insert, (6) mini whisk, (7) straws, (8) ice crusher, (9) ice bucker and tongs.

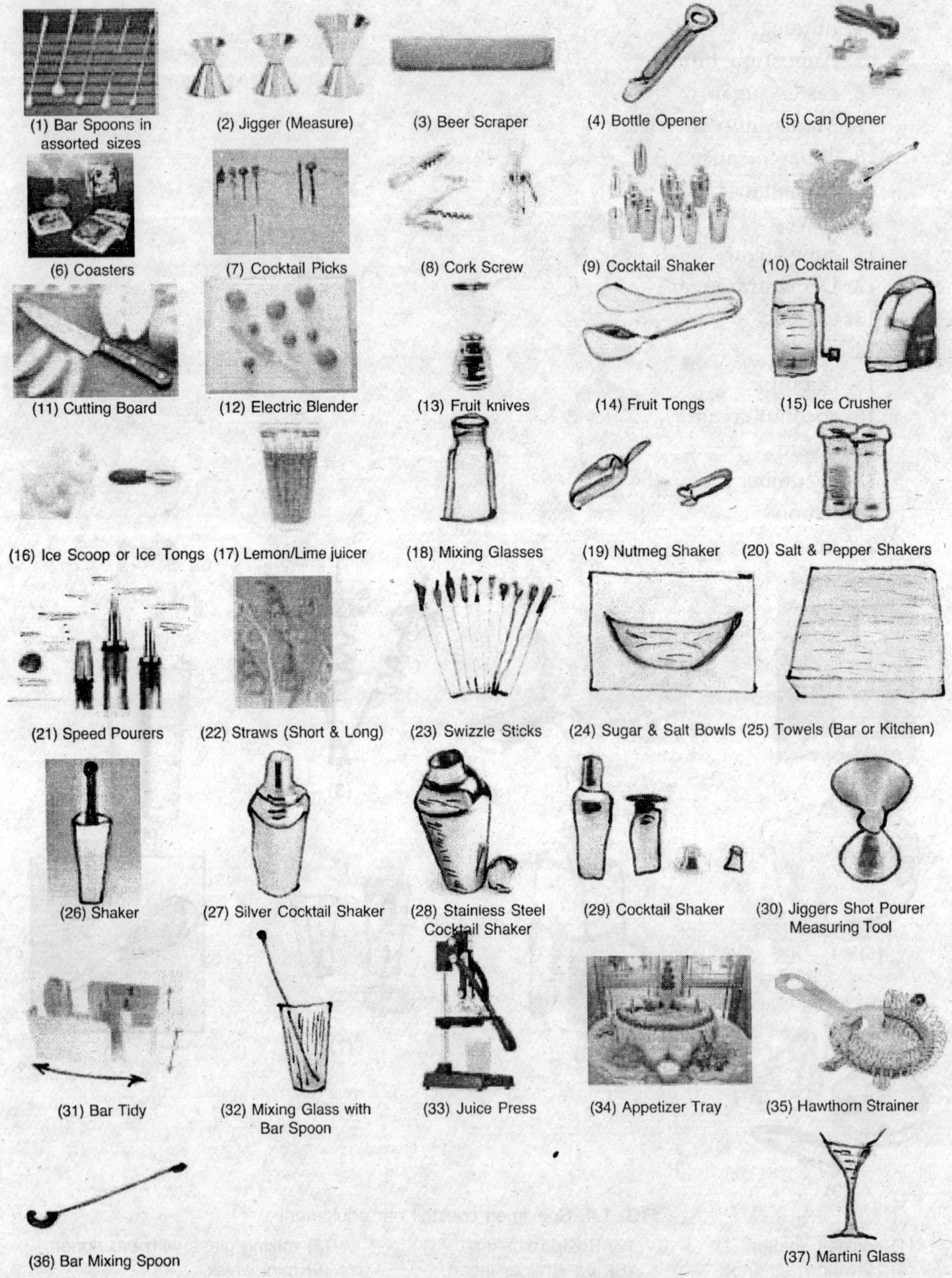

FIG. 1.5. Specimen bar equipment

Glassware

The choice of the right glass is a vital element if the cocktail is to be invitingly presented. Well-designed glassware combines elegance, strength and stability, and should be fine rimmed and of clear glass. All glassware should be clean and well polished.

Planning of the bar

There are certain essentials necessary in the planning of every bar. They are factors that should be given prime consideration when planning for a fixed bar or when setting up a temporary bar for a particular function, some of there are as follows :

Siting

A major factor is the siting of the bar. The position should be chosen so that the bar achieves the greatest possible number of sales.

Area

The bar staff must be given sufficient area of space in which to work and move about. There should be a minimum of 1 m (3 ft 3 in) from the back of the bar counter to the storage shelves and display cabinets at the rear of the bar.

Layout

Very careful consideration must be given, in the initial planning, to the layout of the bar. Adequate storage must be provided, in the form of shelves, cupboards and racks, for the stock required and equipment listed. Everything should be easily to hand so that the bar staff do not have to move about more than necessary to provide a quick and efficient service.

Plumbing and Power

It is essential to have hot and cold running water for glass washing. Power is necessary for the cooling trays, refrigerators and ice-making machines.

Safety and hygiene

Great care must be observed to ensure that the materials used in the make-up of the bar are hygienic and safe. Flooring must be non-slip. The bar top should be of a material suited to the general decor that is hard wearing, easily wiped down and has no sharp edges. The bar top should be of average working height – approximately 1 m (3ft 3 in) and a depth (across the top from the bar to the service side) of about 0.6m (20m).

The preparation work *(mise en place)* relating to dispense bar involves the following :

1. Opening the bar.
2. Remove the liqueur trolley from the bar area.
3. Bar silver requiring cleaning to be taken to silver man.
4. Clean any debris left from the previous day.

5. Checking the stock of appetizers – nuts, gherkins, etc. and replenish stock if required.
6. Make up dishes for tables.
7. Wipe down bar tops.
8. Clean shelves and swab out the bar flour.
9. Check optics.
10. Prepare ice buckets, wine coolers, service trays and water jugs.
11. Check pads and wine lists line up, clean and polish aperitif glasses.
12. Check the liqueur trolley for glasses, stock and bottle presentation.
13. Prepare the bar service top according to the standards of the establishment.

Bar Service Top

It may include a number of items depending upon the standards of the restaurant. Some of these are :

1. Cutting board
2. Fruit knife
3. Fruits: lemon, orange, apples, etc.
4. Cucumber
5. One egg (fresh)
6. Mixing glass spoons
7. Hawthorn strainer
8. Cocktail shaker
9. Whine funnel
10. Glass jar with olives
11. Coloured sugar
12. Angostura bitters
13. Peach bitters
14. Worcester sauces
15. Cocktail sticks
16. Cherries in glass
17. Straws in sherry glass.
18. Tea Strainer
19. Wine coasters
20. Spirit measures
21. Soda siphon
22. Ice bucket and tongs.

Miscellaneous Preparations

Other preparatory work includes :

1. Preparing and laying up the following :
   (a) Display buffet
   (b) Carving trolley
   (c) Sweet trolley.
   (d) Cheese trolley.
   (e) Hors d'oeuvre trolley.
2. Polishing of side plates and fishplates required for laying up.
3. On completion of preparatory work the staff should report back to the headwaiter. The headwaiter must check that the work has been carried out in a satisfactory manner.
4. The headwaiter will reallocate the member of the staff to work involving the laying up of the room.
5. Other works : The order of such work should be as follows :
   (a) Dusting
   (b) Stacking chairs on the tables.
   (c) Vacuuming
   (d) Polishing
   (e) Arranging tables and chairs according to the table plan.
      1. Linen
      2. Accompaniments
      3. Hot plate
      4. Still room
      5. Sideboards
      6. Silver cleaning
      7. Miscellaneous -trolleys.

Display Buffet

The preparation of the buffet table as per the supervisor's instructions.

In a display buffet, generally followings are displayed :

1. Butter dishes and knives
2. Accompaniments
3. Food items
4. Special cutlery and tableware as required *e.g.* grapefruit spoons Under plates for large butter dishes
5. Service spoons and forks
6. Side plates with doilies, if necessary
7. Water jugs and joint knives for pates or mousses
8. Cold fish plates
9. Carving knife.

Trolleys

Carving Trolleys

1. Checking of trolley for cleanliness
2. Check and refill methylated spirit burners
3. Empty the water reservoirs and fill it with boiling water from the still prior to leaving for the lunch break
4. Lay up the bottom shelf only
5. Ensure the sauce and gravy reservoirs are in place under cover. They should be sited beside the platform
6. Lay up for the top shelf : folded linen napkin only
7. Lay up for the bottom shelf : service plate with
   (a) 1 joint knife
   (b) 6 service spoons and forks.
   (c) 2 sauce ladles (set into a folded (pouch) napkin)
   (d) Joint plate with carving knives, fork and steel (the steel placed between plates).

Sweet Trolley

1. Checking the trolleys for cleanliness and polish
2. Place doilies on top two tiers
3. Place on the bottom shelf on a folded slip cloth :
   (a) Sweet plates.

FIG. 1.6. Sweet/Cheese Trolly

(b) Soup plates if fruit salad appears on the menu
(c) Gateaux slice, pastry tongs (in the drawer or on a joint plate)
(d) Service spoons and forks
(e) Joint knives
(f) Sauce ladles (in a folded napkin)
(g) Joint plate for dirty service gear.

Cheese Trolley

1. Check the trolley for cleanliness
2. The top and bottom selves could be laid as follows :
   (a) *Top shelves:*
      (i) Salt and pepper
      (ii) Coaster sugar
      (iii) Flat or dish with biscuits
      (iv) Various cheese on a cheese board
      (v) Knives and forks for cheese service
      (vi) Celery glass on under-plate.
   (b) *Bottom shelf :*
      (i) Side plates.
      (ii) Side knives.
      (iii) Butterdish.

HORS-D'OEUVRE AND OTHER APPETIZERS

Hors-d'oeuvre

Traditionally hors-d'oeuvres are a selection of salads, fish and meats. The selection was served onto a cold fish plate and the cover was a fish knife and fork. The cover nowadays is more likely to be dictated by the type of food being served and its presentation. Oil and vinegar were also traditionally offered but this has become less common because the foods are usually already well dressed. Brown bread and butter is also less often offered, thereby allowing the customer a choice of either butter or alternatives.

Service can be a pre-plated selection or offered as a selection, in individual ravier dishes, from a tray, gueridon or from the traditional hors-d'oeuvre trolley as illustrated in Fig. 1.4.

Common hors-d'oeuvre item include

Salads. Plain or compound. Examples of plain salads include fish and meat salads, cucumber salad, tomato salad, potato salad, beetroot salad, red cabbage and cauliflower. Compound salads include for example, Russian (mixed vegetables in mayonnaise) Andalouse (celery, onions, peppers, tomatoes, rice and vinaigrette), Italienne (vegetable salad, cubes of salami, anchovy fillets and mayonnaise) and Parisienne (slices of crayfish, truffles, Russian salad and bound with mayonnaise and aspic).

Fish. May include items such as anchovies, herring (fresh or marinated) lobstrer, mackerel (marinated, smoked or fresh), smoked eel (filleted or sliced) and prawns (plain, in cooktail sauce or in a mousse).

Meats. Includes items such as foie gras, ham (raw, boiled or smoked) and salami of all sorts.

FIG. 1.7. Hors-d'oeuvre trolley

PREPARING TABLES AND CLOTHING UP

Table laying is a group exercise. Food and beverage establishments offering waiting service either use dinning tables covered with a cloth or polished tables on which plates are places with or without an undermat. The waiter first obtains the clothes or mats. If mats are to be used they should be placed on the table exactly where the plate, bowl, glass etc. are later to be set. Before laying the cloth, one must be sure that the table is in its proper place, in line with other tables. It must be correctly angled and that it is steady so that it is not again to be handled, once the cloth is on. The table covered with a cloth should be of the type fitted with baize or felt. This is to deaden noise of plates, cutlery and glass placed on them; keep the cloth impression to hand without slipping; and cushion the guests wrists from sharp edges of the table. If required a loose silence cloth (of baize or felt) covering the tabletop may be used as an under-cloth. This under cloth can be kept in position with clips or card. The tablecloth should be right side up. The fold should be centered on the table with the points at the corners so that the cloth hangs evenly over the table legs. Table clothes are normally screen-folded (*i.e.* to form a 'W') with the face side outside. The aim is laying a cloth is to cover the four table legs with the four comers hanging about 8 or 10 cm (3 or 4") from the floor.

Guidelines Preparing Table and Clothing UP

1. Check that table is correctly positioned and firm
2. Place felt over the table
3. Choose the correct size of the tablecloth
4. Stand centrally between the two legs of the table
5. Placed the folded cloth on the table with the open edges towards you and the main folds facing away from you
6. Open the cloth across the table so that its woven edges (the selvedge edges) and its inside double fold lie facing you and with the two double folds facing away from you
7. With thumbs uppermost take the top flap of cloth between you thumbs and first finger and take the central folds between the first and second finger
8. With arms spread out the width of the table, move the cloth to the far edge of the table away from you
9. Release and drop the bottom flap (which is lying loose) over the far edge of the table
10. Allowing rest of the cloth to lie on the table, release your hold on the centre folds and gently unfold the cloth, drawing it across the table towards you until the tablecloth is opened and the table covered
11. Inspect to see that the drop is even all around and the cloth covers drape the legs
12. To adjust the cloth, stand squarely between the table legs and with arms out stretched, pull square
13. The corners of the tablecloths should cover the edge of the table
14. The overlap should be even all around the table : 30 - 45 cm (12 - 18 in).
15. The crease of the tablecloth should all ran the same way in the room.
16. If two table clothes are necessary to cover a table then the overlap of two table clothes should face away from the entrance to the room. This is for presentation purposes of both the room and the table.
17. The chairs should be placed in their correct position.

The table-cloth should be the right side up; this side is always more highly laundered and the hem is always on the underside of the cloth. The folds should be centred on the table with the points at the coners so that the cloth hangs evenly over the table legs.

Tablecloths are normally screen-folded (that is to form a 'W') with the face side (more glossily laundered) outside. This facilitates putting on the cloth. The aim in lying a cloth is to cover the four table legs with the four corners hanging about 8 to 10 cm (3 or 4") from the floor. When laying the cloth, care must be taken to avoid creasing it as this greatly spoils the general appearance of a table.

Technique for Laying a Table cloth

The following are steps to be taken in cloth laying :

Step 1 : Check that the table is correctly positioned and firm.

Step 2 **:** If felt is not already fitted, place felt over the table.

Step 3 **:** Choose the correct size of tablecloth.

Step 4 **:** Stand centrally between two legs of the table.

Step 5 **:** Place the folded cloth on the table with the open edges towards you and the main folds facing away from you.

Step 6 **:** Open the cloth across the table so that its woven edges (the selvedge edges) and its inside double fold lie facing you and with the two double folds facing away from you.

Step 7 **:** With thumbs uppermost, take the top flap of cloth between your thumbs and first finger and take the central folds between the first and second finger.

Step 8 **:** With arms spread out the width of the table, move the cloth to the far edge of the table away from you.

Step 9 **:** Release and drop the bottom flap (which is lying loose) over the far edge of the table.

Step 10 **:** Allowing the rest of the cloth to lie on the table, release your hold on the centre folds and gently uphold the cloth, drawing to across the table towards you until the table cloth is opened and the table covered.

Step 11 **:** Inspect to see that the drop is even all round and that the cloth carners drop the legs.

Step 12 **:** To adjust the cloth, stand squarely between the table legs and with arms outstretched, pull square.

Step 13 **:** The chairs should then be placed in their respective positions.

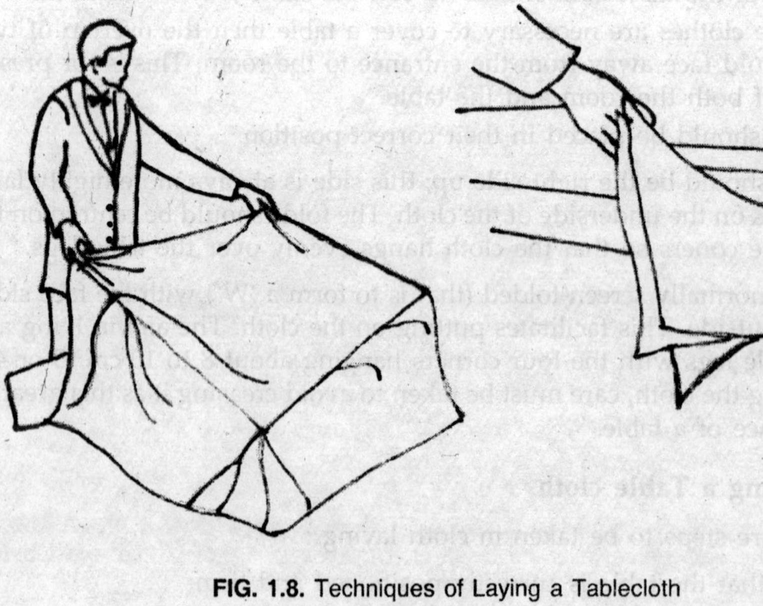

FIG. 1.8. Techniques of Laying a Tablecloth

Techniques for changing a Table cloth during Service

When a soiled tablecloth has to be changed during service, the following method should be adopted. Any articles on the table should be cleared to the sideboard, never placed on chairs or on the next table. The soiled cloth should be brushed, if necessary, on to a crumb tray or plate. The routine below aims to ensure that the felt-covered top of the table is not exposed during cloth changing. (See After 1.9).

Step 1 : Select the correct size tablecloth.

Step 2 : Stand as for laying a cloth.

Step 3 : Place the new cloth on the far side of the table in the same way as for laying a cloth.

Step 4 : Open the new clothe and hold it as previously described.

Step 5 : Stretching across the table, hold the loose flap of the tablecloth clear of the far edge of the table.

Step 6 : Release the lower flap and release the double fold held between the thumb and first finger. This allows the cloth to fall lightly (usually on to the chair on the far side).

Step 7 : Without relinquishing hold of the clean one, pinch the soiled cloth at the outer edges of the table between the palm and fingers to pick it up.

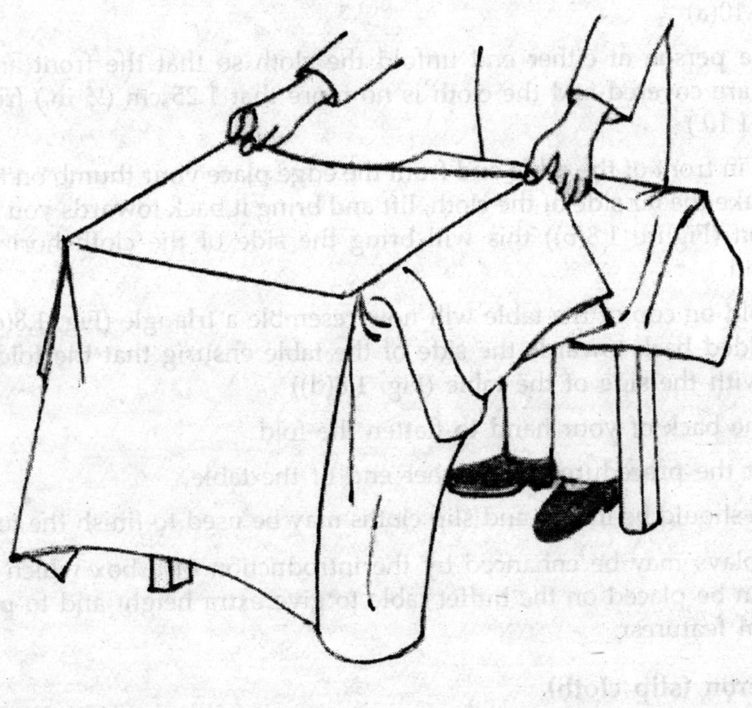

FIG. 1.9. A Technique of changing the tablecloth. The soiled table cloth is drawn towards the waiter who at the same time pulls the clean cloth across the table so that the table top is always covered.

Step 8 : Draw the soiled cloth towards you, gently shaking the clean cloth over the table.

Step 9 : Inspect the clean cloth for correct drop and alignment.

Step 10 : Place the soiled cloth a way in the dirty linen receptacle.

DEALING WITH SPILLS

Water, wine, sauce or similar moist matter can be spilled on the cloth. For such spills as sauce, take a small plate with a knife or spoon to the table and remove the sauce by scraping when the sauce is removed, cover the stain with a piece of white paper or menu card (in some cases slip a card also beneath the cloth). This prevents any marking of the clean slip cloth (napperon) or table napkin (if the stain is very small), which should then be neatly unfolded and laid over the card or paper.

Process of Boxing a buffet tables

The buffet should be cavered with suitable cloths, making sure that the drop of the cloth is with in 1-25 cm (½ in.) from the ground all the way around the front and sides of the bufet. If more than one cloth is used, the creases should be lined up, and where the cloths overlap one another the overlap should be facing away from the entrance to the room. The buds of the buffet should be 'box' pleated, thereby giving a better overall presentation of the buffet. The following procedure should be followed :

1. with assistance, open the screen fold along the buffet table from end to end (Ref. fig. 1.10(a)
2. with a person at either end unfold the cloth so that the front and sides of the table are covered and the cloth is no more that 1.25 cm (½ in.) from the ground (Fig. 1.10.)
3. stand in front of the cable and from the edge place your thumb on the front corner and take the far side of the cloth, lift and bring it back towards you in a semi-circle motion (Figure 1.8(b)) this will bring the side of the cloth horizontal with the ground.
4. the fold on cop of the table will now resemble a triangle (Fig. 1.8(c)) this should be folded back towards the side of the table ensurig that the folded edge is in line with the side of the table (Fig. 1.8(d))
5. use the back of your hand to flatten the fold
6. repeat the procedure at the other end of the table.

All creases should be in line and slip cloths may be used to finish the top of the table.

Buffer displays may be enhanced by the introduction of a box which has been box-clothed. This can be placed on the buffet table to give extra height and to provide display space for special featuresr.

Using a napperon (slip cloth)

When a tablecloth is only lightly stained, it may (as a measure of economy) be covered with a napperon (or slip cloth). This may often allow the same cloth to be used several times during one service.

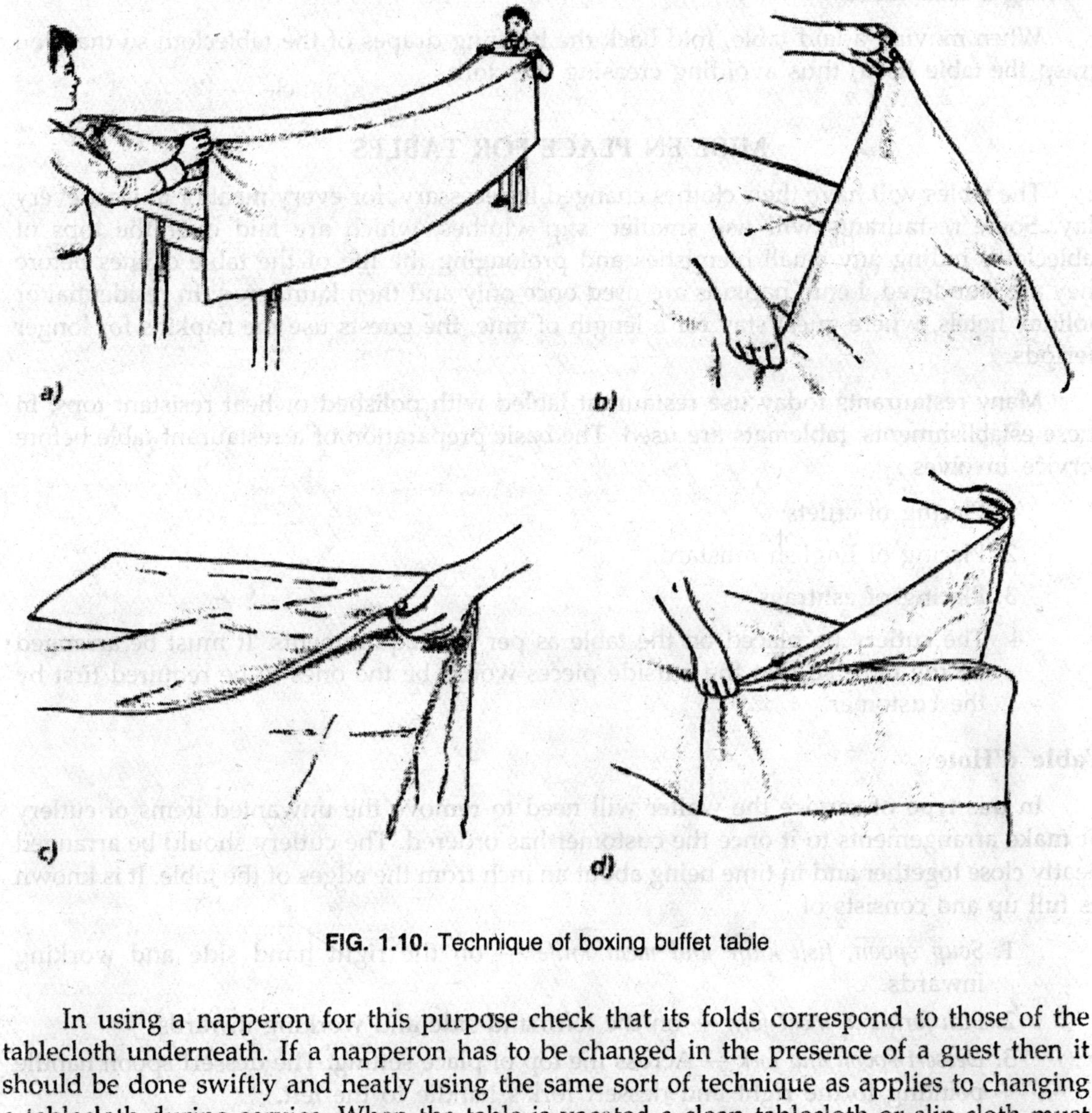

FIG. 1.10. Technique of boxing buffet table

In using a napperon for this purpose check that its folds correspond to those of the tablecloth underneath. If a napperon has to be changed in the presence of a guest then it should be done swiftly and neatly using the same sort of technique as applies to changing a tablecloth during service. When the table is vacated a clean tablecloth or slip cloth must be laid before the table is offered to another party.

Relaying covers during service

The flowers, cruet and other items are replaced on the table and the table laid with the cutlery, one cover at a time, from a cloth covered salver.

During service, cutlery should never be carried in the hand, even in a cloth, but always on a salver or large plate, which has been covered, with a napkin to deaden any noise.

The relay silver should be arranged neatly on the salver with the spoons and forks tucked underneath at right angles on either side. This facilitates handling, allays noise, possible accident, and looks neater.

Moving a laid table

When moving a laid table, fold back the hanging drapes of the tablecloth so that you grasp the table itself, thus avoiding creasing the cloth.

MISE EN PLACE FOR TABLES

The tables will have their clothes changed if necessary, for every meal or at least every day. Some restaurants will use smaller 'slip' clothes, which are laid over the tops of tablecloths hiding any small blemishes and prolonging the life of the table clothes before they are laundered. Lenin napkins are used once only and then laundered. In residential or holiday hotels, where guest stay for a length of time, the guests use the napkins for longer periods.

Many restaurants today use restaurant tabled with polished or heat resistant tops. In these establishments, tablemats are used. The basic preparation of a restaurant table before service involves :

1. Placing of cruets.
2. Placing of English mustard.
3. Placing of ashtrays. ·
4. The cutlery be placed on the table as per the requirements. It must be arranged on the table so that the outside pieces would be the ones to be required first by the customer.

Table d'Hote

In this type of service the waiter will need to remove the unwanted items of cutlery or make arrangements to it once the customer has ordered. The cutlery should be arranged neatly close together and in time being about an inch from the edges of the table. It is known as full up and consists of :

1. *Soup spoon, fish knife and meat knife* — on the right hand side and working inwards.
2. *Fish fork and meat fork* — on the left hand side and working inwards.
3. *Dessert spoon and fork* — Across the top of place setting. The dessert spoon handle pointing to the right and dessert fork's handle to the left.
4. *Side knife* - On the side plate at a slight angle towards the customer

   OR

   Place across the top of the place setting, in line with the dessert spoon and fork or next to the meat knife, depending upon the particular restaurant's customs.

A La Carte

In this type of service, only cutlery is placed on the table, apart from the side knife, will be on an *hors d 'oeuvre* or fish knife or fork. With this type of service the waiter will lay the correct cutlery on the table once the customer has decided on his meal and given his order.

1. ***Hors d'oeuvre plate :*** A medium sized plate is sometimes positioned centrally at each *or Liner or show plate* place setting on the table, helping to correctly space the cutlery. This serves a decoration purpose and could be used, if appropriate, for the service of the customer's first course.

2. ***Badged plate :*** Must be laid on the table so that the emblem or name of the *crockery etc.* establishment is facing the customer.

3. ***Side plate :*** Placed at the left side of this place setting or 'cover' and a wine glass on the right hand side, just above the knife. On the round tables the waiter must always be sure that he lays the place setting between the legs of the table.

4. ***Napkins (linen/paper) :*** Is positioned at each place setting. These are usually placed in the centre on the 'show plate' if this is used or at the left hand side on or above the side plate.

5. ***Flowers :*** Small bowls with some form of low-level flower arrangements are usually the most convenient for restaurant table use.

NAPKINS

Now a days, elaborate napkin (serviette) folding is less fashionable. Modern taste favour napkins — simply folded on the cover plate to reveal any monogram or design in the desk-mask. Folding of napkin is undertaken for two basic reasons. Firstly, to present the guest own personal table napkin in the cover and thus enhance the table and secondly, to aid in the presentation of food. Size of the napkin should be as per the requirement. It should be square in shape having well-starched linen.

Napkin Folds/Serviette Folds

There are many forms of serviette and each one has special names, such as :

1. Cone (Cornet or pointed cap)
2. Clock combe
3. Bishops mitre
4. Prince of Wales
5. Rose
6. Cockscomb
7. Fan — Free standing;
   — Triple wave.
8. Simple folds — Folding in half for a triangle.
   Folding into one or more simple rolls.

1. A Corent

It is also known as cone or pointed cap. It is popular because it is useful for giving height and importance to a table. This practice is not always noticed by guests and may be dropped during unfolding, a universally approved as the role is method of folding :

Step 1 : Open a square napkin as the table

Step 2 : Fold it in halfway from you

Step 3 : Refold in half-length wise so that seveledge edges are on the top

Step 4 : Fold the side's to touch in the middle

Step 5 : Fold under the right and left-hand corners as indicated by the dotted lines shown. In Fig. 1.11 (b).

Step 6 : From the top right hand side, point 'A' turn and roll towards the centre as shown Fig. 1.11 (c)

Step 7 : Repeat this roll on the opposite side from point 'B'.

Step 8 : Press the rolled part into place so that the napkin will stand up.

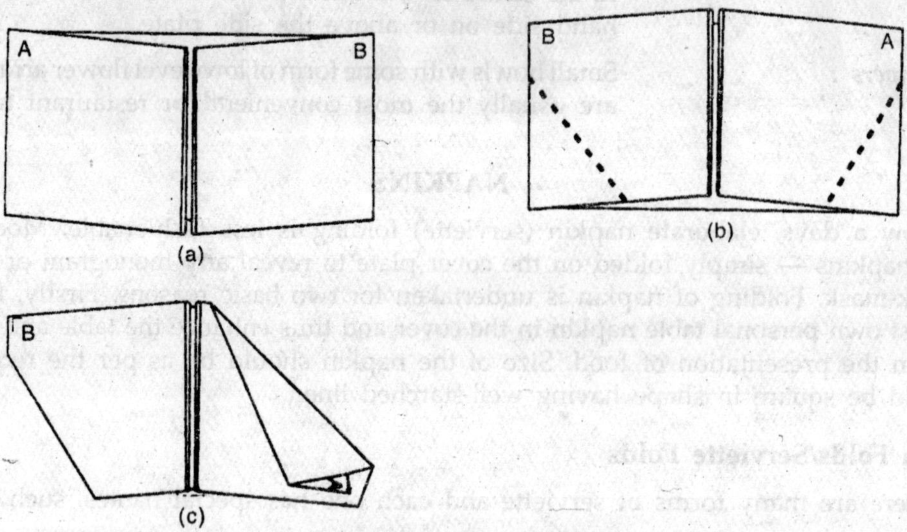

FIG. 1.11. A Cornet Style-1.

Cornet Style

Step 1 : Fold napkin into three equal parts, ABC

Step 2 : Fold part C at C_1.

Step 3 : Curl over into the shape of a cornet by holding C at C_1 and making point of the cone come at the fold between A-1 land B.

Step 4 : Fold part A, holding at point A_1 and take over to meet point D.

Step 5 : Turn up a sufficient fold at point A, so that the napkin will stand erect.

2. Bishop's Maitre

The classic maitre is one fold requiring a large napkin (66-cm/26 inch.) square.

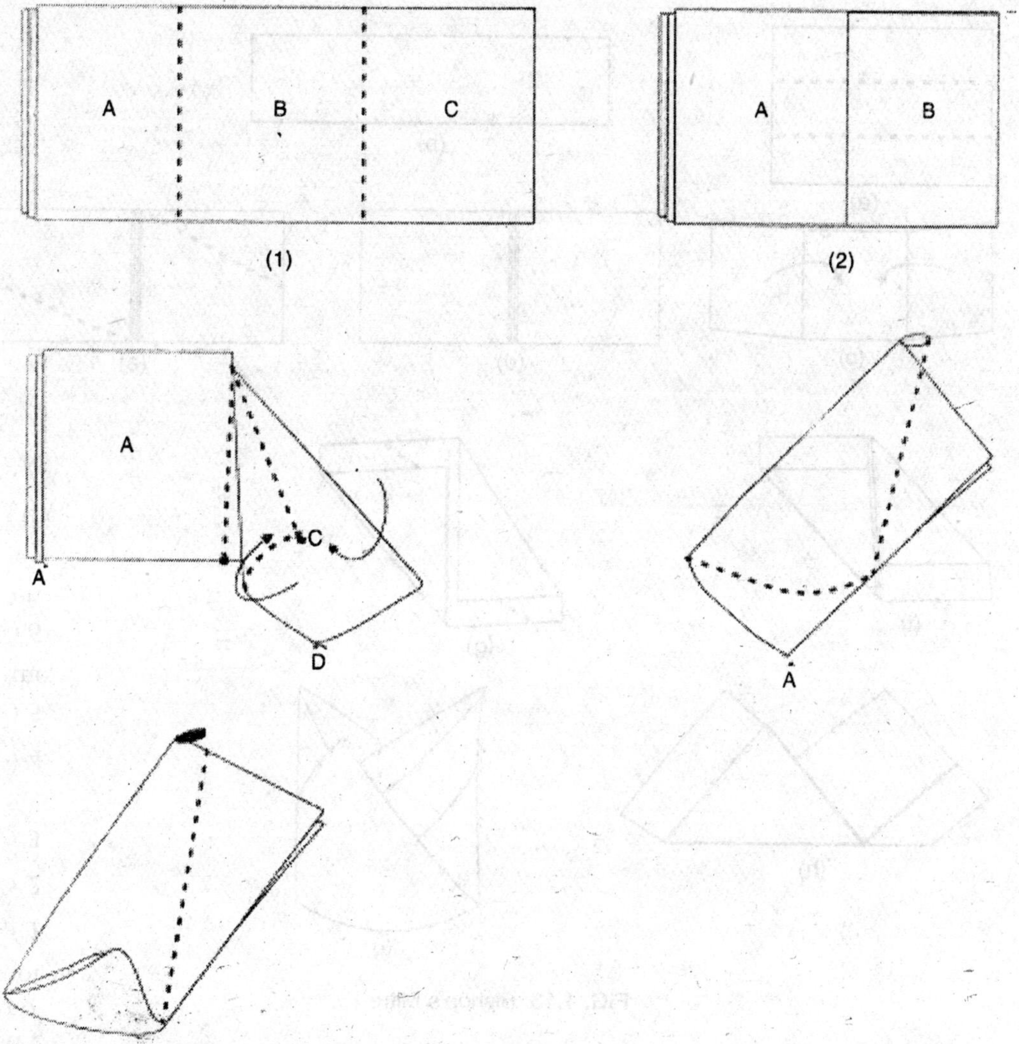

FIG. 1.12. Cornet style-2.

Method :

Step 1 : First crease the square napkin into three as indicated by dotted lines in Fig.1.13 (a)

Step 2 : Fold the lowest third over the middle one.

Step 3 : Turn the top one inward and insert it between the first two.

Step 4 : The resulting fold of the three thickness' is a rectangular shape as shown in Fig.1.13(b)

Step 5 : Crease this strip equally into four parts.

Step 6 : Open them out so that they are lying flat on the table so as to enable the two ends sections to be fitted and folded over as given in Fig. 1.13(c)

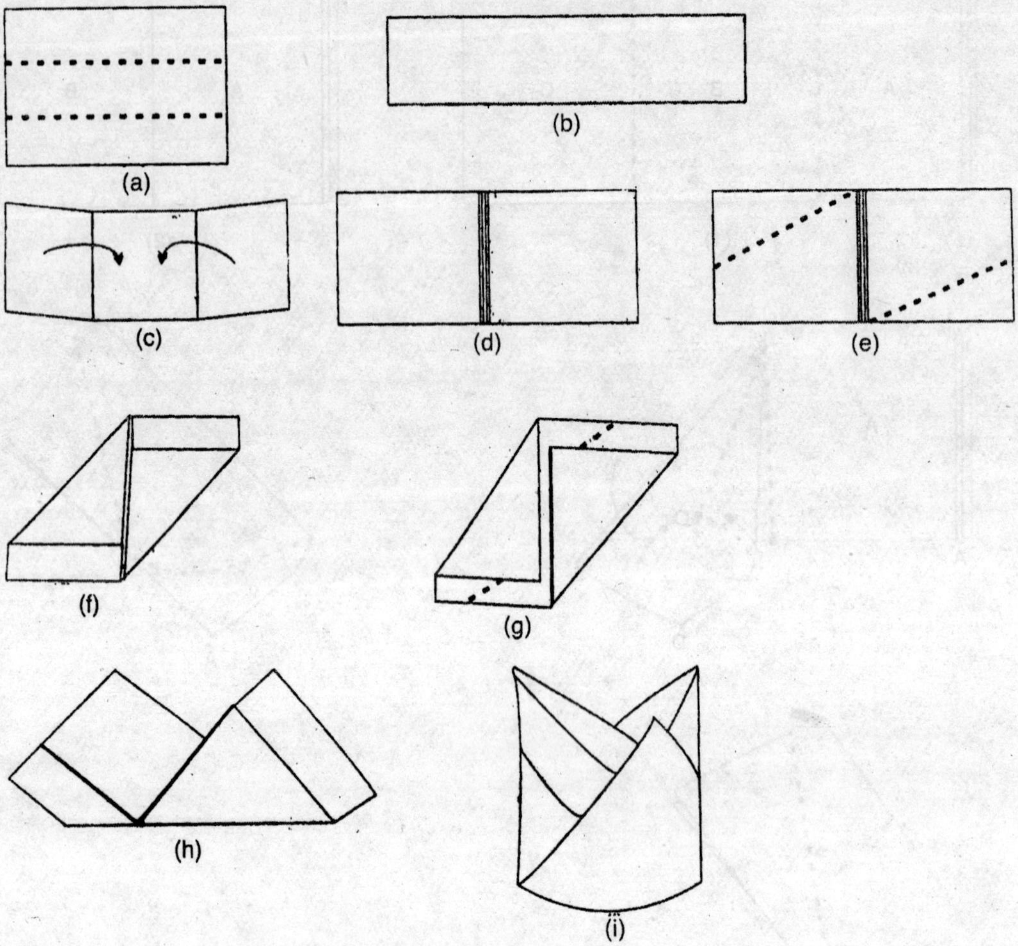

FIG. 1.13. Bishop's Mitre I

Step 7 **:** Fig. 1.13(d) Indicates how they are folded over so that the original ends of the strip have been brought together and now lie touching at the middle.

Step 8 **:** Next, grasp the strip firmly to prevent it gaping and so that the corners are creased, as shown by dotted lines in Fig. 1.13 (e)

Step 9 **:** Now, fold them over as illustrated in Fig. 1.13(f)

Step 10 **:** Crease the napkin diagonally along the middle, as indicated by the dotted lines in Fig.14(g)

Step 11 **:** Now, fold the napkin along the crease so that the two triangles emerge towards and are not turned inwards.

Step 12 **:** The napkin should now appear as shown in Fig. 1.14 (g) (the bottom line in Fig. (g) being the dotted line as shown in Fig. 1.14 (e)

Step 13 **:** To complete the design, grasp' the farthest point on the left (see Fig.1.18) and bring it up with a circular action so that its ends can be tucked into the pleats of the triangle seen towards the right. This provides the left-hand edge of the maitre.

Step 14 : Finally, take the farthest point on the right as shown in Fig.1.14 (i) and in the same way fold into the pleats of the left hand edge.

Step 15 : These steps, as given above, complete the mitre so that it showed appear as in Fig.1.14 (i).

Bishop's Maitre

1. Lay the napkin out flat in front of your (Fig. 1.12(a)
2. Fold it in half, straight side to straight side (see Fig. 1.14(b)
3. Take the top right corner and fold it down to the centre of the bottom line (see fig. 1.14(c)
4. Take the bottom left coner and fold it up to meet the centre of the top line (see fig. 1.14(d)
5. Turn the napkin over so that the folds are now face down (see fig. 1.14(e)

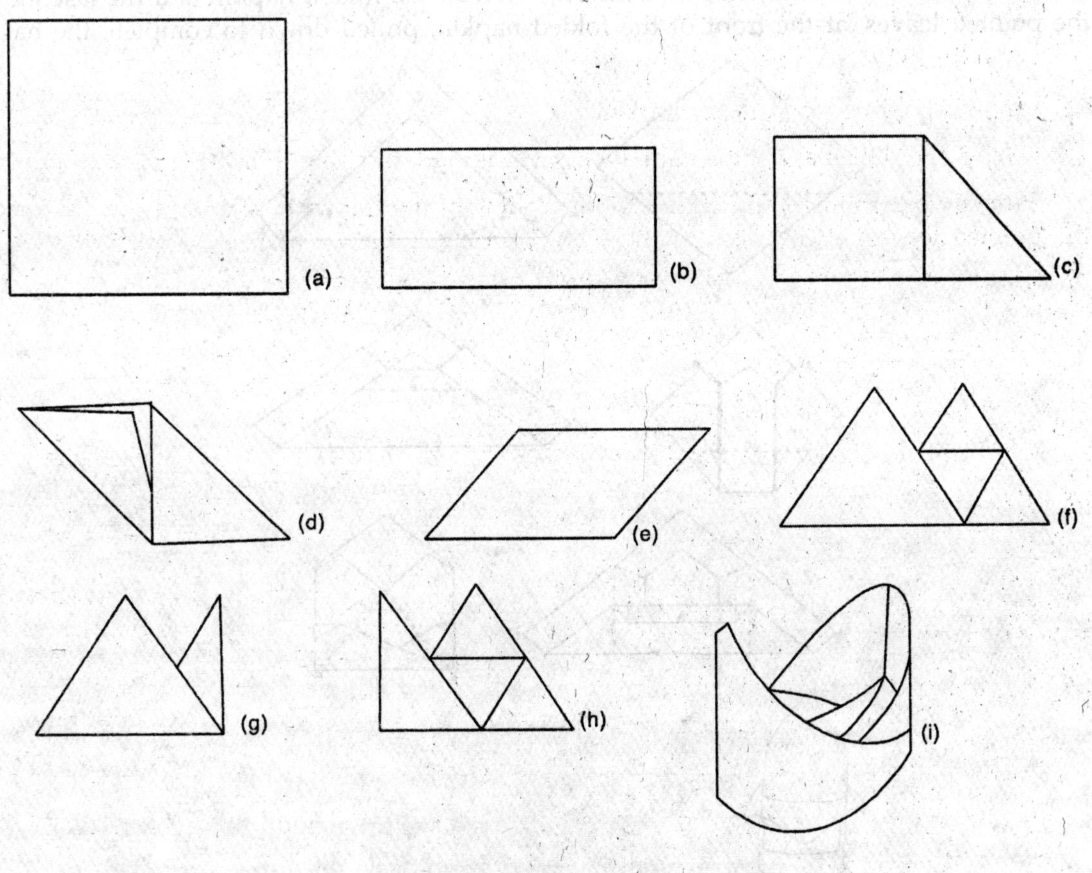

FIG. 1.14. The Bishop's Mitre II

6. Take the topline (edge) and fold it down to meet the base line (bottom edgs), leaving the two peaks pointing away from you (see fig. 1.14(f)
7. Take the bottom right-hand side and fold it cender the flap on the left side make scere it tucks right under the flap for a snceg fit (see fig.1.14(g)).
8. Turn it completely over see (fig. 1.14 (h)
9. Again take the bottom right hand side and fold it under the flap on the left side. Now stand the napkin up by pulling the sides of the base out until it is circular in shape (see fig. 1.14(i))

Bishop's Hat Style

Step 1 : Open napkin out and fold at dotted line.

Step 2 : Fold at dotted lines A and B.

Step 3 : fold base upwards at dotted line C.

Step 4: Fold down portion marked D.

Step 5 : Fold the base of the napkin backwards, and fold point E into the pleat of point F.

Step 6 : Next illustration shows the rear view of the folded napkin and the last shows the pointed leaves, at the front of the folded napkin, pulled down to complete the hat.

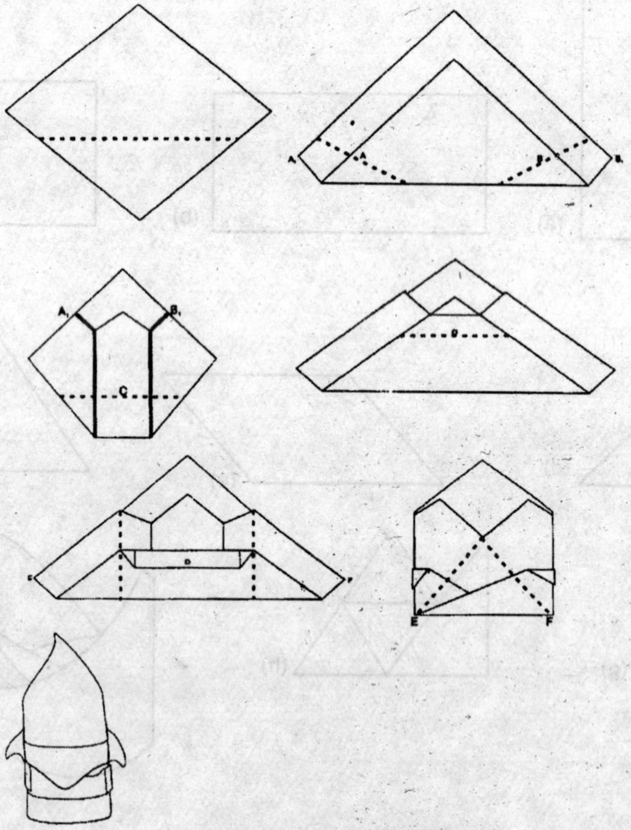

FIG. 1.15. Bishop's that

Mitre Style

Step 1 : Fold napkin in half and then fold at dotted lines (Fig. 1.16.) A and B at points. B_1 A_1

Step 2 : Turn napkin over and place horizontally.

Step 3 : Fold down at dotted line C, releasing point of flap D. fold at dotted line E and tuck $\in_1$ behind flap of δ

Step 4 : Turn napkin over and repeat, placing point D-1 behind flap of E.

Step 6 : Open napkin so that it will stand erect.

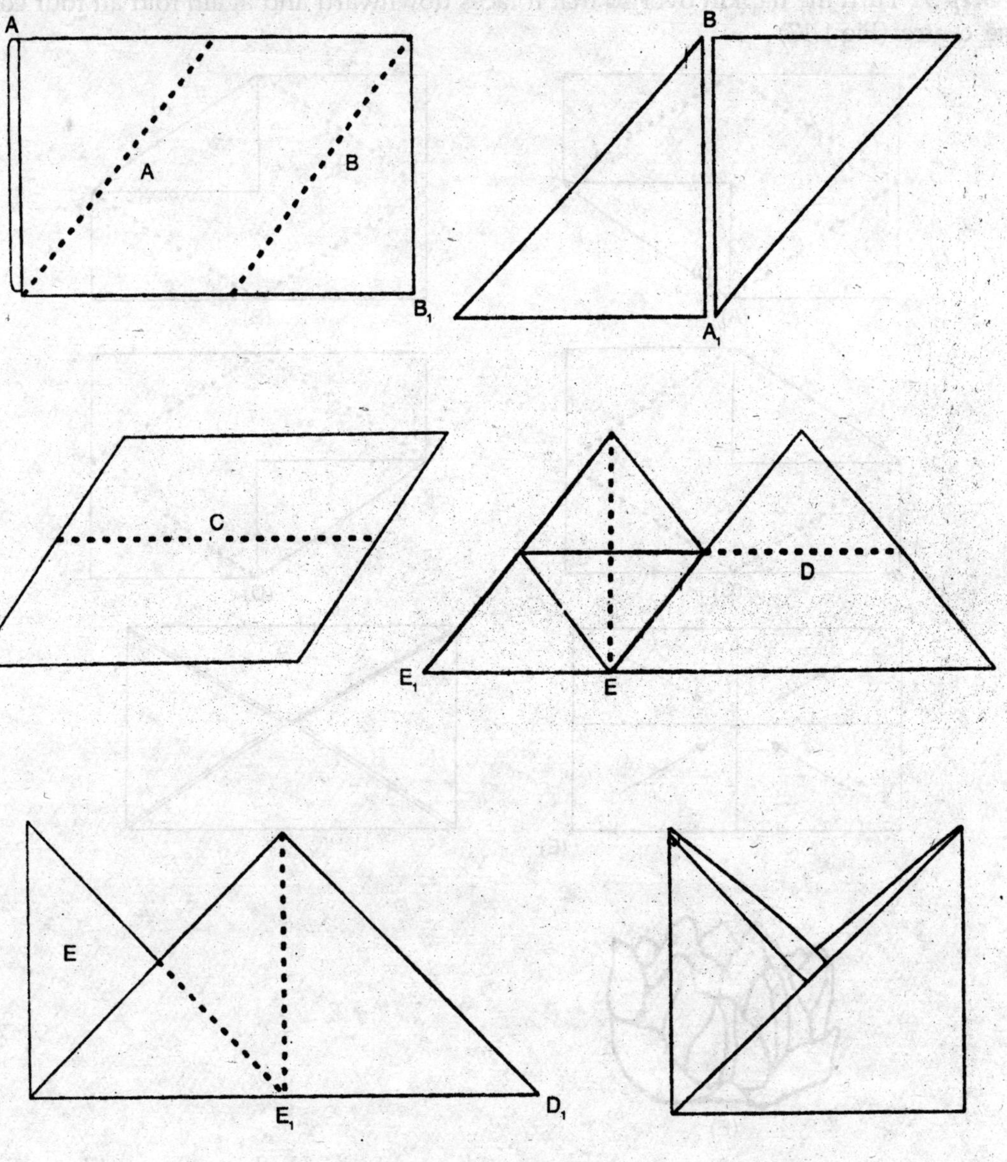

FIG. 1.16. Mitre Style

5. The Rose Style

This type of napkin is mainly used for presenting round dishes or tumblers

Method:

Step 1 : Open flat the square napkin on the table.

Step 2 : Fold the corners to the centre (Fig.1.15A)

Step 3 : Repeat this folding (Fig.1.17B)

Step 3 : Repeat this folding (Fig. 1.17C)

Step 4 : Repeat a third time (Fig.1.17D)

Step 5 : Turn the napkin over so that it faces downward and again fold all four corners to the centre (Fig.1.17)

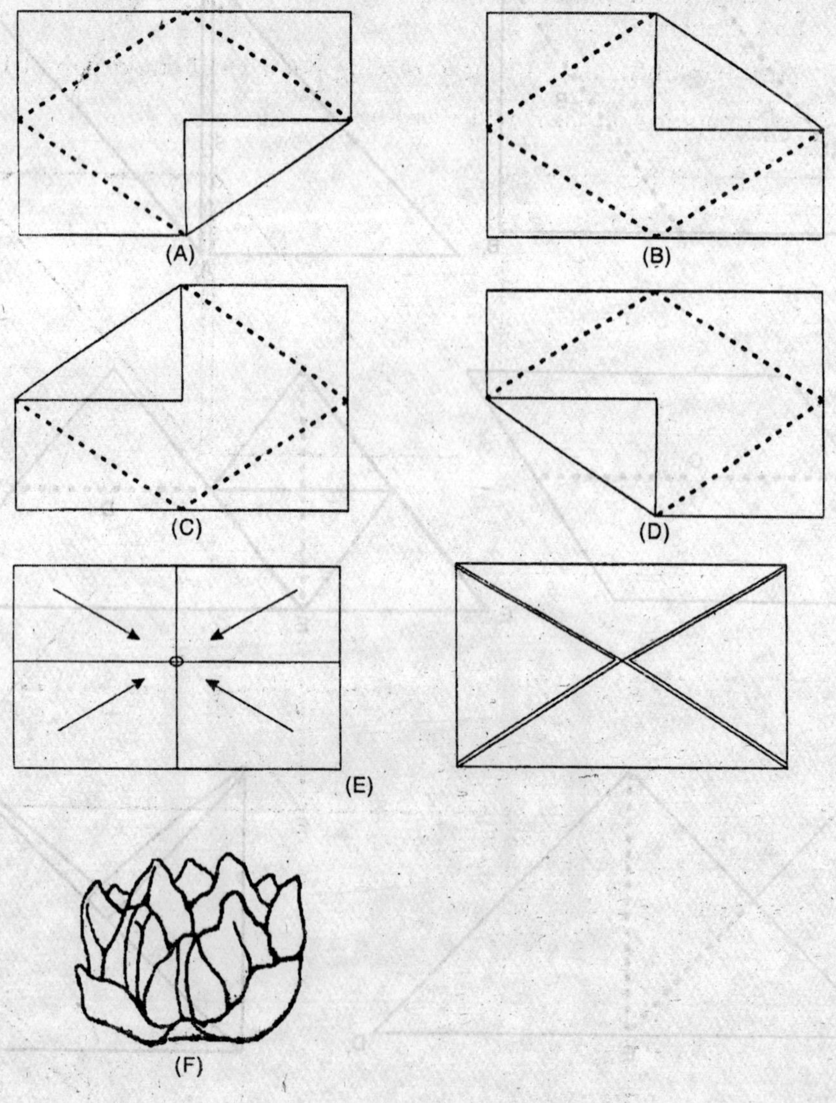

FIG. 1.17. The Rose Style I

Step 6 : Using a small cup or simply the fingers, hold the centre firm (Fig.17E)

Step 7 : Now, pull up the twelve corners from underneath so that a petal appearance results (Fig.1.17F). Corners are usually folded only twice to the centre before turning the napkin over. One set of corners is then pulled up, the napkin reversed again and the single corner turned.

4. Cockcomb

Step 1 : Open the napkin into square shape.

Step 2 : Fold it in half.

Step 3 : Fold it in half again to make a square.

Step 4 : Rotate the square so that it now forms a diamond shape in front of you. Make sure that the four single folds are at the bottom of the diamond.

Step 5 : Fold the bottom corner of the diamond to the top corner. You will then have a triangular shape in front of you, with the four single folds on top.

Step 6 : Take the right side of the triangle and fold it over on the centre line.

Step 7 : Do the same with the left-hand side.

Step 8 : Tuck the two lower triangles (A&B).

Step 9 : Under the main triangle.

Step 10 : Fold the two triangles (C&D) down from the centre line and hold it together. The four triangle folds should now be on the top and at the peak of this fold.

Step 11 : Hold this narrow fold firmly, ensuring the four single folds are away from you. In turn, pull each single fold up and towards you.

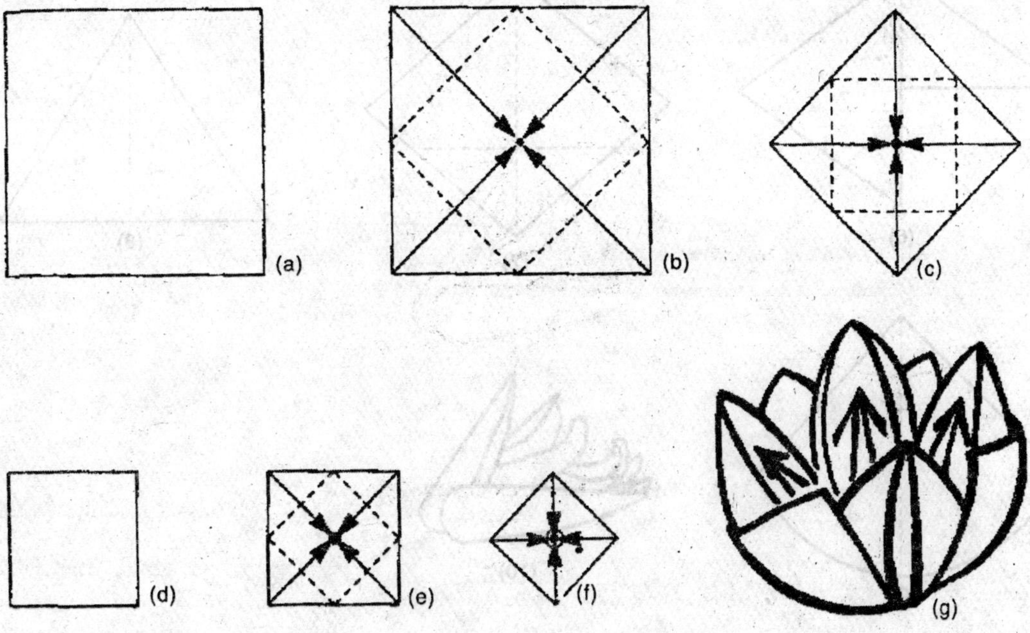

FIG. 1.18. The Rose II

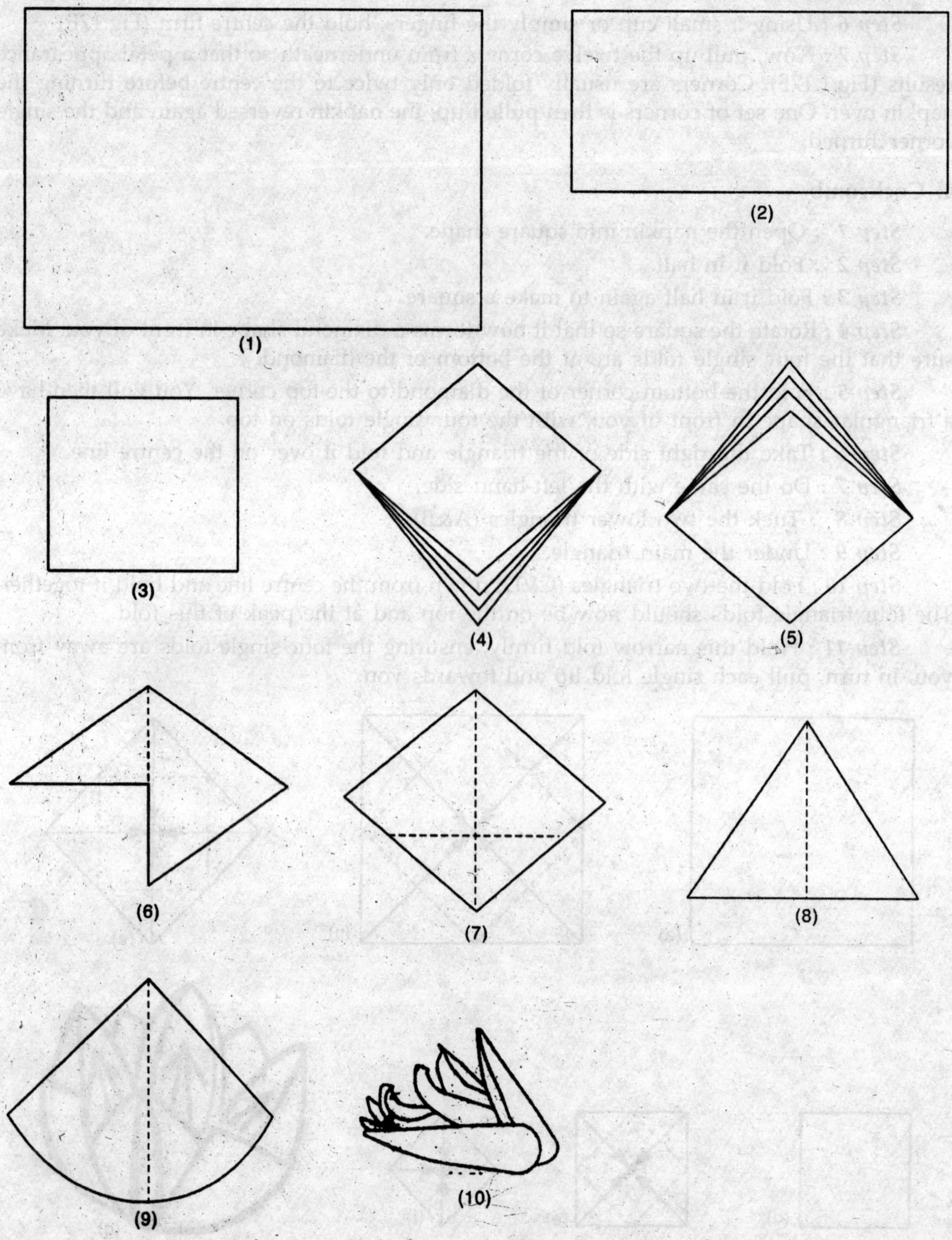

FIG. 1.19. Cock Comb Style.

5. The Fan

There are two types of fans :

(a) Simple fan
(b) Treble pleated fan.

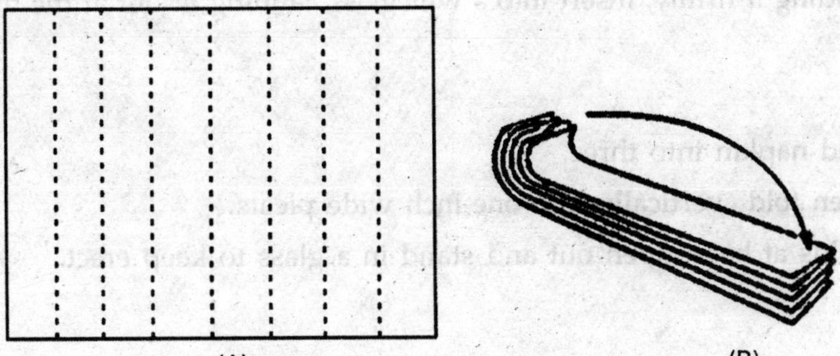

FIG. 1.20. Simple Fan

Simple Fan

Method:

Step 1 : Take a well-starched napkin.

Step 2 : Fold the napkin in three lengthwise.

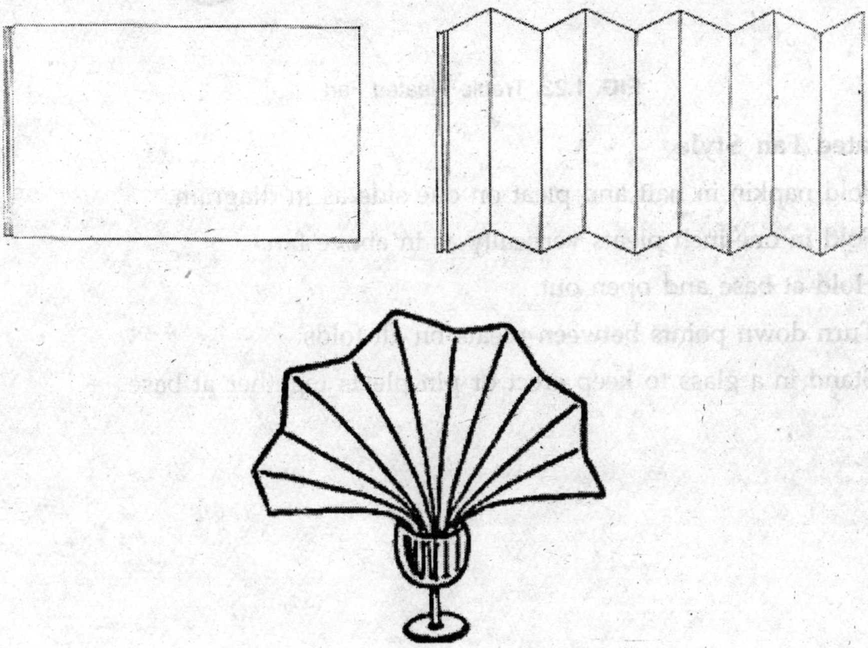

FIG. 1.21. Simple Fan

Step 3 : Pleat half of it evenly to the centre.

Step 4 : Then pleat from the other side also to the centre so that the pleats face each other.

Step 5 : Firmly flatten them down.

Step 6 : Holding it firmly, insert into a wineglass, fanning lit out at the top as given in Fig. 1.21

Fan Style

Step 1 : Fold napkin into three.

Step 2 : Then fold vertically into one-inch wide pleats.

Step 3 : Holds at base, open out and stand in a glass to keep erect.

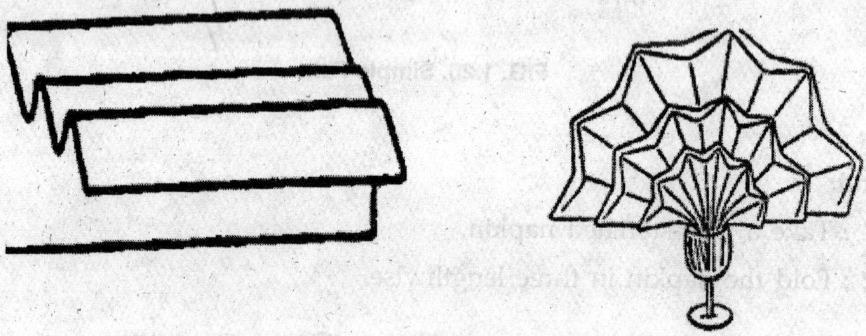

FIG. 1.22. Treble Pleated Fan

10. Treble Plated Fan Style

Step 1 : Fold napkin in half and pleat on one side as in diagram.

Step 2 : Fold in one-inch pleats vertically as in above fan.

Step 3 : Hold at base and open out.

Step 4 : Turn down points between pleats on all folds.

Step 5 : Stand in a glass to keep erect or pin pleats together at base.

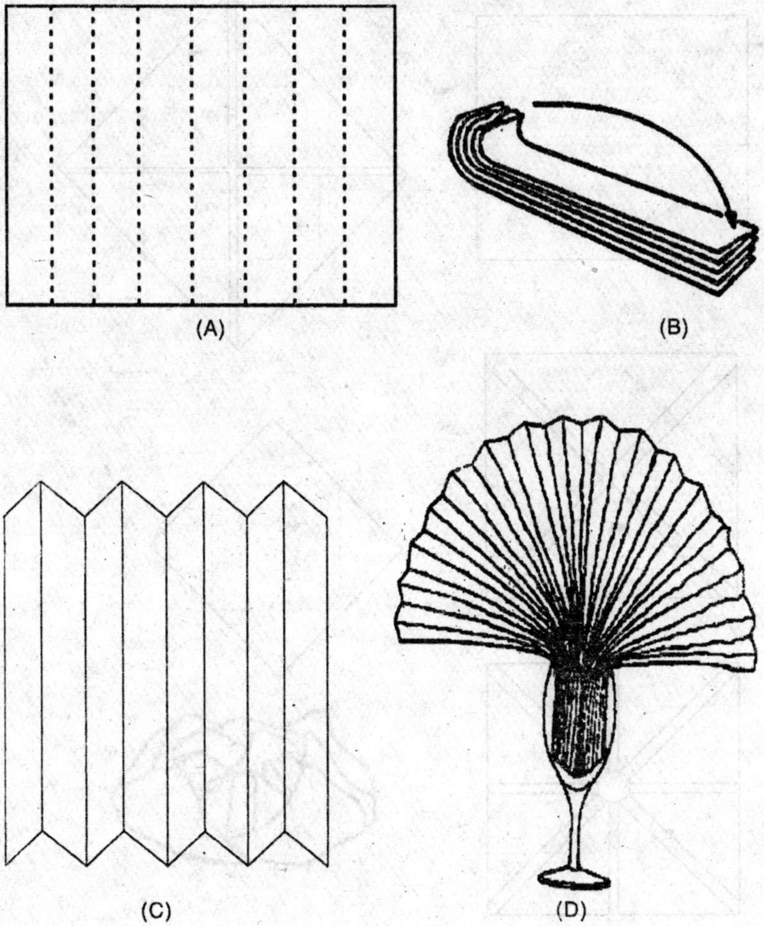

FIG. 1.23. Fan Style.

11. The Water Lily Style

Step 1 : Open napkins out and Fold corners into the centre.

Step 2 : Fold corners into the centre a second time and again a third time.

Step 3 : Turn napkin over and fold corners into the centre.

Step 4 : Hold down the points of the napkin firmly at the centre and pull out each of the points that are folded underneath to give the completed water lily.

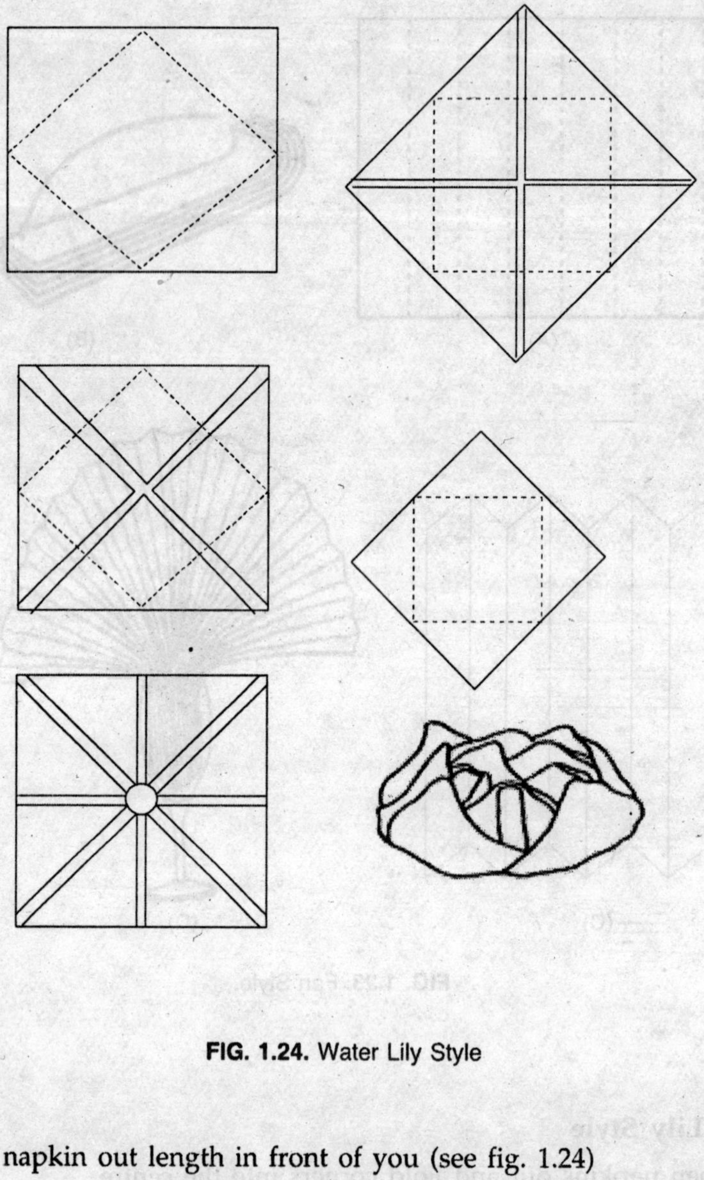

FIG. 1.24. Water Lily Style

Cone :

1. Open the napkin out length in front of you (see fig. 1.24)

2. Take the top left corner and fold it diagonally on to the right ed of the centre line (see fig. 1.24.

3. Foldthe bottom squarce on to the top tringle (see fig. 4)

4. Take the two points at the top right corner by placing year chand inside napkin and fold them back to words you as for as posseble (see fig. 1.2d)

5. Full the base out so that it is circular and placiet in the centre of the conver (see fig. 1.24 (e))

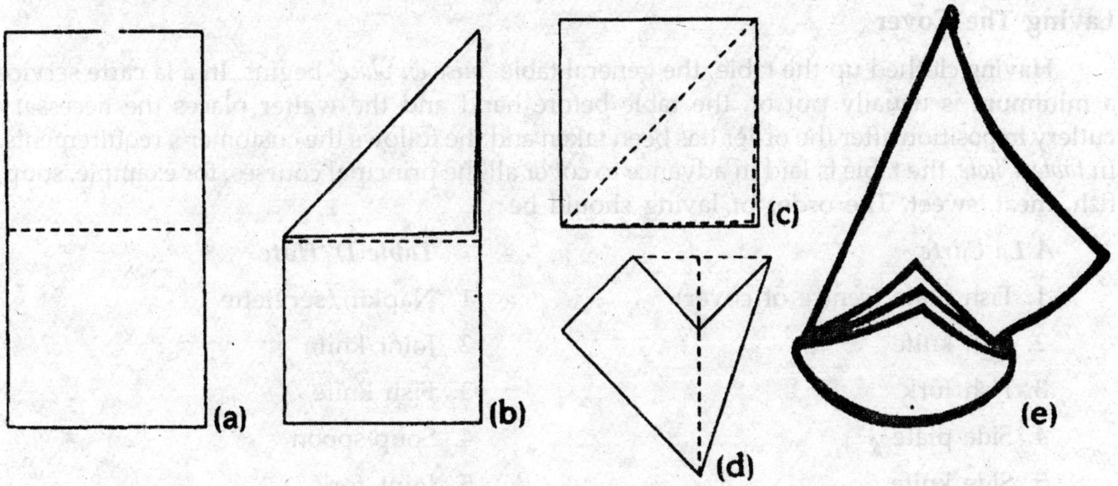

FIG. 1.25. The Cone

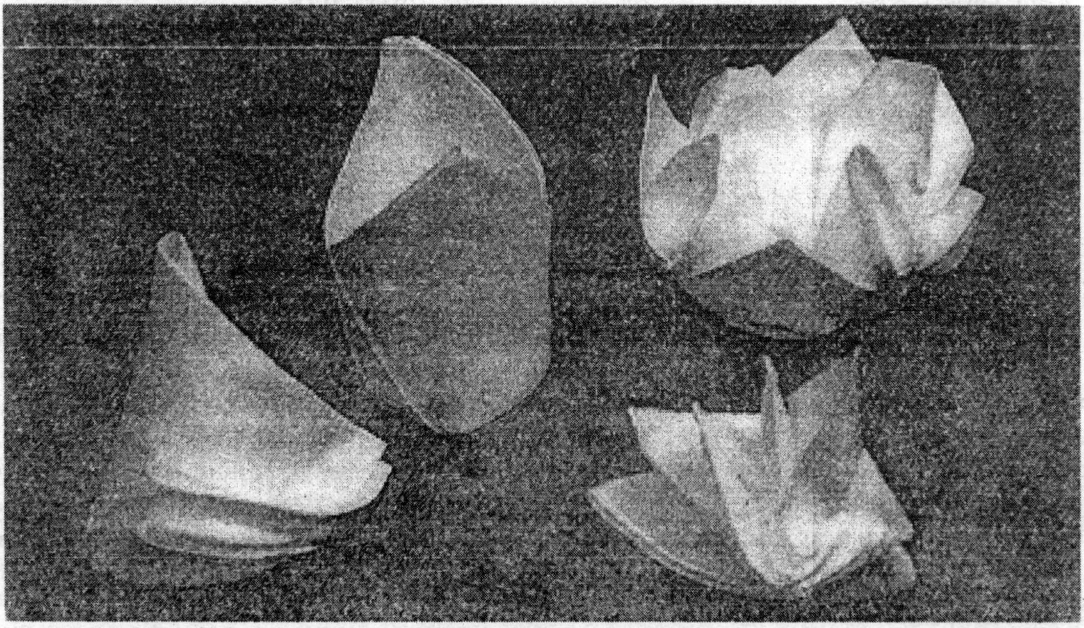

FIG. 1.26. Sample of different Napkin Folds

THE COVER

There are two definitions of the term 'cover'. Firstly, it means how many guests a restaurant or dining room will seat, or how many guest will be attending in certain cocktail party, *i.e.*, total number of guests. Secondly, it refers to the space setting when laying a table in readiness for service. In other words, a cover denotes the entire necessary cutlery, flatware, crockery, glassware and linen necessary to lay a certain type of place setting for a specific meal.

Laying The Cover

Having clothed up the table, the general table *'mise en place'* begins. In a la carte service a minimum is usually put on the table before hand and the waiter places the necessary cutlery in position after the order has been taken and the follows the customer's requirements. In *table d 'hote,* the table is laid in advance to cover all the principal courses, for example, soup, fish, meat, sweet. The order of laying should be :

A La Carte

1. Fish plate (centre of cover)
2. Fish knife
3. Fish fork
4. Side plate
5. Side knife
6. Napkin / serviette
7. Paris goblet
8. Wine glass

Table D' Hote

1. Napkin/serviette
2. Joint knife
3. Fish knife
4. Soup spoon
5. Joint fork
6. Fish fork
7. Sweet fork
8. Sweet spoon
9. Side plate
10. Side knife
11. Paris goblet
12. Wine glass

A LA Carte Cover

A la carte cover is normally laid in a good class restaurant, dinning room or hotel in readiness for service of either luncheon or dinner. This cover follows the principle that the cutlery and flatware for each course will be laid just before each course is served. The traditional cover, given below, therefore represents i. cover for hors-d'oeurre, which is the first course in a classic menu sequence. There are now a variety of differing approaches to what is laid for this form of service. This can include using large decorative cover places and a side plate and knife only, or replacing the fish knife and fork with a joint knife and fork. It should consist of the following :

1. Fish plate
2. Serviette
3. Fish knife
4. Fish fork
5. Side plate
6. Side knife
7. Wine glass.

FIG. 1.26. Example of a Typical 'A LA CARTE COVER'

Table D'Hote Cover

This is a place setting normally laid in a good class restaurant, dinning room, hotel, medium-sized hotel or departmental store, in readiness for service of either luncheon or dinner.

1. Serviette
2. Soup spoon
3. Fish knife
4. Fish fork
5. Joint knife
6. Joint fork
7. Sweet spoon
8. Sweet fork
9. Side plate
10. Side knife
11. Winegg lass.

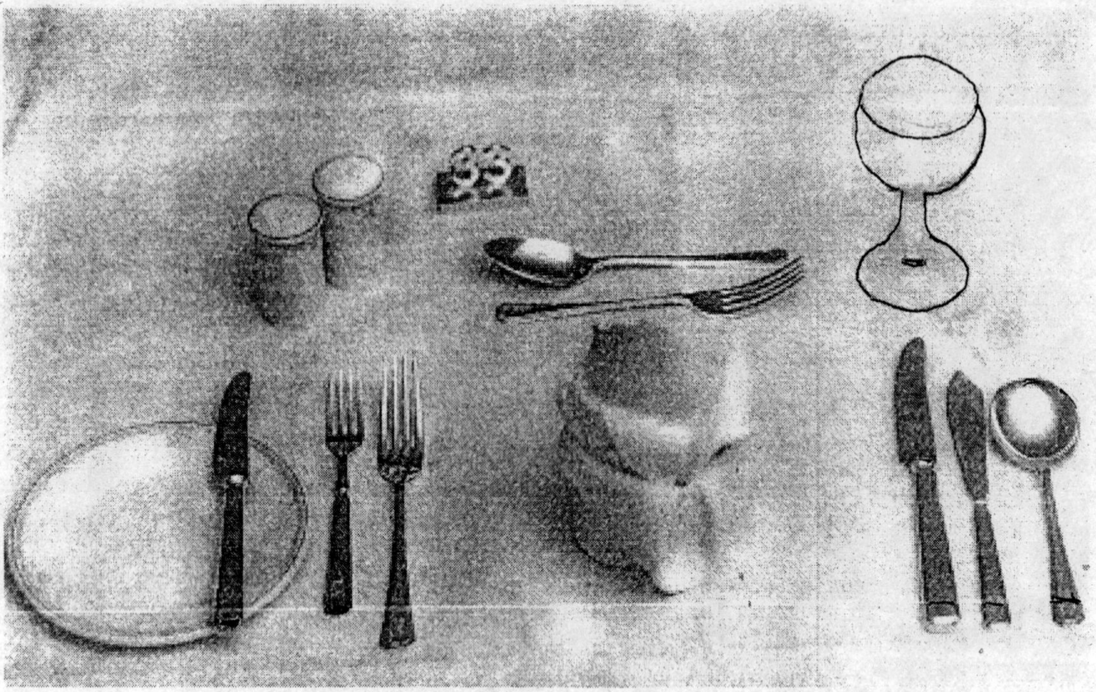

FIG. 1.27. Example of a Typical Table d'Hote Cover

This cover follows the principle chat the cutlery and flatware for each course will be laid just before each course is served. The traditional cover, given below, therefore represents i. cover for hors-d'oeurre, which is the first course in a classic menu sequence. There are now a variety of differing approaches to what is laid for this form of service. This can include using large decorative cover places and a side plate and knife only, or replacing the fish knife and fork with a joint knife and fork. It would consist of the following:

Once the table is clothed-up it should be laid in readiness for service.

- If an a la carte cover is being laid then the first item set on the table should be the fish plate in the centre of each cover
- If a table d'hote cover is being laid then the first item to be set on the table should be the serviette or sideplate in the centre of each cover
- If the sideplate were laid in the centre of each cover it would be moved to the left-hand side of the cover once all the cutlery and flatware had been laid. The purpose of initially placing something in the centre of the cover is to ensure that the covers are exactly opposite one another and that the cutlery and flatware of each cover are the same distance apart .
- Cutlery and flatware should be laid from a service salver or service plate. An alternative to this is to use a service cloth and hold the items being laid in the service cloth, giving a final polish before setting the items on the table.

In some instances a cutlery trolley is used for scoring the cutlery and flatware and this should be pushed around the cables and then the cutlery and flatware laid after the final polish with the waiter's cloth.

When laying a table d'hote cover, the cutlery and flatware should be laid from inside to the outside of the cover. This ensures even spacing of the cover and normally lessens the chances of having to handle the items laid more than is necessary.

After the covers have been laid, the cable lay-up should be completed by che addition of the following items :

1. Cruets
2. Ashtrays may be laid upon request from the customer depending on the establishment policy.
3. Table numbers
4. Table decorations

The waiter must ensure that where applicable all cuclery and flatware is laid 1.25 cm (1/2 in.) from the edge of the table and that badged crockery has the badge or crest at the head or top of che cover. The glass after polishing should be placed upside down at the top right-hand corner of the cover. Once the covers have been laid the table accompaniments should be placed on the table according to the custom of the house.

Where an a la carte cover has been laid, the cutlery and flatware required by the guest for the dishes he/she has chosen will be laid course by course. In other words there should not, at any time during che meal, be more cutlery and flatware on the table than is required by che guest at that specific time.

If decorative cover places are used for an a la carte cover it is common for che first course places to be placed on this place. The first course and rhe cover plate are then removed when the First course is cleared.

Table Accompaniments

Complete the table layout by the addition of the following items. The table accompaniments for both *'a la carte* 'and *table d'hote* cover are same as given below :

1. Cruets — salt, pepper, mustard and mustard spoon
2. Ashtrays
3. Table numbers
4. Table decorators/vase of flowers.

Ensure that all cutlery and flatware is laid 1.25 cm (1/2 in.) from the edge of the table and that badged crockery has the badge or crest at the head or top of the cover. The glasses after polishing should be placed upside down at the top right-hand corner of the cover. Thereafter, accompaniments should be placed on the table according to the custom of the house. In some establishments, following items are placed on the table' prior to the service to complete its lay up :

1. Roll basket
2. Melba toasts

3. Gristicks
4. Cayenne peppers
5. Pepper mill
6. Butter pats.

General Guidelines for Laying a Cover

1. Place 'show plates' (entree plates) at each cover about 5 to 10 mm (1/4 to 1/2 in.) from the edge of the table and centre to the chair.

2. Clean polished cutlery should be carried on a salver covered with clean cloth when guests are present during service. Handling only at the base, place the cutlery at the correct position round the table. Follow the following procedure :

(i) Knives on the right or forks on the left with space between them determined by the 'show' entree plate.

(ii) Set the cutlery in the order in which items will be used. The first to be needed by the guest are laid in the outer position.

(iii) Place knife with the sharp edge turned to the cover plate.

(iv) Place forks with prongs turned up away from the cloth.

(v) If a 'show plate' is not used, the distance between the inside knife and fork should be a good 250-mm (9-in.).

FIG. 1.28. A — Table Setting

(vi) Sweet or dessert silver spoon and forks, when set are laid horizontally at the top of the cover and should also be about 250mm from the table edge.

(vii) Thus, the space should be about 250 mm square.

(viii) Those knives, forks and spoons set at the right and left side of the cover should be near one another but without actually touching and about 10 mm (½ in.) from the edge of the table (except for fish forks on *table d'hote* cover).

(ix) Spoons are placed at right of the first knife to be used (unless an *hors d'oeuvre* knife and fork are laid). However, except at functions a knife and fork for *hors d' oeuvre* is not usually laid on the table, but brought on a napkin - covered plates as required).

(x) Dessert spoons and forks are set for *table d'hote* service and functions and are then placed horizontally at the head of the cover.

(xi) No knife, fork or spoon should be laid unless the meal requires it, that is, do not lay covers until the menu has been studied.

(xii) Tableware should not be spread out. Cutlery should be grouped closely.

Basic single cover for luncheon or dinner with single glass is given in fig. 1.27. Note the position of the water or red wine glass which is always above the tip of the meat knife.

FIG. 1.29. A Table Setting, a cover showing aditional wine glass

A similar basic cover showing additional wine glasses. Three glasses may be laid diagonally as shown but if six different glasses are to be laid they should be arranged in a triangle (with the sherry glass at the near point to the guest and the wine to he used first on the right of the triangle, the others to the left).

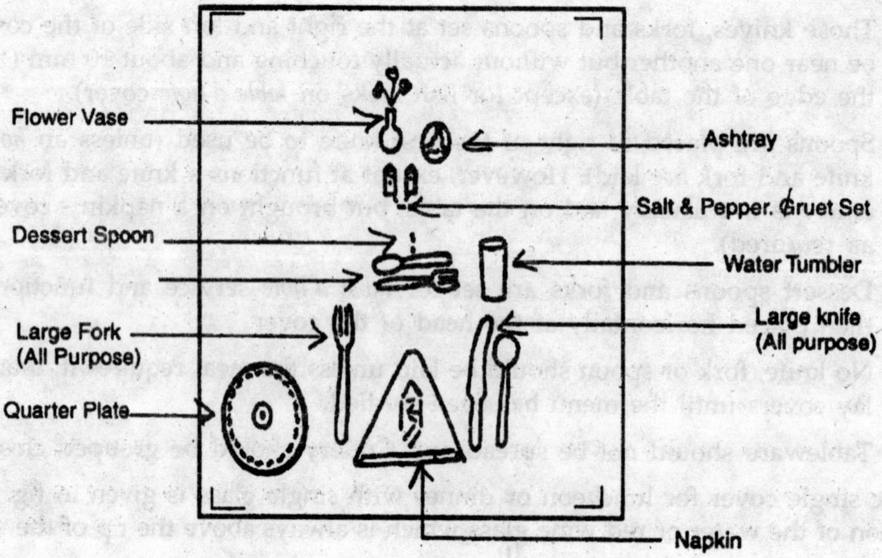

FIG. 1.30. Standard Restaurant Cover

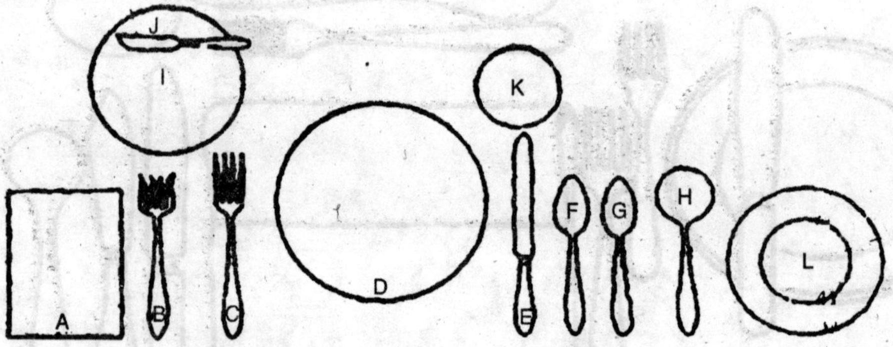

FIG. 1.31. Table Diagram of a Cover

A. Napkin
B. Salad Fork
C. Dinner Fork
D. Service Plate
E. Dinner Knife
F. Teaspoon
G. Teaspoon
H. Soup Spoon
I. Bread and Butter Plate
J. Bread and Butter Knife
K. Water Goblet
L. Coffee Cup

BREAKFAST COVERS

The *breakfast covers* divided into two types. These are:

1. Full breakfast cover
2. Continental breakfast cover

Cover for a Full Breakfast

The full breakfast consists of a number of courses, usually three or four, with a choice of dishes from within each course, as shown on the specimen full breakfast menu above. The cover will therefore include some or all of the following :

1. The cover laid is a table d'hote cover without the soup spoon
2. The positioning of the items is for the convonience at the guest

FIG. 1.32. Example of a Full Breakfast Cover

3. Joint knife and fork
4. Fish knife and fork
5. Sweet spoon and fork
6. Side knife
6. Sideplate
7. Tea or breakfast cup, saucer and teaspoon
8. Slop basin
9. Tea strainer
10. Sugar basin and tongs
11. Stands or underplates for teapot/coffee pot and hot water jug/hot milk jug
12. Salt, pepper
13. Caster sugar in shaker
14. Napkin
15. Ashtray (depending on smoking policy)
16. Table number

FIG. 1.33. A breakfast tray laid for a continental breakfast

FIG. 1.34. Room service tables

QUESTIONS AND ASSIGNMENTS

Objective Type

Q. 1. Choose the correct answer:

(a) The type of service characterized by the serving of guests from huge platters of food by a waiter is :

(i) American service (ii) French service

(iii) English service (iv) Russian service.

(b) The type of service in which the menu number of guests and time of service are predetermined in advance is a (an)

(i) Banquet (ii) Buffet

(iii) Family style dinner (iv) English style dinner.

(c) Smorgasbord service is similar to :

(i) Banquet service (ii) Buffet service

(iii) French service (iv) English service.

(d) A side stand is

(i) Tray stand (ii) Coat rack

(iii) Storage and service unit (iv) Waiter and waitress lounge.

(e) When food on a menu is a la carte, it is :

(i) Served from a cart (ii) Served with a beverage

(iii) Priced to include an entire meal (iv) Listed as single item and priced separately from other food items.

(f) Juices, fruits and seafood items are examples of foods included in the following category:

(i) Appetizer (ii) Salad

(iii) Dessert (iv) Entree.

(g) Closing the dinning room involves duties such as :

(i) Asking the remaining guests to leave.

(ii) Setting up the tables for the next morning business

(iii) Discarding voided checks

(iv) Turning off all heating equipment such as roll warmers and coffee urns.

(h) The sequence of serving the courses during a meal is as follows :

(i) Appetizer, dessert, entree, salad

(ii) Salad, appetizer, entree, dessert

(iii) Entree, appetizer, salad, dessert

(iv) Appetizer, salad, entree, dessert

(i) To serve booths

(i) Serve the guest farthest from you first with the hand farthest from the guest

(ii) Serve the guest farthest from you with the hand closet to the guest.

(iii) Serve the guest closet to you first with the hand farthest from the guest.

(iv) Serve the guest to closet to you first with the hand closet to the guest.

(j) When serving more than one table, choose the order of serving the following foods from your tray so that proper food temperatures will be maintained :

(i) Ice cream, crackers, hot rolls

(ii) Crackers, ice cream, hot rolls

(iii) Hot rolls, crackers, ice cream

(iv) Ice cream, hot rolls, crackers.

(k) Two ways a guest check may be presented to the customer are :
   (i) Face up on the table on a face down on a tip tray
   (ii) Face up on the table and a face down up on a tip tray
   (iii) Face down on the table and face down on a tip tray
   (iv) Face down on the table and face up on the tip tray.

(l) French service is characterized by -
   (i) Food being plated in the kitchen.
   (ii) Food being dished up on plates by the host.
   (iii) Foods being cooked in front of guest and served by two waiters.
   (iv) Goods being served from large platters by one waiter.

Ans : (a) i; (b) i; (c) ii; (d) iii; (e) iv; (f) i; (g) ii; (h) iv; (i) i; (j) iv; (k) i; (l) iv. (BHM)

Q. 2. Fill in the blanks with correct word or words to complete the sentence :

(a) A section of the dinning room that has a seating for a dozen or more guests at tables, booths or counter seats and is assigned to one waiter or waitress is a (an)............

(b) A second table cloth or padding beneath the top cloth is called a (an)..............

(c) A left-over seasonal dish, chef's specialty is called a (an)............

(d) Condiments, decorative garnishes and foods that complement the entree are called.............

(e) A method of taking orders in which your simple check the designated section is called a (an)............

(f) Making suggestions benefits the restaurant by increasing the size of the check and benefits the server by increasing the size of the ....

(g) If guests at a table order beef burgundy, filet mignon, lobster Newburg and ribs of beef, you would submit the ....order to the kitchen first, followed the other three orders, so all four orders are done at the same time.

(h) Clear dishes from the ....of the guest with the ....hand.

(i) Stack dishes on trays so that they are ....

Ans : (a) Station; (b) soliner; (c) specialty; (d) accompaniments; (e) checking system; (f) tip; (g) Beef burgundy; (h) right, right: (i) safe. (BHM)

Q. 3. Fill in the blanks with correct word or words :

(a) Size of a four covers square table is ....

(b) Name five banquet tools: (1)......... (2)........ (3)...........(4)..........(5)..................

(c) Banquet Memorandum means .... (Function Sheet/Banquet Diary/Function Prospectus).

(d) Capacity of Margarita (a stemware) is .... (5 oz/oz / 6 oz).

(e) Air space at top of a wine barrel due to evaporation or leakage is called

(f) In a formal banquet toasting is done at the beginning of dinner or at the middle with rest course or at the end of dinner. (Choose the appropriate one).

(g) Henry Charpentier accidentally invented flambe dish in the year ....

(h) For a buffet service of 300-pax total space required would be .... sq. ft. (BHM)

Q. 4. Fill in the blanks :

(a) Capacity of Jeroboam is ....

(b) Standard dimension of a cover is ....

(c) Length of the tablecloth for a 30-ft. long table is ....

(d) Champagne bottles are racked in a special rack called ....

(e) Cabernet Sauvignon is the most important variety of grapes grown in ______.

(f) Crepe suzette was invented by .... in the year ....

(g) Trolleys are fitted with Casters /Castors /Coasters (chose the correct word).

(h) .... sugar is used to make banana flambe.

(i) French term for junior station waiter is ....

(j) Length of the top table for seating 15 people is 30′ 40′ 45′ 50′ (chose the correct one).

(BHM)

Q. 5. Answer briefly:

(a) How many metres of table cloth material required to stitch 100 tableclothes for 36" × 36" table and 50-table cloth for 36" × 60" table, if the table cloth selected is of 54" width?

(b) What are the accompaniments for Tomato Juice and Fruit Juice ?

(c) List the items in a room service tray to serve tea for 2-persons.

(d) Name 10-properietory sauces used in the restaurant and explain why they are not recommended to be served in the sauce boat.

(e) Explain the service of espresso coffee. (BHM)

Q. 6. State whether the following statements are True or False:

(a) A bad occupancy ratio is better indication of capacity utilization from room occupancy.

(b) A room occupancy percentage is the same thing as a house count.

(c) Liquidity ratio is an indicator of a bank balance of a company.

(d) Current ratio expresses a relationship between CA & CL.

(e) The higher the room occupancy the higher the average room rate.

(f) Industrial canteens have English service.

(g) For Airline catering the cooking is done in the galley.

(h) *Maitre d' hotel* is the French term for Headwaiter.

(i) The capacity of teacup is approx. 200 ml. [BHM]

Q. 7. Identify the Staff requirements for a five star hotel coffee shop (service staff only) and prepare a duty roaster for two weeks with the following assumptions :

(a) 100-covers divided into 4-stations

(b) Seat turnover : for break-fast (Buffet only)

(c) 1.5 lunch , dinner and evening snacks - 1 each;

(d) After dinner snacks - 0.5

(e) Hours of operation :

Breakfast	:	07.00 to 11.00 hrs.
Lunch	:	11.00 to 15.00 hrs.
Evening snack	:	15.00 to 19.00 hrs.
Dinner	:	19.00 to 24.00 hrs.
And Midnight snacks from	:	0000 to 0700 Hrs.

Assume additional′ data, if required. [BHM]

Q 8. Answer the following :

(a) If the allowance along the cover is 2 feet per person, the member of people who may be seated at a round table 3- feet in diameter is .... ?

(b) What is the correct overlap of a tablecloth allowed all around the table? The size of a tablecloth to fit a table 2' 6" (76 cm) is .... ? [BHM]

Essay Type

Q. 9. Draw the layout of a still room connected to a restaurant of 150-covers and is open for 3-major meals. In not more than 50-words explain the importance of a still room. [BHM]

Q.10. Name three pieces of equipment, which would come under each of the following headings :

(a) Cutlery, (b) Flatware, (c) Hollowware.

Q. 11. Name six napkin folds.

Q. 12. State two reasons why it is necessary to write out a 'retour'/enplace food check.

Q. 13. What would a slip cloth be used for ?

Q. 14. With the help of a neat diagram explain the functions of a sideboard.

Q. 15. Answer the following :

(a) Advantages of a serving position in a food arid beverage establishment.

(b) Qualifications for a serving position.

(c) Knowledge of the organizational setup of personnel in a restaurant.

Q. 16. (a) Observe the waiters/ress in a food and beverage establishment/restaurant in five-star hotel and note whether the appearance of the servers is satisfactory or unsatisfactory.

(b) Arrange a group discussion and decide the rest course of action to handle the following situations :

(i) You have come down with a bad cold the night before you have to go to work.

(ii) You are an above-average server and feel the policy of sharing tips equally with fellow workers is unfair.

(iii) The chef has made a mistake on your order.

Q. 17. You are requested to design a waiter/ress self-evaluation sheet. List both personality and appearance qualifications for serving position down the left side of the paper sheet and think of other qualifications you can add. At the bottom of the right hand side, a list a rating scale of poor, fair, good and excellent. Rate yourself by checking the appropriate column for each qualification. Set the goal to improve yourself in all areas not marked good or excellent

Q. 18. Define the following terms: -

(a) Special

(b) Silencer

(c) Side stand

(d) Station

(e) Study of menu.

Q. 19. Explain the methods of food preparation and preparation times. Why may preparation times vary from one restaurant to another?

Q. 20. Discuss the advantages and disadvantages of cabinet doors for concealing the shelves of a side stand.

Q. 21. Explain the procedure for keeping he side stand replenished on a routine basis.

Q. 22. Explain the several methods of assigning station to servers.

Q. 23. Assuming that you are employed in a restaurant, list all the closing duties that you can think of or that must be done in your restaurant. Post these in the kitchen and make regular habit of checking them off at the end of the day.

Q. 24. Study a menu of an Indian restaurant and consult with the chef in order to do the following :

(a) Identify the main ingredients of each food item.

(b) Describe the methods of food preparation for each food item.

(c) Identify the preparation time necessary to cook or prepare each food item.

(d) Name the meal accompaniments that go with each food item.

Q. 25. Visit some of the local restaurants and study their menu. Identify the following parts :

(a) Items those are a la carte.

(b) Items that are table d' hote.

(c) Grouping of food and the number and kind of sections in each group.

Q. 26. Visit a local restaurant in a hotel of your locality and list the opening duties and divide them among the servers who work in the morning hours. You may rotate groups of duties so as the waiter/ress can be responsible for a variety of jobs on different days.

Q. 27. Ask one trainee to demonstrate how to place a tablecloth on a table in a professional manner. Repeat this process with the centre items on the table. Then have the trainee demonstrate how to remove the tablecloth with and without centre items on the table. Now have all trainees try this procedure.

Q. 28. Differentiate between :
(a) English and American Service.
(b) KOTand BOT
(c) Crockery and Cutlery
(d) *Mise-en-place and Mise-en-scene.*

Q. 29. Calculate the space required for a 120-pax format comb shape seating arrangement with a neat drawing of the arrangement in which the top table has 11-covers. [BHM]

Q. 30. Differential between *(any five):*
(a) Mise-en-place and Mise-en-scene
(b) Chef de rang and Chef de etage
(c) Sommelier and Aboyeur
(d) Continental Breakfast and English breakfast
(e) Cona coffee and Espresso coffee
(f) Brunch and Supper.

Q. 31. Make a comparative study of having a cashier with the system of having servers keep their own receipts. Discuss the advantages and disadvantages of each situation.

Q. 32. French service is characterized by -
(a) Food being plated in the kitchen.
(b) Food being dished up on plates by the host.
(c) Foods being cooked in front of guest and served by two waiters.
(d) Goods being served from large platters by one waiter.

Q. 33. Compare the cuisine of Punjab with Kamataka, Tamil Nadu and Kashmir. Limit your answer within 250-words. In three or four lines each, explain the following :
(a) Hollandaise
(b) Sorbet
(c) EPNS
(d) Garnish
(e) Canape
(f) K.O.T.A.
(g) Gueridon
(h) Baise.

Q. 34. Discuss the view that successful catering today seems to rely increasingly on the use of statistical and financial analysis to the extent that, managers can no longer afford the time to develop their personal flair and traditional skills. [HCIMA (London)]

Q. 35. As catering Manager of a food and beverage unit of your choice, suggest steps you would take to increase and sustain the volume of profitable business.

Q. 36. Examine current trends in food production and service. To what extent do you feel technology will influence the catering industry in the future? [HCIMA (London)]

Q. 37. To what extent do you judge that in order to satisfy profit targets today, the catering industry has misjudged long-term consumer, expectations by reducing 'service' so drastically that it could never be reintroduced ? [HCIMA (London)]

Q. 38. What are the problems that you are likely to face as a Caterer, specializing in off premises catering? What steps would you take to counter these problems? [BHM]

Q. 39. As a private party caterer, you are required to prepare an indent (list of raw materials with quantities) for a silver wedding anniversary for a group of 500 (five hundred) People. The function is in the evening on an open ground during the month of December. What are the factors that you would consider while preparing the indent? Give reasons. [BHMs]

Q. 40. Make a duty roster showing duty schedule for one week for the following staff of a specialilty restaurant operating only for Lunch and Dinner. One Manager, Two Sr. Captains, Five Captains and Twelve Stewards. [BHM]

Q. 41. Make a duty roster showing the various *mise en place jobs to* be carried out by different waiting staff of a restaurant on daily basis. [BHM]

2 Food and Beverages Service Techniques

After learning this lesson, you should be able :

1. *Describe and practice various types of service producer; such as*
   (a) *French Service*
   (b) *Russian Service*
   (c) *English Service*
   (d) *American Service*
   (e) *Buffet Service*
   (f) *Salad bars*
   (g) *Counter/Cafeteria Service.*
2. *Understand the procedure of laying the tables.*
3. *Understand and practice the procedure of carrying plates;*
4. *Know the procedures of relaying tables;*
5. *Explain the techniques of booking procedure in a restaurant;*
6. *Practice the reception procedure, method of taking order, servicing guest, silver service procedure, plate and dish clearance;*
7. *Explain the procedure of presentation of bills;*
   (a) *Understand and practice the procedure of breakfast preparation*
   (b) *Practice the service of afternoon tea,*
   (c) *Reception tea, lounge service, floor service, mini bar, lounge service, hospital tray service and airline tray service.*
8. *Damanstrate*

The present trend in food and beverage service is the elimination of unnecessary staff and hence doing away with the formalities that are labour consuming. The forms of service, generally depends on :

1. The type of establishment.
2. The type of customers to be served.
3. The time available for the meal.

4. The turnover of customers expected.
5. The type of menu presented.
6. The cost of the meal served.
7. The site of the establishment.

TABLE 2.1

Typical Food and Beverage Service Methods and their characteristics

Categories	*Table Service*	*Assisted Service*	*Method of Self-service*	*Service single Point*	*Specialized or in situ service*
1. Food & Beverage Service Area	Customers enters area and is seated ↓	Customers enters area and usually seated ↓	Customer enters ↓	Customer enters ↓	where the customer is ↓
2. Ordering/selection	From menu ↓	From menu buffet or passed trays ↓	Customer selects itenison to a trays ↓	Orderes at single point ↓	From menu or predect ermined ↓
3. Service	By staff of customer ↓	Combination of both staff and customer ↓	Customer carries ↓	Customer carries ↓	Brought to the customer ↓
4. Dinning consumption	At laid cover cover	Usually at laid cover	Dinning area or take away	Dinning area to take away	Where served customer
5. Clearing	By staff	By staff	By staff or customer	By staff or customer	By staff or customer

SERVICE OF FOOD AND BEVERAGES

The term *'service'* in relation to food and beverage means bringing means bringing the food and beverages to the table and attending to the guests' needs throughout the meal. It includes :

1. Bringing the food and beverages in an efficient manner that combines proper serving techniques and courteous attention to the guests.
2. Being prepared to handle unusual circumstances, safety and sanitation in the establishment; and
3. Suitable handling of the payment *i.e.* settlement of bill.

FIG. 2.1. Carrying a loaded oblong tray

The usual practice is to serve firstly the women and elderly people unless the party consists of a host entertaining friends. In the later case the service should start with the guest of honour at the host's right. The service should continue around the table counter clockwise.

Table wines are brought to the table and opened at the time they are opened. Wines are served as other beverages. Serve all food (soups, salads, entrees and desserts) from the left of the guest with your left hand support the dish with your left fingers underneath the plate and your thumb on the rim and place it on the centre of the cover.

The **first course** to be served is the appetizer. Appetizer is a food item served before the meal. Examples of appetizer are *Shrimp cocktail, oysters on the half shell, fruit or juice.* This first course is placed on a smair plate called an under liner and centered before the guest.

The soup may be served as a **second course** or it may be served in place of the appetizer. It is served in a small, handless cup or saucer. A soupspoon must be provided if it is not furnished with the table setting. Serve the soup in the centre of the cover with the soupspoon on the right side of the saucer.

The salad is the **next food** served. It is placed on the left of the corner allowing space in the centre for the entree.

The **fourth course** is the entree, which is the main part of the meal. First be sure, the table is properly set for the entree selected. Dinner rolls may be served, with the salad course and as an accompaniment to the entree. Condiments such as sauce should be brought to the table when requested. Serve the entree in the centre of the cover. Next refill the glasses.

The **fifth and the last course** is the dessert, the dessert fork or spoon should be brought with the food item and placed to the right of the dessert plate.

Replenish coffee and water and place clear ashtrays and matches on the table.

All foods should be served from the left of the guest and dishes should be placed with the server's left hand. Always serve at the convenience of the guest, even if, you must break the rules of proper service. Serve all beverages (water, milk, coffee and all alcoholic beverages) from the right of the guest with your right hand. Place beverages (milk and tea) to the right of the cover and pour beverages such as coffee or wine without lifting the cup or glass from the table. When pouring hot beverages use a clean, folded napkin in your left hand and shield the guest from the hot container.

When all the guests at the table have finished the course, immediately, thereafter clear the dishes. Generally, the guests will place fork and knife parallel to each other on the plate, which is an indication that the course is finished, otherwise, if in doubt, ask the guests if they have finished. Then remove all soiled dishes and utensils completely before serving the next food item.

Clear dishes from the right of the guest with the right hand. Move from guest to guest in a counter clockwise direction around the table. In addition to dishes, pick up all cracker wrappers and soiled silver. Clear soiled dishes to a nearby tray stand. Stack the dishes on the tray so that they are well balanced and safe for you to carry to the kitchen.

Before serving the last course, *i.e.* dessert, you should remove all dishes except water glasses and coffee cups and crumb the table. Crumbing the table is the process of sweeping loose food particles into a clean plate or other container with a clean, folded napkin to make the table look more presentable.

You can save time by saving steps whenever possible. Never walk back to the kitchen empty handed. Take dirty dishes back to the kitchen on your way to pick up food.

Always serve hot foods hot and cold foods cold. Pick up and serve foods in the order that will maintain this temperature quality. For example, when serving several tables, pick up salads and crackers first and hot soups or cold ice cream last on the same tray. Likewise, serve the hot soup or cold ice cream first and the salad and crackers last.

Guests need you by a look, gesture or remark and you should respond promptly to their needs. Therefore, do not avoid the guests. Allow little delay between courses and keep your eye on the guests as you serve others in your station. Special attention should be given after you have served the entree. When the guests begin to eat the main course, check back to ensure that all entrees are as ordered, satisfactory and complete.

Occasionally, you may encounter customers who need special handling such as very young, intoxicated, handicapped or ill guests. They require special care and attention. Be sure to watch the guests' belongings. Possessions such as purses, parcels and coats should be kept in sage place until the guest is better.

Better the service, fewer the complaints. Do not take offence, when customers complain. Valid complaints are the restaurant's feed back and should be used to improve service in the future. Some complaints can be prevented before they occur. Avoid arguing with customers. Always use tact and courtesy and respect their opinions. A good procedure for handling complaint should be based on the following points :

1. Listen,
2. Restate,
3. Agree, and
4. Handle.

Develop a routine with other waiters/resses for a smooth running operation. Use all means to make your restaurant a safer place to work. Every employee in the restaurant has the responsibility to maintain sanitary eating conditions for guest. Try your best to prevent food contamination in the restaurant.

When the guests indicate they have finished their meals you should complete the check and present it to the left of the host. There are two methods of presentation of a bill; firstly, the check may be placed face down on the table. Thank the guest and make brief departure remark like 'You may pay the cashier' and 'Come back again, soon'. The guest then pays the cashier. The second alternative, generally used in many restaurants is, the check may be presented face up on a tip tray and the host pays the waiter. When the host pays to the waiter, he takes the tray, checks and pay to the cashier and return all change on the tray to the table; thanks the guests and invite them back again.

Today payment is made by credit cards in lieu of cash — Master cards. Diner's cards, American Express, Visa, etc. These cards should be signed by the card-holder. To use the card, place it in the addresser or stamping machine with the credit slip on the top and slide the bar over both to imprint the slip. List dinners, tax and bar total on the slip and total the amount. Adding on a tip is upto the card-holder. Bring the pen and have the guest check and sign the slip. Then compare the signature with the one on the credit card to be sure they are identical and return the credit card.

Electronic Service

In this age of information and technology, many hotels have improved their food and beverages services by introducing the latest techniques such as electronic computers. These computers are installed in dinning room areas such as server terminals, visual displays, printers, and cash drawers, change dispensers and hand held order pads. The system merely enhances service; it should in no way replace the server or change the courteous service by the waiter/ress.

Computer hardware in the restaurant is the back office computer hardware operated by the manager and dinning area computer hardware run by the servers. Server terminals are points of sale machines with a keyboard; they are connected with the back office control processing unit and are used to enter information, such as date, number of guests at a table and food and beverage orders, into the system. The CPU in the manager's office determines exactly what is done with this information by the way it is programmed. Several terminals may be placed at convenient locations in or near the dinning room, at the cashier's station to replace the traditional cash register and in the bar.

The server terminal may have a keyboard that is preset, that is, dictates each key to a specific menu item. By touching the preset key for the menu items wanted, the description and price are instantly recalled from the system memory. For expanded menu pricing, traditional menu items can be stored in the CPU and accessed by use of an automatic price look-up feature. Server terminals may function themselves or they may be equipped with other hardware attachments such as visual displays, printers, and cash drawers and change dispensers.

The visual display is a video screen that attaches to the server terminal. The items entered on the terminal keyboard by the server are projected line by line on the display. In this way, the server can verify the information put into the terminal. Step by step instructions may also be programmed to appear on the screen to guide the servers in using the terminal correctly. A display may also be useful at cashier's stations or bars where management wants to have the guest see the items ordered on the amount owed.

Printers, imprint information on food and beverage orders, guest checks, receipts and management reports. Menu items, quantity, preparation, meal accompaniments and other information can be clearly described on paper. Printers can be installed in bars and kitchens at the cashier's station and in the manager's office. The CPU is programmed to route items ordered by the server to the chef or bar tender who can fill the order as it comes off the printer in the work area. Guest checks or the printer in the dinning room at a cashier's station can imprint tab receipts. Management reports are stored for management use and are printed when they are accessed in the manager's office.

In hand held order pad is a small cordless computer terminal used by server to take order from guests. It replaces the traditional order book or pad. It is connected by radio transmission to larger terminals and printers so that orders placed on them are immediately sent to the bar and kitchen. A server can also check on orders or have immediate feed back on wine in stock. Hand held order pads are recommended for busy bars, terraced dinning rooms beach and post side service, and deck service on cruise ships and dinner theatres with short transmissions for serving drinks.

Clear used items immediately from a vacated table. Replace cruets, flowers and clean ashtrays at the same time, if a cloth is soiled, and needs changing, do so at once. Reset covers as soon as possible. Check the chairs are clean and free from crumbs when you are cleaning the table.

TABLE SERVICE

Different types of table services are in current use. Some of which are :

1. French service

2. Russian service
3. English service
4. American service
5. Buffet service
6. Salad bars
7. Counter/Cafeteria service

The space allotted to each customer is known as *'cover'*. Depending upon the type of restaurant, the space varies and ranges from 24 to 36 inch. The edge of the table, counter seat or a booth is called the edge of the cloth; setline is one inch from the edge of the cloth. All silverware and chinaware setting wherever possible, is set starting at the setline,

1. ***Dinner Plate*** : It should be placed one inch from the edge of the table.

2. ***Knife*** : It should be placed to the right of the dinner plate with the sharp edge of the blade turned towards the dinner plate with the tip of handle placed one inch from the edge of the table (set line).

3. ***Cup and Saucer*** : These should be placed to the right of the teaspoon, with the handle of the cup towards the right hand side of the consumer. Cups may be inverted, if the arrangements are for service at a later time, but preferably be turned before service.

4. ***Goblet*** : It should be placed above the knife one inch from above the tip of the blade.

5. ***Bread and Butter Plate*** : It should be placed a the top of the fork (about 2-inch above the lines of the fork). Butter knife should be placed neatly across the butter plate with the sharp edge of the knife facing the customer. Also, the handle of the knife should be towards the right hand side of the customer.

6. ***Napkin*** : It is placed on the left of the fork. This may vary depending on different factors. The napkin may also be placed on the plate or silverware may be wrapped in it and placed either at the left side of the plate or on the plate. One of the methods of placing napkin is to place it in such a way that the free hemend of the in napkin is facing towards the left hand side of the guest. This provides the customer or food server easy access to the napkin for unfolding without inconvenience or embarrassment. Folding of the napkin to suit the theme or decor of the restaurant is highly desirable.

Care should be taken that the napkin is folded in such a way that it can be unfolded easily without interfering with the other table settings. If the person serving is required to place the napkin on the guest's lap, the napkin should be picked up with the left hand and evenly spread on the lap.

7. ***Dinner Fork*** : It should be placed on the left of the dinner plate with the edge of the fork handle one inch from the table. The fork should be placed upside down — the tines of fork should always point upwards. More than one fork may be desired for each setting, in which case, they should preferably be arranged on the left side of the dinner plate and set according to the sequence of courses on the menu for which these forks are to be used.

8. ***Salt and Pepper shakers*** : These should be placed between bread and butter plate and goblet.

Setting the Table : *Checklist*

The following guidelines will help in getting ready for service and properly attending to patrons :

1. Tables and chairs should be placed in their correct positions.
2. Table should be well levelled.
3. The size of the tablecloth should be checked.
4. Corners of the tablecloth should cover the legs of the table and should not fall between the table legs.
5. The overlap of the tablecloth should be even all around the table.
6. The tableclothes should be positioned on the-tables so that the creases are parallel in the room.
7. When two table clothes are used to cover a table, the overlap should face away from the entrance to the room.
8. All cover should be symmetrical.
9. The cutlery and the flatware should be cleaned/polished and given final touches before setting on the table.
10. Once the cover is laid, the other tables' accompaniments should be set.

Guidelines for Service

1. All food service is to be made from the left-hand side of the guest with the left hand.
2. A place with meat or a main entree should always be placed directly in front of the guest.
3. All beverages are served from the right hand side of the guest with the right hand.
4. All food dishes are removed from the right hand side of the guest.
5. All beverages are removed from the right hand side of the guest with right hand.

The changes in this procedure are advised only if it is in convenient to follow or is not in line with the theme and style of the food and beverage operations.

Table Service Procedure : *Checklist*

Rapid food and beverage service is highly desirable whether it is room service or in the adjoining restaurants, since guests are normally on a very tight schedule. The following procedures are recommended for maintaining food and beverage services that are of uniform quality.

The Menu

Study the menu thoroughly. The host or hostess will give you a list of menu items, an explanation of what each item is and the abbreviation that you will use on the order card.

Final Menu Check List (for each dish)
↓
Name & spelling of dish
↓
Country of origin
↓
One line description of dish
↓
To be served in which plate (crockery)
↓
Accompaniments with dish
↓
Time of preparation
↓
Photograph of each dish

FIG. 2.2. Flow Chart of Check List for Final Menu

Table Assignment

The host/hostess will give you your table assignments. Check the tables in your area to be sure that they are completely and properly set :

1. Each place setting should have silver, bread and butter plate, napkin and cup and saucer.
2. Each table should have an ashtray, salt and pepper shakers, sugar bowl and cream pitcher
3. At the last minute, place iced water glasses at each place setting.
4. At your tray stand, keep a water pitcher and a service napkin for wiping up spills.

Seating of the Guests

The host/hostess will seat the guests and will give each guest a menu or till the guests which table to take and you will give the guest the copies of the menu.

Taking the Order

After the guests have had enough time to read the menu, ask them what they would like. Write the orders on the cards, using the correct abbreviations. Be sure the orders are complete including beverages. There should be separate card for each guest. Collect the menus from the guests and return them to the host or hostess.

How to Serve?

Everything with the left hand side of the customer with the exception of the beverage. The beverages are served with the right hand on right hand side of the customer.

Service of the First Course and Salad

Soups are to be served on an under-liner. Place soupspoon or cocktail fork on the right, outside the silver already placed.

After the first course is served, pick up the salads from the kitchen and serve. If a salad dressing is to be passed, bring it with you.

When all the guests have finished with the first course, clear the dishes. On you tray stands, stack dishes according to size. After you have cleared your table, take the dishes to the dishwashing unit through the exit door.

Service of the Main Course, Rolls and Beverage

While the orders are being set up, assemble your beverage order. Take beverage and roll baskets from the kitchen to your stand.

Return to the kitchen and pick up your food orders. Set the tray of hot food on the tray stand. Carry two dinner plates to the double. Place the first dinner plate in front of the customer with your left hand, then transfer the second dinner plate to your left hand and serve the second guest. Serve hot rolls immediately after dinner plates have been served to everyone.

Rolls

Roll baskets are held with your left hand and offered to each guest from the left. After everybody has been served, return the roll basket to the tray stand.

Beverage

Serve after the rolls have been served. Keep water glasses filled. Stay near your tables as much as possible so that you will be available should your guest desire any service. Pass rolls the second time while the guests are still eating the main course.

How to Clear?

Clear everything with left hand from the left side of the customer with the exception of the beverage. When all customers at your table have finished eating, you may clear the table :

1. If the dinner knife has not been placed on the plate by the guest, pick it up and place it across the centre of the plate.
2. Pick up the dinner plate with your left hand; transfer it to the right hand, holding it behind the customer.
3. Pick up the salad plate and place it on the top of the dinner plate.
4. Pick up the bread and butter plate and place it on the top of the salad plate.
5. Place the dirty dishes on your tray that is located on your tray stand.
6. Repeat the above process until the dishes on the table have been cleared.
7. Clear everything except cups and saucers, water glasses, sugar bowl, creamer, ashtray and silver for dessert.
8. Salt and pepper shakers must be cleared.
9. Take the dishes to the dishwashing unit.

Dessert Service

Pick up the dessert orders and necessary under-liners. Place any necessary silver (if there is none on the table) for dessert on the right side of the customer.

1. If the dessert is on a plate, use a salad fork.
2. If the dessert is on a dish, use a spoon. When serving pie, plate the place so that the point of the slice of pie faces the guest. Refill coffee cups. Complete the check.
3. Place the check on small check trays facing down and leave it with the customer.
4. Guest will pay you; get the correct change from the host/hostess and bring the change back on a small tray to the customer.
5. After guests leave, clear the table of all dishes and linens. Wipe tables with clean cloth.

Taking Dirty Dishes to the Dish room

When taking dirty dishes to the dish room, stack dirty dishes according to size, *e.g.* salad plates in one stack.

Miscellaneous Instructions

When you are not busy, assist other waiter/waitress. Keep dinning room free of soiled dishes and trays. Follow one traffic pattern: use one door of dinning room for going into the kitchen and the other door for going out of the kitchen into the dinning room, whenever possible. Always leave your station and table clean and orderly. Return any silver linen or food, which has been left on the service stand, to the proper place. Wipe off the top of each service stand at the end of the meal period.

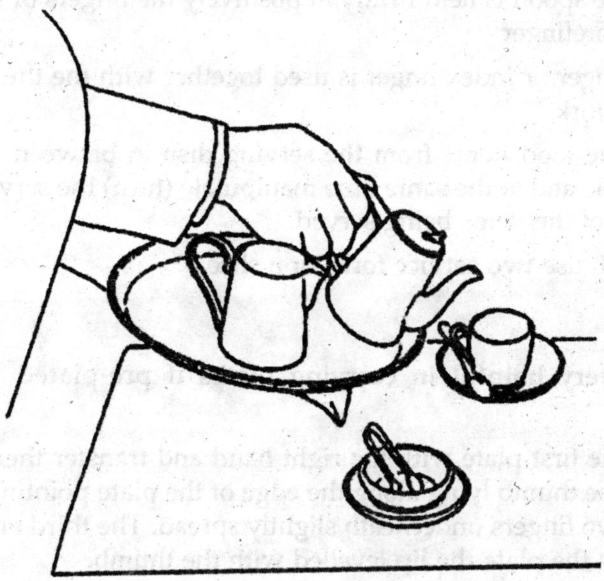

FIG. 2.3. A Traditional Coffee Service

As given in the Fig. 2.2. the waiter inclines the pot downwards making a pivot of the part of the base exactly under the spout. The pivot point remains on the tray.

TECHNICAL SKILLS FOR FOOD AND BEVERAGE SERVICES

In relation to table service assisted service and room service, there are six basic technical waiting skills :

1. Holding a service spoon and fork
2. Carrying plates
3. Using a service salver
4. Carrying glasses
5. Carrying trays.

Techniques of holding a Service Fork

The Purpose of revence and fork is to enable the waiter to perve food from a flat or dish on to the customer's plate quickly and to present food as the plat well you may case and practice following genidelines.

1. The end of the service spoon and fork should be positioned in the centre of the position of
2. the serving hand.
3. The service fork should be positioned above, or on the top of the service spoon.
4. The service spoon is held firmly in positively the fingers of the serving hand other than the forefinger
5. The forefinger or index finger is used together with the thumb to hold the handle of service fork.
6. Pick up the food items from the serving dish in between the service spoon and service fork, and at the same time manipulate (turn) the service fork to mould with the shape of the items being served.
7. If required, use two service forks or a slice.

Carrying Plates

This skill is very helpful in carrying plates if pre-plated foods as well as for carrying :

1. Pick up the first plate with the right hand and transfer them to the left. Hold the plate by the thumb lying along the edge of the plate pointing across the body, and the first two fingers underneath slightly spread. The third and fourth fingers stand up outside the plate-the lip levelled with the thumb.
2. Position the second plate on the left hand. The second plate will rest firmly on the forearm and the third and fourth fingers.

Using a Service Salver

A service salver consists of a round silver salver with a serviette set on it. It may be used :

1. Carrying clean glasses and removing dirty glasses from a table.
2. Removing clean cutlery, flatware from the table.
3. Placing clean cutlery, flatware on the table.
4. Placing coffee service on the table.
5. As an under flat when silver serving vegetables.

Carrying Glasses

Glasses should be placed upside down on the service salver. When placing them on the tables hold the stem and place the glass at the top right hand corner of cover and the correct way up. This ensures that the boil of the wineglass is not touched.

Carrying Clean Cutlery and Flatware

Cutlery and flatware should always be carried on a silver salver when it is to placed or removed from the table. The blade of the knives should be placed under the arch in the middle of the forks and if carrying dessert spoons or forks the pangs of the fork should go under the arch in the middle of the spoon.

Carrying Coffee Service

When taking coffee service to a table, the side plate may be stacked in the pile on service salver, the coffee saucers in another. All the demitasse together and all the coffee spoons laid flat on the service salver. When the waiter is at the table the coffee service is placed down from the right hand side, having first set a Coffee saucer on a side plate, a demitasse on the saucer with a coffee spoon on the coffee saucer and to the right of the demitasse. He/she goes to the right hand side of each guest and completes this simple operation. Coffee is served from the right.

Silver Serving Vegetables

An under flat should be used to hold either one large vegetable dish or number of smaller ones depending on the guest orders. This is usually done when silver serving vegetables are potatoes.

Using a Service Plate

A silver plate is a joint plate with serviette upon it. It helps in

1. Removing clean cutlery and flatware from the table.
2. Placing clean cutlery and flatware on the table.
3. Cleaning side plates and side knives.

Crumbing down after the main course or any other stage of the meals, if necessary; and cleaning accompaniments from the table as and when necessary.

Cleaning

1. ***Carrying clean cutlery and flatware :***

2. ***Cleaning side plates and knives :*** Clear the dirty side plates and side knives after the main courses. Take a service plate to the table to stack small items. The side plates are stacked one upon another with all the debris in a separate file and the side knives laid flat upon the service salver.

3. ***Crumbing down :*** After the main course have been consumed and all the dirty items of equipment cleared from the table, the waiter brushes any crumbs and other debris lying on the table cloth on to the service plate with the aid of either the folded service cloth or a small brush used for this particular purpose.

4. ***Clearing accompaniments :*** The service plate is also used to clear items such as the cruet, cayenne pepper, pepper mill or other accompaniments which are not already set on an under plate.

Carrying of Wine Glasses

1. ***Carrying by hand :*** The wine goblets should be positioned between alternative fingers as far as possible. These should only be carried in one hand, allowing the other hand to remain free to steady one self in case of emergencies. They can be carried about the room and set in their correct position on the table without the bow of the glass being touched.

2. ***Carrying glasses on a silver salver :*** Use the service cloth on the palm of the hand, with the service salver placed upon it. The wine goblets placed upside down on the service salver to avoid dust settling in them. It is easier to remove the clean and polished wine goblet by the base, and set in on the table without touching the bowl of the glass that is to be holding the wine.

For clearing the dirt wine goblets from the table, the first dirty goblet should be placed on the service salver nearest the holding hand. Use the thumb over the base of the first glass cleared to hold it steady whilst clearing further glasses. As the dirtying are cleared, they should be placed on the secvice salver firstly nearest the holding hand, working out to fill the service salver as more glasses are added.

Carrying Trays

For the correct method of holding and carrying a tray is to position the tray lengthwise into the forearm and to support it by holding the tray with the other hand. The tray is organized in such a way that the heaviest items are nearest the carrier. This helps in balancing of the tray. These trays are used for :

1. Carrying food from the kitchen to the restaurant sideboard.
2. Serving in room and lounges.
3. Clearing from sideboard.

4. Clearing from table (when the customer is not seated on the table).
5. Carrying equipment.

Inter Personal Skills

1. ***Showing customers to their table*** : Always walk with them on their place.
2. ***Seating customers*** : Ladies first descending in age unless the host is a lady.
3. **Handling coats/wraps** : Handle with obvious care.
4. ***Handling menus/wine list to customers*** : Offer the list and wait for the customer to take it.
5. ***Opening and placing napkins*** : Offer carefully, do not shake it like a duster, place it on the customer's lap after saying 'Excuse me' to the customer.
6. ***When offering water, rolls*** : Say, for example, 'Excuse me Sir/Madam, would you like a bread roll?
7. ***Offering accompaniments*** : Only offer them if you have them at the table.
8. ***Serving and clearing*** : Always say 'excuse me' before serving or clearing and 'Thank you' after you have finished with each customer.
9. ***Explain food and beverage items*** : Use, terms the customer understands (not to use technical terms). Use terms, which make the item sound attractive *e.g.* 'Casserole' not 'stew' 'creamed' or puree potatoes' not 'mashed'. Don't use abbreviations *e.g.* 'veg.'.
10. ***Addressing customers*** : Only when standing next to them. 'Sir/Madam' should be used when name is known *e.g.* Mr. Pali, Sir; Miss Sadai, Madam. First names should be used in less formal operations where the customer explicitly indicates that this is acceptable. If the customer has a title, then, appropriate use should be made of the correct forms of address.

Use greeting words 'Good Morning' and Good Evening' upon receiving customers or when the member of staff first comes into contact with the customer. When in conversation with customers :

1. Don't talk to other members of staff without first excusing themselves from the customer.
2. Don't interrupt interaction between customers and staff, but should wait until there is a suitable moment to catch the attention of the member of staff so that they may excuse themselves from the customer first.
3. Don't serve customer while carrying on conversation between them.
4. Don't talk across either to each other or to customers.

In Figure 2.4 the position of the first finger, which is inserted between the spoon and the fork giving initial leverage and enabling the food to be firmly held. The second finger supports the spoon. Handles of both spoon and fork rest in the centre of the palm where they can be kept *'locked'* with case.

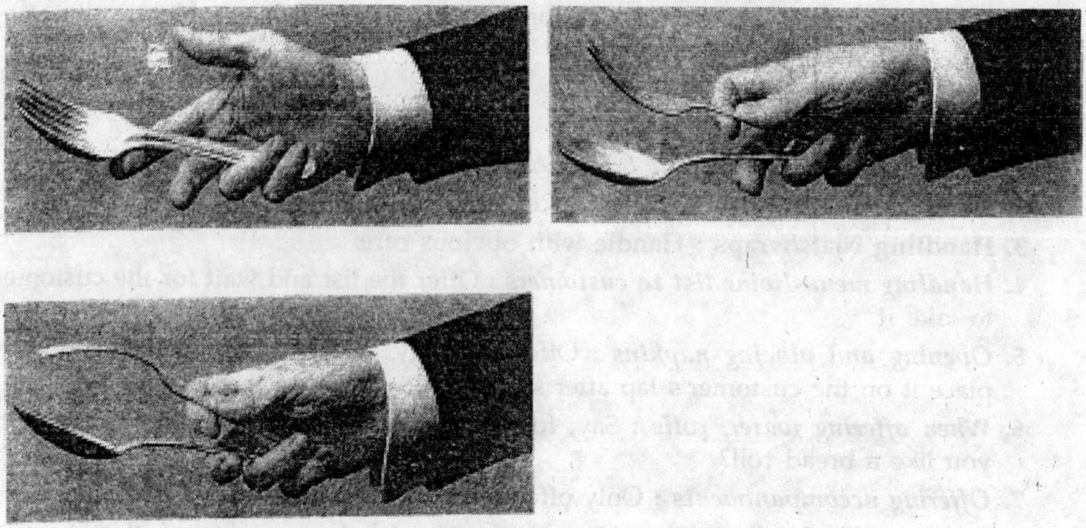

FIG. 2.4. The technique of holding the serving spoon and fork.

In using the serving spoon and fork to serve a round object such as a potato, the fork is inverted to follow the shape of the food. The serving dish is correctly positioned low down, almost touching and slightly overlapping the guest's plate.

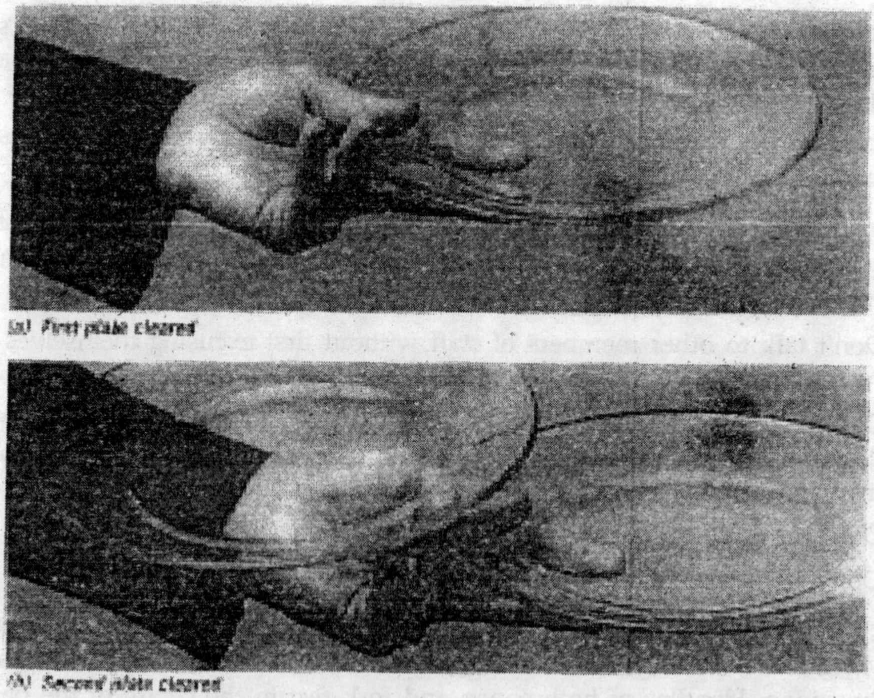

(a) First plate cleared

(b) Second plate cleared

FIG. 2.5. The technique of hand positions when clearing plates

Note the position of the first finger, which is inserted between the spoon and the fork, giving initial leverage and enabling the food to be firmly held. The spoon is supported by the second finger. Handles of both spoon and fork rest in the center of the palm, where they can be kept 'locked' with ease.

Soup Service

With ladle in right hand, stir soup gently and serve as given in figure 2.6.

FIG. 2.6. A Technique for serving soup from a tureen

TABLE 2.2
Examples of Soup Service

Soup	*Accompaniment*	*Cutlery & Crockery*
1. Artichoke	Chopped chervil and croutons	Soup spoon and soup plate
2. Borscht	Sour cream	Soup spoon and soup plate
3. Bouillabaisse	Toast	Soup spoon fish cutlery and soup plate
4. Consume cold, en glee	Lemon wedge	Cup and dessert spoon
5. Consume hot, en tasse	Pain grille or paillettes	Cup and dessert spoon
6. Green Pea	Croutons	Soup spoon and soup plate
7. Minestrone	Grated Parmeasan cheese	Soup spoon and soup plate
8. Onion	Flutes and grated cheese	Soup spoon as for marmite
9. Petite marmite	Flutes, grated cheese	Served in earthenware Individual marmites with dessert spoon.
10. Turtle	Buttered brown bread and lemon (formerly accompanied by small glass of cold milk punch)	Cup and dessert spoon (when en tasse) or soup plate and soup spoon.
11. Vichysoisee (Cold)	Toast Melba	Cup and dessert spoon.

Food And Beverage Service Preparation–*Booking Procedures*

1. When customer makes booking in person, then say, 'Good Morning Sir/Madam, how may I help you?
2. When the telephone rings, lift the receiver and say 'Good morning' .... (name of the establishment) may I help you?
3. Inquire about the following information —

   Day........ Number of covers........

   Date........ Any special request.......

   Name..........
4. On receiving this information, repeat it all as confirmation to the customer.
5. If a cancellation is being received then again confirm to cancellation with the customer by repeating his/her request over the telephone and then ask if he can make a booking for any other occasion in place of cancellation.
6. At the end of the call for booking one should say 'Thank you for your booking, we shall look forward to see you'.

Proper records of all bookings should be made in a Booking Sheet/Booking Register. This register contains the following information :

1. Restaurant name.
2. Day and date
3. Number of maximum covers
4. Name of the customer
5. Telephone number
6. Time
7. Total number of covers
8. No remaining
9. Remarks
10. Signature of the booking assistant.

RECEPTION PROCEDURES IN A RESTAURANT

Actual allocation of table depends on whether a table is pre-booked. Otherwise it is conditioned by the member of vacant places at the time of entry, the size of the party and as far as possible, the wishes of guests themselves. Customers, especially those on their own, tend to like 'back protection'; that is having their back to the wall, a corner or an alcove. Others seek table with status or amenities, that is, with views by windows or in raised alcoves.

A pleasant welcome to a guest can gain a sale, a poor welcome will loose a sale. First impression counts. Therefore, the management and staff start when a guest enters a restaurant and when he or she should be received and show to a suitable seat usually by the headwaiter.

(a)

(b)

FIG. 2.7. Silver service of soup from an individual soup tureen

The guests are first received at the entrance to a restaurant's cocktail bar or lounge. Here in aperitif is taken and the meal and accompanying wines may be selected. In America, a hostess or greater is consigned restaurant reception work on the basis of personality, intelligence and aptitude. Greeting phrases may, of course, be varied to suit the occasion. A stranger need to receive the old traditional greeting.

'Good morning (or afternoon or evening/Sir or Madam'. 'How many are there in your party please? Where guests' names are known, they may be used.

Having received an answer, the headwaiter leads the way to a suitable table. He then helps the ladies to be seated. He slightly draws the lady's chair from the table and as he seats about to seat herself, slide the chair gently forward and calls the head wine butler and section headwaiter to attend the guests.

A station headwaiter acknowledges customers with smile and greetings the same way as was done on arrivals. In America, a captain or station waiter introduces himself by saying 'I am... I'm your Captain (or waiter) for tonight.' or' Hi ! I am.......from......and I am your waiter for tonight.'

In Britain and on the continent such informality is not widely practiced. Social conditions make anything acceptable provided it makes guest feel welcome.

When evening dress is worn, ladies should be assisted in removing their wraps or stoles, which they might want to be placed over the chair back. In a party of several people a waiter attends first to the lady guests unless the gentleman accompanying them do so. If any guest is smoking, ensure that an ashtray is placed on the table.

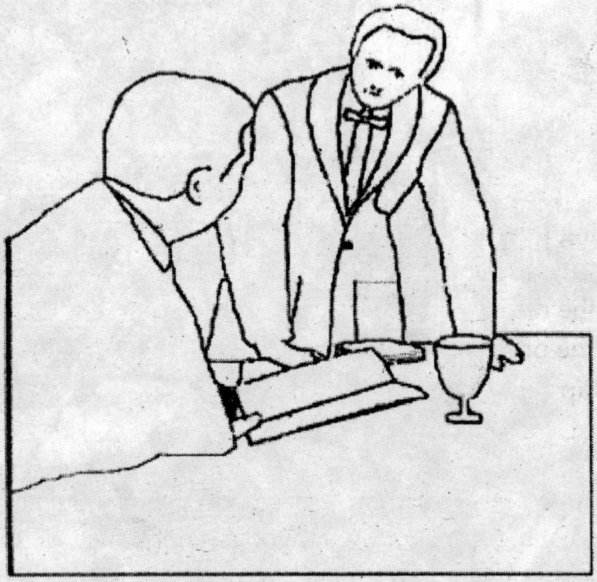

FIG. 2.8. Unsuitable stance of a waiter in front of a guest

It may be necessary for a covers to be added to, taken from, a table. Sometimes a party turns up with one guest less than originally quoted. In such cases, the waiter must remove the spare cover laid on the table. The cover should be removed in the correct manner using a service plate or service salver. The position of other covers needed may be adjusted and table accompaniment re-positioned.

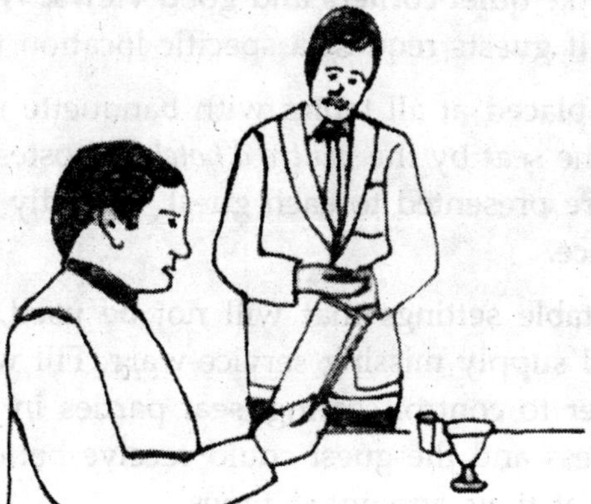

FIG. 2.9. The Correct Stance of a Waiter When Taking an Order

Arrival of Guest of initiating the Service

The procedure of reception of guest and initiating service could be grouped under the following heads :

1. Greeting the guest
2. Seating the guest
3. Approaching the guest
4. Taking orders
5. Conversation with the guest
6. Answering queries
7. Making suggestions
8. Timing the meal
9. Placing the order in the kitchen
10. Picking up orders from the kitchen.

Greeting the Guest

Generally, guests are greeted and seated by the *maitre d'hotel*, hostess, headwaiter or headwaitress. Approach guests with words of greetings such as 'Good evening'. Guests will inform you when they have reservation. When they do not have reservations, you may ask them 'How many are in your party?' When there appears to one person, ask 'Table for one?' Takes clean menus and lead the guest to the tables.

Seating the Guest

When women are in the party, a *maitre d' hotel* or headwaiter seats one or more of them in the set with the best view. The hostess/headwaiter/ress pulls out the women's chair to indicate where they can be seated, but does not actually seat them. Utilize tables according to party size; large families' at large tables and couples at smaller tables for two called *deues*. Young people like quiet corners and good views. Well-dressed people may be placed in central positions. If guests request a specific location try to accommodate them.

When patrons will be placed at all tables with banquette seat on one side, the table may be pulled away from the seat by the *maitre d'hotel* or hostess so guests may be seated easily. Now, open menus are presented to each guest. Friendly conversation is carried on throughout this initial service.

At this time, remove table settings that will not be used, bringing junior chairs or high chairs for children and supply missing service-ware. Fill water glasses or have them filled by a bus boy. In order to control seating, seat parties in different stations to avoid the burden on the waiter/ress and the guest could receive better service. Give preference to guests with reservations at their appointed times.

Approaching the Guest

Now, approach the guests after they had time to look at the menu. If you have not seated them, greet them with a friendly 'Good evening' and 'would you like a cocktail?' In some restaurants, there is a practice to announce your name and that you will be served for the meal. If required, inform the guests about unlisted specialties. After a few minutes, ask 'May I take your order?' If you have seated them, approach them again with a pleasant, 'Are you ready to order now?' Usually the host or hostess of the party orders for his or her guests. Being the spokesperson, she/he will address the server for the entire group. She/he takes the seat at the head of the table. Approach the host or hostess first from the left, and if he or she does not wish to order for the others, begin taking the order from the next person to the right. If you are busy with another table when the newest party of guest is seated in your station, you may approach the new group and tell them you will be with them shortly.

TECHNIQUES OF ORDER TAKING

While taking orders from the guest, stand erect to the left of the guest with the order pad supported in the palm of your hand and a pencil. Never place your book/order pad on the table to take an order. Make a mental note of the first person that orders. Proceed taking order counter clockwise around the table. Take the order completely. Generally you would like to ask questions to the guests, such as :

— Whether drinks should be iced ?

— Choice of salad dressing

— Choice of vegetable

— How meat should be cooked ?

— Sour cream or butter on baked potatoes
— How eggs should be cooked ?
— When to serve coffee.

When you take order, use abbreviation known to the kitchen staff, for example, 'ch' for chicken, 'ff' for French fries, 'Caf' for Coffee, 'r' for rare cooked etc.

If you like, repeat the order back to the guests for their confirmation. Now collect the menu from each guest after you write his or her order. There are three main methods of taking orders in the restaurant:-

1. ***A checklist system*** **:** In this system, the waiter/ress checks off the designated selection on a pre-printed list of menu items. This method is suitable for start order and most popular in fast food establishment.
2. ***A guest written down*** **:** Each guest is supplied an order pad and a pencil. The guest writes down his/her order. The server collects the order and takes them to the kitchen. This is suitable for restaurant having elaborate luncheons.
3. ***A waiter/ress written orders*** **:** This method is most suitable for restaurants having large dinning rooms, having *table d'hote* listings.

The server may take the order directly on guest checks. The bar order is recorded on the back and the food order is recorded on the front of the check or the bar order may be taken on the separate check. The food check is placed on a rotating wheel or other device in the kitchen and filled by the chef or in turn with other orders. It is returned to the server when he picks up the meal from the kitchen. Then the bar total is added to the good total and the check is presented to the guest for payment.

Alternatively, a server can write an order to note the selections on a pad of paper, carbon copies are made or part of the order are then re-written for kitcnen staff. The original order retained by the waiter/ress, who uses it to serve cocktails, appetizers, salads and other items. After the meal, the waiter/ress summarizes the order on a guest check and presents the check to the guests for payment. This system of taking order is suitable for multi-unit kitchen.

Brief and positive comer stations with guests about menu items, food suggestions, opinion about the whether, etc. are pleasant part of the waiter's job. The waiter should also be prepared to answer the guest queries about the food, the restaurant, the community and even the state. Therefore, he/she should know about hours and address of the restaurant menu and ingredients of each dish, general menu of other dinning room and coffee shops, historical facts about the restaurant and community, event and attractions in the community, area and state.

You may make suggestions by recommending food, beverages and services, to make the meal more enjoyable to the guests. You may suggest cocktails, orders that complement the entree, beverages, desserts and after dinner cordials. After taking the complete order, the waiter/ress should submit the order in accordance with the length of time necessary to prepare the entree. In a single unit kitchen, the chef sees that the entire order is already at the same time. In a multi-unit kitchen, the server coordinates the meal. He should submit these orders in separate stages so that they are ready at approximately the same time and thus assuring that the hot foods is hot and cold foods are cold. Dessert orders should be submitted and picked up immediately after the meal.

The system of communicating the orders to the kitchen staff varies among restaurants depending upon their size, type of kitchen and type of service. In some restaurants, the order is orally communicated to the kitchen by entering the kitchen and giving order to the proper chef, who may write the order down.

In larger kitchen, the order written on guest check is given to the chef, who arranges all the orders in sequence. The chef may attach them to a rotating wheel, spindle, or clip device so that all orders will be filled in their turn. Alternatively, the waiter/ress must re-write part of the order for the separate kitchen units.

There are several ways in which the waiter/ress is notified that the order is ready. A lighted number on a wall clock in the dinning room, signals a specific server to pick up an order in the kitchen; or the chef may take the responsibility of orally notifying the server some waiter/ress are supplied electronic devices that signals them when their orders are ready. The waiter should compare the food with the waiter to see that order is complete; it is attractively arranged and garnished. Arrange the food plates on the tray so that they are well balanced to carry to the table in the restaurant.

How to Take the Order ?

The server takes a guest's order on a traditional order pad. The waiter/ress proceeds to a server terminal to record the order and open the guest's account. Each server is given can identify key a code number or authorizing card that must be used to activate the server terminals in the dinning room. The server then enters the identity key number or card to sign into the system. The waiter/ress punches in the table number, number of guests in the party and check number and then inserts the check into the printer.

The server then keys in the order and pushes the correct number as per the menu or simply pushes a present menu key on the terminal to enter the customer's menu choice into the system. As food and beverage items are entered, they may be shown on the display for verification. Each entry made contains quantity, description, accompaniments, and preparation instructions and price and prints a guest check, the manager's journal and a kitchen and/or bar-order in one operation. The system also automatically prints the date and time of the order on the guest check.

The server can easily add to the guest's order at a later time from a different terminal. This change is possible because each guest check has a number signs into the guest's account. Some members may also be in the bar code, a code of lines representing that number and can be 'red' by the computer. When that number is read, the previous balance for that number is recalled from memory. As each additional menu item is punched into the terminal, it is sent to the kitchen or bar. The guest check is automatically positioned to the next available print line, and the new information prints on the guest check.

There are some computers where there is a provision to allow the server to follow easy to understand screen prompts for the entire process from entering orders to cashing out their checks.

Printers or display could be installed in the bar and kitchen. As soon as the server punches the customer's order at the server terminal the information is immediately transmitted to the appropriate remote order printer or display and beverage and food orders are filled by the bartender and chef without delays.

In single kitchen establishments, the computer function may identify cold food items in blue ink and hot food items in red ink on the same paper on the kitchen printer. In multi-unit kitchen, one printer can be placed at the hot food production station and another in the cold food section. The stationary is programmed to trigger printing of specific menu items to the designated kitchen printer.

Following preparation a person called an expediter may assemble complete orders and bring them to the dinning room for the waiters and waitresses. This assistance helps facilitate efficient service and reduces kitchen traffic. In a restaurant without an expiator, the server is notified that the order is ready, picks it up from the kitchen and servers the meal.

Thus the terminal records all items ordered, adds tax on taxable items and totals the guest check. At the end of the meal, the totaled guest check its presented to the guest for payment when the guest has paid, the server takes the payment to a cashier's station or acts as a cashier and settles the check.

The server must insert the guest check back into the terminal, press the key and validate each check total as a proof of settlement. This applies regardless of whether the transaction is settled by cash or credit card. When settlement is completed, the guest account is closed. The shift cashier keeps all receipts of settlements and balances them at the end of the day. In case there is no cashier, the server keeps the money, checks and credit slips collected as payment. As the waiter/ress keys each order into the computer, the amount of the item is automatically and immediately charged to that server's account. The computer calculates all the drinks and menu items, puts in appropriate taxes and totals the guest checks. At the end of the shift the server cashes out completely balancing the receipts in his or her pocket with guest check totals calculated by the computer.

Method of taking different Orders

Aperitif Order

Aperitifs are generally taken in adjustment cocktail bar, lounge or anteroom and the meal and wines are selected there. The station waiter and wine waiter greet the customers and initiate the service. When food and beverage (wine) orders remains to be taken at table, the head wine butler comes first, greets and inquires if an aperitif is required.

Presentation of Menu

As soon as guests are seated the menu should be presented. On taking the aperitif orders the section headwaiter approaches the host from the left, unfolds the guest's napkin and offers it to him. He pledges menu in front of him and allows time to study it. (Menu is already placed on the table before the guest and not handed to her). A waiter can, during this time, be offering bread rolls and send his commies with appropriate checks to the stillroom for butter and Melba toast. It is customary for a waiter to place fresh butter on the table pass bread rolls and fill water glasses.

Taking the Order : Food Items

The waiter will approach the guest from the left. He should inquire 'May I have your order, Sir/Madam'. When there is a host, his instructions are to be taken, otherwise, receive order, as guests are ready. The waiter would like to inquire about such dishes as grilled steaks and chops. 'How do you like cooked. Sir — rare (underdone), medium or well done?

Inform customer about the cooking time. For *table d'hote* meals or when no cooking time be allowed, the first course should be served as soon as possible.

In recording an order, a waiter should fold his serving cloth into a neat pad on which to rest his book. There are four methods of taking food and beverage orders as given in Table 2.3. In case electronic system is operation the actual check may not be written but communicated electronically to VDUs or print out machines.

TABLE 2.3
Typical Methods of Taking Food and Beverage Orders

S.No.	*Method*	*Description*
1.	Pre-ordered	(i) Individual - room service breakfast (ii) Hospital tray system (iii) Functions.
2.	Service With Order	(i) Take order, (ii) Serve customer (iii) Require payment according to the order *e.g.* bar service and take away method.
3.	Duplicate	(i) Take order (ii) Top copy to supply point Second copy for service and billing.
4.	Triplicate	(i) Take order (ii) Top copy to the supply point (iii) Second copy to the cashier for billing. (iv) Third copy is retained by the waiter as a Means of (v) eference during service.

The waiter should write in the corner of the next unused sheet of his order pad the number of the table being served. He records in abbreviation forms the dishes that are ordered. Information normally required on an order include :

1. Waiter's code number/station number

2. Table number
3. Number of guests
4. Details of dishes
5. Price and type of meals ordered
6. Date.

Taking the Order of Wine

By the time the food order was been taken, the wine butler has served the aperitifs. He presents the wine list to the host from the left, advises the customer on choice of wines to match food order.

Passing Orders to Kitchen

The food checks made are handed over to appropriate part of the kitchen or whoever is accepting the orders. The aboyeur (kitchen clerk) calls out the order, then files the waiter's check on his series of spikes where it remains until the order is completed. The *chef de partie* on hearing the order from the aboyeur responses by calling out equally loudly to acknowledge their acceptance of it.

TABLE 2.4.
A Typical Sequence of Serving Guests

S.No.	*Guest*	*Sequence of Service*
1.	In a Party of Two	One lady and another gentleman - **Serve the Lady First**
2.	In a Party of Four	Two ladies and two gentlemen - **Serve the Lady on the Right of the Host First** **Then the Lady on His Left** **Thereafter, the Gentleman opposite to the Host** **Finally, serve the Host**
3.	In a Party of Six	Three ladies and three gentlemen **The Host and Hostess will sit facing each other** **The Lady on the Right of the Host is served First** **Then the Lady on the Left of the Hostess** **Next, the Gentleman on the Right of the Hostess** **Then the Gentleman on the Left of the Hostess &** Finally, serve the Host
4.	In a Large Party	With a host rather than a Chairman Serve First, the Guest of Honour who is sitting on the Right Of the Host (in a fix-mixed party, it is usually a lady). Then the Guest on his Left Then the Host himself The other waiter on the **Top Table** of the large party of this Kind starts with:

(Contd...)

First guest on the right of the guest of honour.

The hostess is served last in a party of ladies and the last of anybody.

This may be summarized as follows:

(i) The guest of honour is served first.

(ii) A lady in a party takes precedence over a male guest of honour.

(iii) A lady in the company of men is served first.

(iv) Older people precede younger.

***Exception* :**

Banqueting, where each waiter serves his station in order of seating irrespective of precedence.

House Custom of Food Service

The guiding principle for food service should be interpreted and conditioned always by the application of the 'house rules' of any particular restaurant to which side of clearance shall be adopted. But once a decision is taken, observance of it should be total.

Silver Service

This service is offered from platter to plate. It is also known as French service.

Flow of Work in Silver Service

↓

Server takes the order in a K.O.T.

↓

Punch the order in Micros/Software

↓

Place the dinner plate in front of guest

↓

Food comes in platter (individual dishes)

↓

Individual serves the dish from platter

↓

It is always served from left hand side

↓

Put the platters 'in centre of-table

↓

Refill the platters as & when required

↓

Clearance

↓

Check

↓

Farewell

FIG. 2.10. Flow chart of sequence of silver service procedures in serving meals in a restaurant.

Service of Course and Dishes – Service Sequence

The food and beverage service staff should be on duty well before the service is due to commence in order. Check the following :

1. Sideboards have all equipment necessary for service.
2. Tables are laid correctly.
3. Checking of the menu and full understanding of the dishes, methods of cooking, garnishes, the correct covers, accompaniments and mode of service.
4. Allocation of stations and other duties.
5. The staff is dressed correctly in a clean and well-presented uniform of the establishment.

General Service Procedures and Techniques

The service techniques and procedure should be evolved on the basis of following objectives :

1. To meet the customers' needs
2. To aid waiters to operate productivity and profitability, and
3. To merchandise the food and beverages.

A sensible food and beverage merchandising should be so blended with tradition and innovation that the forms of service are best oriented to guests' needs. In practical situations any technical slip is either not noticed by the guest or it is overlooked if the waiter's conduct is agreeably attentive in other aspects.

Service of Food : Procedure

Food service procedure tends to vary according to different establishments – idea of efficiency and convenience. Once it was widely accepted that in a table and assisted service food service should be from the left and to clear from the right. All beverages both alcoholic and non-alcoholic are served from the right. There are one or two exceptions to this rule; for example, it may depend on the position of table and the guest seated at the table. Also side plate, being on the left-hand side of place setting or cover are more easily covered from the left thus avoiding stretching in front of the guest.

Now, it is believed that clearing food plates from the right is hazardous to glasses on the table and ackward when guests are drinking with the increase in plate service; it has become common to serve plated goods from the right.

In Europe there are broadly two main styles with deviations in some establishments. There are

- Continental style
- English style.

Basic procedures for both the continental and English practices are summarized as follows :

TABLE 2.5.
Basic Procedure/or Continental and English Service

Continental Style	*English Style*
1. Place clean plates and glasses from the guest's right.	1. Plates or utensils for food are placed from the left.
2. Place coffee cups and saucers (with under plate) from the guest's left.	2. Food is served from the left.
3. Serve food from the guest's left.	3. Used food plates are cleared from the left
4. Serve drinks (including wine and coffee) from the guest's left.	4. Glasses are placed from the right.
5. Clear all used items, that is, plates, cups and glasses from the right.	5. Drink is served from the right.
	6. Used glasses are cleared from the right.

The usual procedure is that foodservice should be from the left, with drink and glass service from the right. The food clearance is done from the right. However, many prefer that clearing food plates from the left as clearing there from the right is hazardous to glasses on the table and serves ackward when guests are drinking. In European style of service we find two procedures in common use :

1. Continental style of food beverage service.
2. English style of food and beverage service
3. House style of food and beverage service.

FIG. 2.11. Silver service of vegetables

Continental Style of Service

This style is observed in most of the European countries *e.g.* France and Switzerland. The procedure is as under :

1. Place clean plates and glasses from the guest's right.
2. Serve food from the guest's right.
3. Place coffee cups and saucers (with under plates) from the guest's left.
4. Serve drinks (including wine and coffee) from the guest's right.
5. Clear all used items, that is, plates, cups and glasses from the right.

British/English Style of Service

These are traditional British butler and service standards of English clubs and these procedures are most observed and practiced in the higher circles of society. The procedure followed under this system is as given below :

1. Plates or utensils for food are placed from the left.
2. Food is served from the left.
3. Used food plates are cleared from the left.
4. Glasses are placed from the right.
5. Drink is served from the right.
6. Used glasses are cleared from the right.

House Style (*Tradition*) of Service

Each hotel or restaurant may adopt its own custom/rule of the house as determined by the management. You may decide either right hand or left hand clearance. There should never be a mixture of right hand or left hand clearance. Guidance should be interpreted and conditioned always by the application of the house rules as to which side of clearance shall be adopted. Once a decision is taken, observance of it should be total; except when guest's convenience is involved.

Beverages Service Sides

1. Beverages are served from the right.
2. Coffee cups (on saucers and under-plates), sugar (unless it is on the same salver as the coffee itself) and bread are also placed before are offered to the guest from the left. Because coffee is served from the right, it seems illogical to place coffee cups and saucers from the left.

FOOD AND BEVERAGE SERVICE AIDS AND TOOLS

Uses of Waiter's Service Cloth

1. Presenting a dish.
2. In putting on plates.
3. Polishing glasses

4. Polishing cutlery
5. Polishing plates, etc.
6. Wiping spillage from a plate or cup rim
7. Wiping the under side of a dish before placing it on a table.
8. Handling dishes – hot or cold
9. Carrying dishes and trays when the neatly folded service cloth as a pad protects the hand from what is being carried.
10. Wiping fingers to avoid slipperiness, before clearing.
11. When not in use (when standing at the sideboard), carry the service cloth neatly folded on the left forearm.

Service Spoon and Fork

Skill is required to manipulate a spoon and fork. Sometimes such as small boiled potatoes, peas or some other vegetables are served better using only a spoon. Observe the following guidelines when using service spoon and fork :

1. Take a clean set of service spoon and fork for each dish.
2. Never use them again to serve another table
3. Don't use a fork without a spoon except in instances
4. Never use two spoons
5. Never use the same spoon and fork for both potatoes and green vegetables.
6. In lifting food, take care that the portion does not slip from the dish on to the customer's plate.

Silver Service Procedure

The service technique detailed below is applicable to all silver and stainless steel. Similar techniques may also be applied when serving in this style from copper, oven proofs crockery or other ware.

Check the Food

Check the food items about to be served as regards to the following :

1. It is the right order;
2. Portions are adequate;
3. The dish is neat and clean.

Hot and Cold Dishes

If some customers are to be served with hot dishes and others with cold dishes, always serve cold dishes first.

Presentation of Dish

1. Each dish must be presented at the table prior to serving from it.
2. First show it to the host for his approval and to confirm it is the ordered.

3. If it is not visible to the rest of the party, present it also at the other end of the table.
4. When making presentation, lift the cover of the dish so as to avoid condensation dripping onto the carpet or tablecloth. At the sideboard invert the cover to avoid marking the sideboard cloth.
5. If a high-class service, deep dishes be always presented on an under dish or liner.

How to carry a Dish?

1. Carry on oval dish length wise on the palm of your hand.
2. Protect your hand with a service cloth folded into a neat pad.
3. Don't handle dishes, hot or cold, without a service cloth.
4. For large dishes, stretching out the fingers for better control.
5. For extremely large and heavy dishes, allow one end of the dish to rest on the wrist gripping the other end with the fingers.

Serving from Dish

1. Food should be portioned in advance on a silver dish.
2. Place on it a spoon and fork for service.
3. Stand on the guest's left, feet together, with the dish on the palm of yours left hand (protected by the pad of folded waiter's cloth).
4. Advance your left foot forward.
5. Bring the dish down to the level of the guest's, plate just over the rim, the dish being perfectly level.
6. Take the spoon and fork on your right hand to serve food onto the plate.
7. Lift the food with the spoon, with the fork gently keeping it firm.

Service from the Large Flat Silver

1. Ensure that guest's plates are hot and clean.
2. Protect yourself and the plates with a service cloth when carrying a pile of hot plates.
3. Stand on the guest's left.
4. Serve with care to avoid spilling gravy or sauce on the plate's rim.

Serving from Deep Hollowware (*e.g.* Cocolte or Vegetable dish)

1. Check that a dish is an under dish
2. Ensure that guest's plates are hot and clean.
3. Serve with care and avoid spilling on to the rim of the guest's plate.
4. Use a separate spoon and fork for each dish and avoid mixing the contents.
5. Bring down the dishes close to the guest's plate as possible.
6. When there is more than one dish on your under liner turn the under liner as necessary, to bring each dish in turn in line with the plate.

Plate Handling

1. Before placing, check temperature and cleanliness of plates before they reach a table (rather than wipe them in front of guests).
2. For hot courses plates must be hot; for cold courses cold.
3. Hold a pile of plates on the left hand (not between thumb and fingers), which is covered with one end of the waiter's cloth.
4. On approaching the right (or left) of the customer, gently wipe the plate with other end of the cloth before placing.
5. Pick up the plate with the tips of the thumb and fingers of the right hand.
6. Keep the plate horizontal, lower it into position.
7. Continue this procedure, finishing with the host.
8. Plate may be placed as per the house custom — from guest's right or guest's left.

Use of Under Plates

1. Under plates are used for hollow items such as soup plates, coffee cups and saucers and butter plates.
2. Use of under plates exhibits table etiquette and presentation style.
3. Use of under-plates help avoid drips and/or contact of product with waiter's hand.
4. For some food in coupes or similar containers (*e.g.* grapefruits, ice creams, etc.) place a doily and an under plate under the container.

Serving Large Items

1. **Fish :** If the fish portion is too big for easy service with spoon and fork, serve it across the middle with the spoon.
2. **Omelet :** When serving an omelet, cut-off the extreme tips with the spoon before serving. If an omelet, large fish portion or other item has to be cut into several portions, check before hand exactly how many to avoid unequal portioning.

Position of Food on the Plate

1. Arrange food appetizingly when placing on the plate.
2. Fish and meat is served lower centre with vegetables on one side and potatoes the other.
3. Separate sauces and/or accompaniments at the right hand side (2 o'clock position).
4. When serving sauce, do not pour it over the food without ascertaining guest's wishes.
5. Arrangement on the plate should seek to reproduce the effect achieved by a chef on the silver dish.

Meals in Progress

1. Observe the meals progress.
2. Notice right away what is missing from the table.
3. Keep an eye on guests.

4. Seek a customer's permission before removing sauces, cruet or any other item from his table when required for another table.
5. Check that a customer can reach required items like salt and pepper.
6. Check whether the butter dish contains butter.
7. Pass rolls again each time a guest has finished the one on his plate or check that the plate or dish containing toasts Melba is never empty.
8. Make sure during service that all dishes are completely served — all sauces and condiments required are passed with a dish and that a customer has the correct cutlery.

Adjusting Covers

1. Bring cutlery before hand as may be required for the dish ordered. Remove unwanted items.
2. Carryout adjustments of a cover without delay - removing or adding cutlery with a service plate, a medium sized plates (fishplate) with a folded napkin.
3. As soon as any course is finished, remove any unwanted items such as cruets, sauces, etc.

Plate and Dish Clearance

1. Used plates and dishes are cleared either from the left or the right as per the house policy.
2. Collect plates when guests signify that they have finished by putting knife and fork together across the plate.
3. Remove used plates directly after all the party is finished leaving the host until last.
4. Give priority to clearing plates first to keep a table tidy and secondly, to keep from a customer any impression that he is forgotten.
5. Pick up the plates with the right hand and transfer them to the left.
6. Hold the first plate by the thumb lying along the edge of the plate pointing across the body and the first two fingers underneath slightly spread.
7. The third and fourth fingers stand up outside the plate – the tips level with the thumb. Place the used fork with the curve upwards.
8. Put the used knife under the curve of the fork and at right angle. This technique is called as the *"FIRST PLATE"*.
9. Place the second plate on your forearm with the under rim behind the thumb joint and on the two extended fingers (with this technique the plate cannot slip forward and the main weight is supported by your forearm).
10. Pick up the knife and fork and gently scrape any remains of food onto the first plate.
11. Place them with the other cutlery on the first plate, fork with fork and knife underforks, as before.
12. Continue the above step round the table in this manner until it is cleared (one person can clear eight plates in this fashion).

13. Now, go to the side table.
14. Take the first plate out of your left hand, (using right hand) and place it on the top of the pile so that the whole pile is completely steady.
15. Shift food from one plate to the other (as far as possible out of guest's vision). The angle of cutlery on the first plate should be such that should anything fall it will do so towards you and not on the customer.
16. At wash up, clear cutlery from soiled plates and places it in the appropriate receptacle.
17. If any dishes have been left on the table for the guests to serve themselves, return any which contain food to the kitchen.
18. Clear used items immediately from a vacated table.
19. Replace cruets, flowers and clean ashtrays at the same time.
20. If a cloth is soiled and needs changing do so at once.
21. Reset covers as soon as possible.
22. Check that chairs are clean and free from crumbs when you are cleaning the table.

Crumbing Down

1. Remove the cruet from the table at the end of the meat course, just before the sweet is served.
2. Remove other remaining items such as unwanted cutlery and empty bottles.
3. Now use a neatly folded table napkin as a brush or a crumb scoop to bring crumbs to the table edge.
4. From the edge brings down gently on to a medium-sized plate.

Finger Bowls : *After the meal and/or after the dessert*

1. Half fill the finger bowl with lukewarm water (in which a lemon slice, rose petal or similar embellishment may be dropped).
2. Place it on the left of the customer.
3. After a finger bowl has been used, a fresh table napkin may be presented.

Sweet Service : *Adjusting the Cover*

1. The fork and spoon laid across the top of the cover be removed down to right and left of the guest cover (without stretching your arm in front of the guest.
2. Follow the procedure for service of sweet, dessert, etc.

Coffee Service

Service Coffee

Presentation of Bill

Present the bill at the end of the service.

TABLE 2.6
A Typical Silver Service Sequence Checklist

S. No.	*Stage of Service* (1)	*Action* (2)	*Explanation* (3)
1.	Lay up	Table preparation	Neat and aligned.
2.	Sideboard	Preparation	Tidy and organized.
3.	Mise en Place done	Check lay up; Collect rolls; Collect butter and water; check Menu, understand the dishes, Methods of cooking, garnishes, Covers, accompaniments and Mode of service.	Cover jug; Headwaiter to check that all staff are dressed correctly in clean & well presented uniform.
4.	Guest arrives	Greeted and seated by the Headwaiter, unfold guest napkin Hand menus.	Hold chair on a to lap. Hold top.
5.	Guests studying Menu	Serve water; serve rolls; place butter dish on table	Pivot from plate from right; unfold napkin on rolls; from left on under plate with doily.
6.	Guests Order	Using pad of folded service-cloth for support; write carefully then adjust cover using service plate.	Split checks and take to Cashier and kitchen, still-room, spike flimsy on sideboard.
7.	Prepare for Starter Course	Collect starter and plates	Check for chambers and heat; Individual soup at table; Tureen and ladle at the sideboard; Hot hors d'oeuvre or hot-plate; Cold hors d'oeuvre-cold plate. **Note:** *Hors d'oeuvre* accompaniments *e.g.* oil and vinegar.
8.	Prepare for Main course	From kitchen collect plates and main course	Check plates are hot & clear. Place on sideboard Put food on hotplate.
9.	Clear Starter From Table	Stack empty plates and dishes as you go from left	Place the stack on sideboards. Long service cloth in left-hand, wipe each plate in turn.
10.	Serve Main Course	Put on plates from left. Serve from left main course dish	On salver with cloth underneath dishes.
11.	Serve Vegetables	Use spoon or fork as required	Separate service gear for each vegetable.
12.	Serve Gravy or Sauce	From left on underplate	Sauceboat lip towards customer. Use ladle or spoon.

(Contd...)

S. No.	Stage of Service (1)	Action (2)	Explanation (3)
13.	Check	Garnishes	Ensure all accompaniments served and satisfactorily.
14.	Main Course Clearance	Water and rolls When guests have finished remove unwanted items, *e.g.*, Cutlery, cruet etc. Clear and Stack on sideboard.	Replenish as needed. Use fork as bridge for knives
15.	Prepare for Sweet	Crumb down Hand menu Re-adjust cover, if required Go to pastry	From left, use open end of napkin to brush; bring down dessert cutlery from cover top to side. Write order, split up checks, *e.g.* coupe/ cheese use semiplate to bring needed items. Collect sweet and plates
16.	Serve Sweet	Put on plates from the left Check	From left, using cloth, check accompaniments, biscuits, etc. all offered from left. Water etc. as before.
17.	Take Coffee Order	Write check; go to still room & collect coffee, milk, sugar, cups, spoons, saucers.	— —
18.	Clear Sweet/Cheese	Remove polates and stack on sideboard	Normally from right (but note house customs may differ); sugar; milk coffee.
19.	Serve Coffee	Place coffee cups before guests from right Request- 'Do you take sugar? 'Do you wish black or with Milk?' Check	Especially ashtray, cover used ashtrays. Clear and replace with new one.
20.	Bill Presentation	Collect bill, check it When requested, collect money. Return to cashier. Return bill, receipt and change Place on table or plate.	Place folded bills on salver in front of client. Leave it on table.
21.	Assisting Departing Guests.	When quests get up to leave help with chairs.	SMLE & SAY— 'THANK YOU'

Relaying of Tables

In a busy day, a number of tables have to be re-laid in order to coup with the inflow of customers. Firstly, the table should be completely cleared of all items of equipment and then crumbed down. If the tablecloth is a little soiled or grubby, a slip cloth should be placed over it. It can then be relaid in approval manner.

A Typical Guidelines for Service of Meal

1. General guidlines

(i) Food is served from the left.

(ii) Alcohol and non-alcoholic beverages are served from the right.

(iii) Dirty items are cleaned from the right.

2. Before the service commences; (*few minutes before*):

(i) Check the sideboards that all equipment is there for service.

(ii) Check that tables are laid correctly.

(iii) Check the menu and have full understanding of the following :

(a) Dishes,

(b) Methods of cooking,

(c) Garnishes,

(d) The correct covers,

(e) Accompaniments, and

(f) Mode of service.

(iv) Allocation of station and duties of restaurant staff.

(v) The headwaiters to check that all the staff are correctly dressed in a clean and well-presented uniform.

3. On Arrival of the Guest : *Greeting of guest.*

(i) The guests enter.

(ii) Guests are greeted by the reception headwaiter.

(iii) Check to see if they have reservation. If not, see if a table is available.

(iv) The reception headwaiter asks if the guests would like an aperitif in the lounge or reception area or prefer to have one at the table.

(v) Guests are taken to their table.

(vi) The reception headwaiter indicates who is the host to the station waiter and then hands over to him/her.

4. Wine Order/Service

(i) The station headwaiter helps to seat them.

(ii) The station waiter unfolds each guest service and places it over his/her lap and turns the wine glasses upto the correct way.

(iii) The sommelier comes to the table to offer the wine list for the choice of aperitif. He/she takes the order.

(iv) Rolls and Melba toast are offered and the butter is placed on the table.

5. First Course Service

(i) Menus are presented to the host and his/her guests .(Allow time to the party to make their choice).

(ii) Recognition of the host is very important.

(iii) The station waiter takes the order of the party through the host and should be ready to offer suggestions and advice on the menu or translate any items if necessary/required.

(iv) The sommelier/wine butler comes to the table to see if any wine is required with the meal, taking the order through the host He/she will be able to advice suitable wines to accompany certain dishes.

(v) The waiter changes the covers where necessary for the service of the first course. The accompaniments are placed on the table.

(vi) Lay the plates and serve the first course.

(vii) Clear the first course in the approval fashion.

6. Fish Course

(i) Lay the cover for the fish course. Place any accompaniments required on the table.

(ii) If wine is to be served with the fish course, the correct glasses should be placed on the table.

(iii) The wine is presented to the host and opened.

(iv) The host tastes the wine.

(v) The guest are served wine, ladies first, the host last. (Three glasses of wine can be obtained from a half bottle and six glasses from a bottle white wine should be served chilled and red wine at room temperature).

(vi) Lay the fishplates and serve the fish course.

(vii) Clear the fish course.

7. Main Course

(i) Lay the cover for the main course. Place any accompaniments required at the table.

(ii) If a wine is to accompany the main course, the correct glasses should be placed on the table.

(iii) Clear dirty wine glasses.

(iv) The wine is presented to the host, opened and then tasted by the host.

(v) Serve the wine to the guests, ladies first, host last.

(vi) Lay the joint plates and serve the main course. (The station headwaiter must ensure everything required is on the sideboard before commencing service of this course otherwise this can disrupt the service and may mean the food is getting cold).

(vii) All cold dishes should be served before the hot dishes.

(viii) Under plates should be used under vegetable dishes and sauce boats. All food served should be piping hot and served hot on joint plates.

(ix) The meat should be served first and placed on the part of the plate nearest the guest or at the bottom of the cover, *i.e.* 6 o'clock. The potatoes, vegetables and any hot sauces and accompaniments that have to be offered, should follow this.

(x) The sommelier should top up the wineglasses when necessary.

(xi) The station headwaiter should offer more rolls, Melba toast and butter, as required.

(xii) Clear the main course to include side plates and side knives, cruets, butter dishes, gristicks and accompaniments. Everything must be cleared in the approval manner.

(xiii) Start the process of crumbing down.

(xiv) Change the ashtray, if necessary.

8. Sweet Course

(i) Offer the menu for guest to choose a sweet dish.

(ii) Take the order.

(iii) Lay the sweet covers and accompaniments.

(iv) The sommelier clears the wine glasses and wine bottle.

(v) Serve the sweet course (cold dishes are served before the hot-dishes).

(vi) Clear the sweet course.

9. Coffee

(i) Take the coffee order.

(ii) The sommelier presents the liqueur trolley.

(iii) He serves liqueur as required.

(iv) The coffee service is placed on the table.

(v) Serve the coffee.

(vi) Offer more coffee at the appropriate time.

10. Bill Presentation

(i) Present the bill.

(ii) Payment is made to the waiter, who has the bill receipted by the cashier.

(iii) It is then returned with any change to the host.

11. Departure of Guest

(i) The station headwaiter sees the guest out of the restaurant.

(ii) Clear down the table.

(iii) Relay the table, if necessary.

CLEARING PLATES

This skill is necessary in carrying plates of pre-plated foods as well as for clearing. To be able to clear correctly ensure speed and efficiency around the table avoids the possibility of accidents and creates minimum inconvenience to guests. In turn it also allows the stacking of dirties neatly and correctly on the sideboard with the minimum delay. The correct clearing techniques enable more to be cleared, in less time and in fewer journeys between sideboard and table. In the long term this speeds up the eating process and allows for greater seat turnover.

Guidelines for Clearing Side Plates

It is advisable to use service salver or plate to clear the side plates. This will allow larger working surface on which the dirty side knives and any remaining debris can be cleared.

1. Dirties should always be cleared from the right hand side.
2. Clear debris from the side plate on to a service plate/salver.
3. Hand position should be appropriate and stack debris correctly and safely.
4. The waiter should be positioned in sideways distance at the table.
5. The waiter picks up the first dirty soup plate on its underplate. He passes the dirty plate from the clearing hand to the holding hand.
6. The dirty plates are held away from the table and the guests.
7. The first dirty soup plate is cleared. It should be held firmly on its under plate with the latter pushed up firmly between the thumb and the first and second fingers.
8. This first dirty soup plate is held firmly as succeeding dirties are built up on this one, meaning there is considerable weight to hold.
9. Clear the second dirty plate on its under plate, cleared and about to be positioned on the holding hand.
10. The soup spoon is taken from the lower soup plate to be laced in the upper soup plate.
11. Thus, the upper soup plate with its two soups poons now placed in the lower soup plate, leaving the underplate behind.
12. Now, clear the third dirty soup plate with its under plate from the right and place it on the upper under plate on the holding hand.
13. Repeat the above procedure each time a dirty soup plate on its under plate is cleared.

Hand Positions when Clearing Plates

1. Figure 2.12 illustrates the initial hand position for the first plate. Care must be taken to ensure that the first plate is held finnly as succeeding dirty plates are built up from here. the second plate will rest firmly on the forearm and third and fourth fingers.

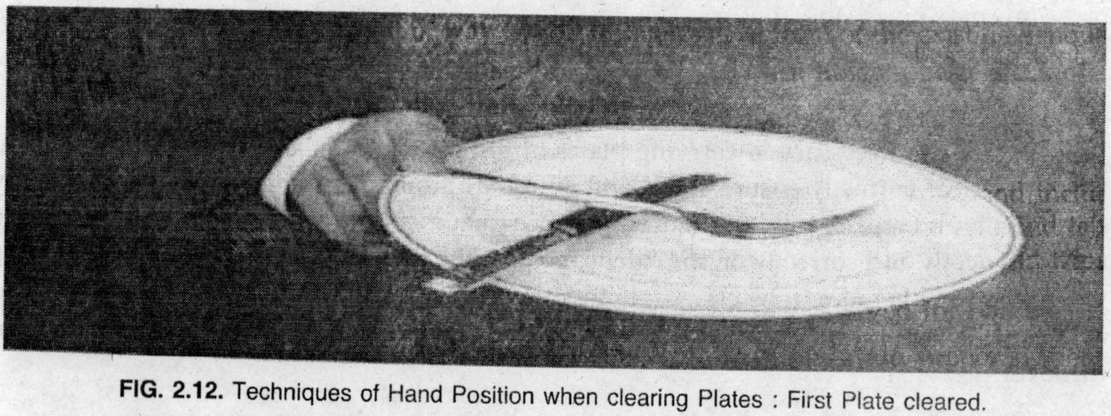

FIG. 2.12. Techniques of Hand Position when clearing Plates : First Plate cleared.

2. Figure 2.13. Shows the second-plate positioned on the left hand

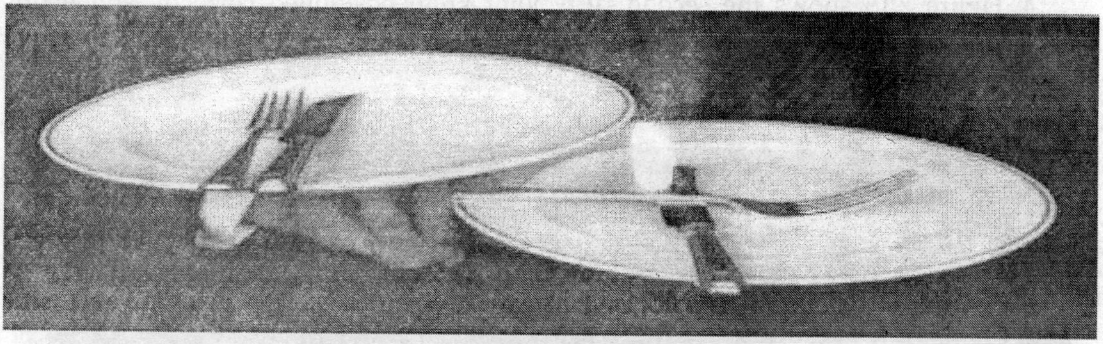

FIG. 2.13. Position on the left hand clearing second plate : Second Plate Cleared.

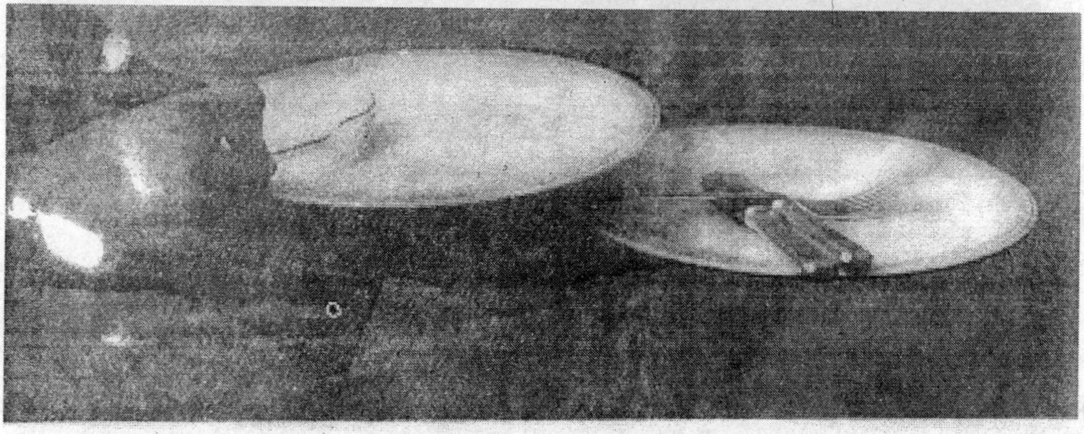

FIG. 2.14. Clearing debris from the upper plate

3. Figure 2.14. Show the second dirty joint plate cleared and positioned on the holding hand.

FIG. 2.15. Preparing to clear the next dirty plate

4. Figure 2.15 shows the second dirty joint knife positioned correctly and debris being cleared from the upper joint plate onto the lower joint plate using the second dirty joining fork cleared.

FIG. 2.16. Cleaning Joint and sideplates in one journey

This procedure is carried out as the waiter moves onto his/her next position (in readiness to clear the third joint plate).

Removing the first plate

This is transferred to the waiter's left hand. Note the position of thumb, little and third finger on top; other two fingers below. The used fork is placed prongs upwards and the knife put at right angles under the bridge part of the fork. An alternative (favoured on the continent is to reverse the fork's position *i.e.* with prongs downwards thus forming a larger bridge under which to slide the knives. Both methods are acceptable. Some waiters find it more secure if the first fork is held by the thumb holding the cutlery plate.

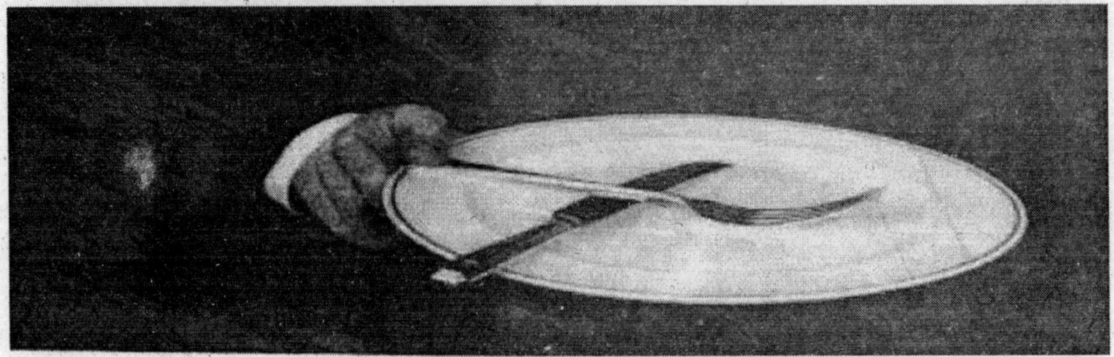

FIG. 2.17. Technique of removing the first plate

Second plate stage

The second plate is balanced on three points formed by the knuckle of the thumb, tips of little and second finger and lower part of forearm (the wrist itself should not be in contact with the plate). Next step is to transfer knife from second plate toi first plate alongside the first knife. Then any food remains on second plate ·e gently scraped with the fork onto the first plate. Carry out this procedure at a safe dista. .e from guests and certainly never over the table.

FIG. 2.18. Clearing Plates : Second plate stage

Stack of cleared plates

Having cleared as outlined above, the waiter now has a neat stack of plates, which do not wobble and are not top heavy. Finally while returning to the sideboard, the waiter will place the first plate (with the cutlery and remains of food) on top of the stack.

FIG. 2.19. Clearing Plates : Stack of cleared plates

Glass plates have been drawn to reveal hand positions. Service cloth normally draping left forearm is omitted for clarity.

Clearing Tables

When the main course had been consumed, the restaurant tables needs to be cleared. Dirty side plates and side knives needs to be cleared. The correct clearing techniques depend on what is being cleared.

(a) First soup plate is cleared

(b) First stage of clearing the second soup plate

(c) Second stage of clearing the second soup plate

d) Second soup plate cleared in preparation for the next

FIG. 2.20. Clearing soup plates

Guidelines/or Clearing Joint Plates

Below are give the guidelines for clearing joint plates :

1. Dirties should always be cleared from the right hand side of the guest.
2. The waiter should position him/herself taking up a sideways stance at the table.
3. Position your hands as given in Fig. 2.19 and clear the first joint plate.
4. The dirty joint plate should be held firmly pushed up to the joint between the thumb and the first and second finger.
5. Position the cutlery and flatware. Hold the fork firmly with the thumb over the end of its handle and the blade of the joint knife placed under the arch in the handle of the fork.
6. Debris and crumbs would be pushed into the triangle formed by the handles of the joint knife and joint fork and the rim of the plate that is nearest the holding hand.
7. The second dirty joint plate be cleared and appropriately positioned on the holding hand.
8. The debris of the second plate/upper joint plate on the lower joint plate using the second dirty fork cleared. This is carried out as the waiter/ress moves on to his/her next position in readiness to clear the third dirty joint plate.
9. Hold firmly all the cleared items and get ready to receive the next dirty joint plate to be cleared.
10. The next step is to clear the side plates in journey to the table and stack them out by one on the second-third joint plates.

[*Note:* The joint plates and side plates can be cleared in two phases].

Crumbing Down

The process of crumbing down should always take place after the main course has been consumed and all the dirty items of equipment cleared from the table. In other words, crumbing starts just after the sweet order is taken and served. The main purpose of crumbing is to remove any crumbs or debris left on the tablecloth at this stage of the meal. The items of equipment used to crumb down are :

1. A service plate (a joint plate with a napkin on it).
2. The waiter's clothe or service cloth.

In a *table d'hote* cover, the sweet spoon and fork should have been positioned at the end of the cover, prior to the commencement of crumbing down, after the main course has been cleared. The procedure for crumbing is as under by the waiter:

1. The process of crumbing down should commence from the left-hand side of the first guest.
2. The waiter places the service plate just beneath the lip of the table.
3. Crumbs and other debris lying on the tablecloth are brushed down towards the plate using a folded napkin or small brush used for this purpose.
4. When this process is over, move the sweet fork from the head of the place setting to the left-hand side of the cover.

FIG. 2.21. Crumbing down. Note the neatly folded service cloth

5. Now, move to the right hand side of the same guest and complete the crumbing down of this place setting.
6. Remove the sweet spoon from the head of the place setting to the right hand side of the cover.
7. Hold the service cloth held under the service plate by the fingers of the holding hand when the sweet spoon and sweet fork are being moved to their appropriate positions.
8. The crumbing down process for one place setting is then completed.
9. Now, commence again the same process of crumbing down of the net place setting, *i.e.* to the left of the next guest. This process will be repeated for next crumbing operations.

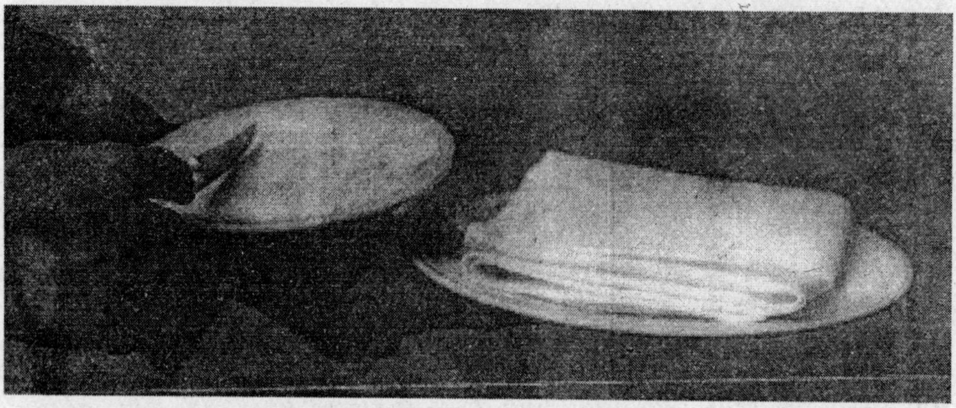

(a) Clearing debris from the sideplate on to a service plate

(b) Hand position having cleared four sideplates

FIG. 2.22. Clearing sideplates

Changing a dirty Ashtray

Changing of dirty ashtray may be carried out at any stage of the meal; whenever so required. The guidelines followed are :

1. Spot the dirty ashtray on the table.
2. Hold a clean ashtray over the dirty ashtray.
3. Place the clean ashtray upside-down on the top of the dirty ashtray.
4. Lift the dirty ashtray, covered by the clean ashtray, from the guest's table. This is done to ensure that no fine cigar or cigarette ash is blown on to the tablecloth.
5. Transfer the dirty ashtray with its cover to the holding hand away from the table.
6. Now place the clean ashtray on the table.

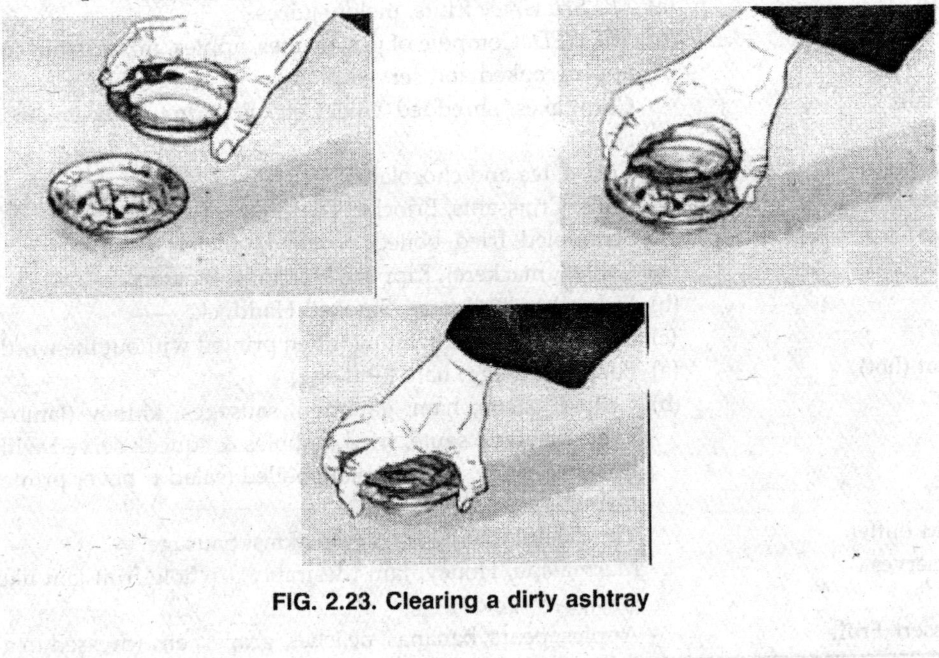

FIG. 2.23. Clearing a dirty ashtray

Closing the Dinning Room

The dinning room should be closed between luncheons and dinning. When closing after lunch, reset enough tables for the anticipated number of dinning guests. At the end of the day, close the dinning room properly. Clean your station, side stand and kitchen area in a clean and orderly condition, ready for business the next day, collect all ashtrays from the tables and empty them into a fireproof container. Remove all salt, pepper, and sugar containers and place them on tray wipe the containers with a clean, damp cloth and refill them. Periodically, the salt, pepper and sugar containers should be emptied and washed.

Take all condiments such as cat sup, mustard and steak sauce to the refrigerator. Creamers and butter containers should be emptied into large containers. The cream may be used for baking or cooking.

Next, strip the tables of their tableclothes. Table should not be set up for the next day because settings gather dust. Instead, assemble all the service ware for the use the next morning on trays and cover them with napkins.

Empty all coffee containers and clean all the coffee equipment. Return unused and voided numbered guest checks to the supervisor. Turn off all heating equipment such as roll warmers and coffee making equipment.

TABLE 2.7

A Typical comprehensive Breakfast Menu Sequence

S. No.	*Order of Course*	*Dishes Available*
1.	Fruit	(a) *FRESH: Grape* fruits, melon, juices. (b) *STEWED:* Compote of jigs, prunes, apples, mixed fruit, cold baked apple (cooked and served plain).
2.	Cereals	Cornflakes, shredded wheat etc. Porridge, Milk cream (hot and cold).
3.	Beverages	Coffee, tea and chocolate.
4.	Bread	Rolls, Croissants, Brioche, Toast, etc.
5.	Eggs	Scrambled, fried, boiled, poached, omelets.
6.	Fish	(a) Grilled, mackerel. Kippers, Herrings, Bloaters (b) Fish cakes. Kedgeree, Smoked Haddock. (c) Fried: plaice, sole, whiting (often printed without the word grilled).
7.	Meat (hot)	(a) Bacon (and egg) ham (and egg). (b) Grilled: bacon, ham, gammon, sausages, kidney (lambs), calves liver. Potatoes: saute, fried, bubbles & squeak served with : Potatoes, saute, fried or plain boiled (salad is never printed on the menu).
8.	Cold Buffet	York Ham, Calves Tongs, Breakfast Sausage.
9.	Preserves	Marmalade, Honey, Jam (desirably a whole fruit jam like cherry, strawberry, etc.)
10.	Dessert Fruit	Apples, pears, bananas, peaches, grapes, etc. (dressed in a basket).

QUESTIONS AND ASSIGNMENTS

Objective Type

Q. 1. Tick mark (√) the answer that best co pletes the statement :

(a) When food on a menu is *a la carte*, it is :
  (i) Served from a cart
  (ii) Served with a beverage
  (iii) Priced to include an entire meal.
  (iv) Listed as single item and priced separately from other food items.

(b) Juices, fruits and seafood items are examples of foods included in the following category:
  (i) Appetizer
  (ii) Salad
  (iii) Dessert
  iv) Entree.

(c) Closing the dinning room involves duties such as :
  (i) Asking the remaining guests to leave.
  (ii) Setting up the tables for the next morning business
  (iii) Discarding voided checks
  (iv) Turning off all heating equipment such as, roll warmers and coffee urns.

(d) The sequence of serving the courses during a meal is as follows :
  (i) Appetizer, dessert, entree, salad
  (ii) Salad, appetizer, entree, dessert
  (iii) Entree, appetizer, salad, dessert
  (iv) Appetizer, salad, entree, dessert.

(e) To serve booths :
  (i) Serve the guest farthest from you first with the hand farthest from the guest
  (ii) Serve the guest farthest from you with the hand closet to the guest.
  (iii) Serve the guest closet to you first with the hand farthest from the guest.
  (iv) Serve the guest to closet to you first with the hand closet to the guest.

(f) When serving more than one table, choose the order of serving the following foods from your tray so that proper food temperatures will be maintained :
  (i) Ice cream, crackers, hot rolls
  (ii) Crackers, ice cream, hot rolls
  (iii) Hot rolls, crackers, ice cream
  (iv) Ice cream, hot rolls, crackers.

(g) Two ways a guest check may be presented to the customer are :
  (i) Face up on the table on a face down on a tip tray
  (ii) Face up on the table and face down up on a tip tray
  (iii) Face down on the table and face down on a tip tray
  (iv) Face down on the table and face up on the tip tray.

Q. 2. Pick the odd one out (stating reasons) and write down that does not fit with the other two :

(a) Fish Plate	Soup Plate	Cheese Plate
(b) Roly-Poly	High ball	Collins
(c) Chef de Rang	Sommelier	Sous Chef
(d) Mise-en-place	a la carte	Plat due jour

(e)	Orange Pekoe	Rombouts	Tisanes
(f)	Hollandaise	Vinaigrette	Mayonnaise
(g)	Consomme	Chowder	Bisque
(h)	Buck Wheat	Shredded Wheat	Wheat flakes
(i)	Croutons	Grated Cheese	Chipolate
(f)	Evian	Ginger beer	Tonic water. (BHM)

Q. 3. Fill in the blanks :

(a) A pleasant............means waiter and waitress will be tactful, courteous and have an ability to smile.

(b) The team brigade is check to denote the t........... ..of s........... ..working together in the dinning room in the same shift.

(c) A form of service, which supplements other system, might often the A.............V..............

(d) All food orders to the *aboyer* showed be .... so that there is ....in calling up a particular dish.

(e) When taking order at the table, recognition, of the ....is an important factor in effective communication.

Q. 4. Fill in the blanks :

(a) .... is the term for the pantry of commercial aircraft.

(b) The first IHC hotel was established in ....

(c) .... is the method of cleaning silver by using aluminum and washing soda.

(d) Another name for eggplant is ....

(e) Restaurant trolleys move with the help of .... (coasters, ball bearings, casters).

(f) Hospital and school catering fall under ....

(g) The analysis at the end of the meal session by a mitre d' hotel is known as...........

(h) Castor sugar and ground ginger are the accompaniments to ....

(i) Cream crackers are .... (pastries, waffles, biscuits, pork rind).

(j) Diameter of a large plate is .... cm.

Q. 5. State whether "True" or False" :

(a) Service lift is known as Dumb Waiter.

(b) Sweet breads are served as an entremet.

(c) Gorgonzola is a blue cheese from Germany

(d) A sideboard is also called a service console.

(e) While laying a cover for spaghetti the fork should be placed on the right hand side of the cover. [BHM]

Q. 6. Fill in the blanks (from the choice given after each) :

(a) Carte du jour is a .... (speciality item, days menu, restaurant trolley)

(b) Plate room is the place for .... (electroplating of cutlery, storing crockery, staff dinning)

(c) Bus boy is a member of the ....staff. (Belt desk, conducted tour, restaurant)

(d) The size of the guest serviette is approximately ....cm. sq. (32, 50, 62)

(e) ....is a stew of white meat. (blanquette, barquette, bisque)

(f) ....sauce is the accompaniment for roast lamb (apple, cranberry, mint)

(g) The capacity of demi tasse is ....cl. (12, 8, 10)

(h) .... is a type of melton, (panier, cantaloupe, potiron)

(i) Dhansak is a speciality ....dish. (Parsi, Bengali, Punjabi)

(j) Sommelier is the ....waiter, (trolley, wine, station).

Q.7. State whether 'true' or 'false':

(a) A mobile pantry can be used in the lobby area.
(b) The tarnish on EPNS cutlery is silver sulphide.
(c) Glass cloth should be made of cotton.
(d) Dumb waiter is a restaurant side-board.
(e) Gorgonzola is a blue-veined cheese.
(f) Petits fours are a type of pastry.
(g) The BOT is an essential control measure.
(h) Cheese is always accompanied by cream crackers.
(i) Cafe complete is coffee with biscuits and brandy.
(j) Bird's nest is the national soup of Ireland.,

Q.8. Fill in the blanks with correct word or words to complete the sentence :

(a) A computer keyboard that is programmed so that each key is dedicated to a specific menu item is called a (an) ....
(b) A machine that imprints information on food and beverage orders, guest checks, receipts and management reports are known as.............Computer point of sale machines with keyboard is referred to..............
(c) A physical component of a computer system that accepts and process the information fed into them at restaurant are called.............

Ans : (a) *preset;* (b) *cash register;* (c) *server terminals;* (d) *server terminals, visual displays, cash drawer.*

Q. 9. How would each of the following adversely affect the average sale in a restaurant?

(a) Deterioration in service standards
(b) Inadequate sales promotion.

Q. 10. As a guest in a restaurant, observe waiter/ress and note down the errors made by the service personnel. Discuss points with other trainees.

Q. 11. Do a role-play exercise serving and clearing dishes from the table. Take terms beings the guest and the waiter/ress.

Q. 12. Define the following terms:

(a) Cover
(b) Underliner
(c) American service
(d) Family style service
(e) French service
(f) Russian service.

Q. 13. Explain the procedure for timing the following entree meal orders in a restaurant with multi-unit kitchen: -

(a) Shrimp souffle
(b) Pork chops
(c) Lamb chops
(d) Red snapper
(e) Chateaubriand.

Q. 14. Pay a visit to a restaurant and kitchen, meet with service and kitchen personnel and agree upon abbreviations for food items on the menu. Make a list and post them in the kitchen.

Q. 15. When a customer does not leave you with a tip

(a) How would you handle the following situations :
(b) Protect the guest from a hot coffee pot when you are pouring coffee at the table.
(c) A guest asks you to take his pate before anyone at the table is finished with the course. [BHM]

Q. 16. How would you handle the complaints when the guest says :

(a) The steak is too rare

(b) The chilly is too spicy

(c) The food is cold

(d) You spilled coffee on me.

Q. 17. The 3-basic types of room service operations are centralized, decentralized and mobile. For a 250-rooms City Hotel, catering mainly to business clienteles, what would be your choice of room service operation? Explain in not more than 150-words. [BHM]

Q. 18. Give French equivalents of *any five* of the following phrases :

(a) Lemon cress

(b) Dinning Room

(c) Mayonnaise based sauce served with fried fish

(d) Corkscrew

(e) Oil and vinegar dressing for salad

(f) Water jug. [BHM]

Q. 19. Explain in about two lines the difference between the following :

(a) Mis en place and mis en scene

(b) Industrial and institutional catering

(c) Counter service and gueridon

(d) Cafe simple and cafe complete

(e) Restaurant and cafeteria. [BHM]

Q. 20. You are a restaurant waiter serving at a table with 10-covers. Whilst silver servicing the soup, a guest accidentally bumped your arm and you spill the hot soup over the table and the dress of a lady guest. In about 10-15 lines describe your reaction to this accident and what method you would employ to rectify it ? [BHM]

Q. 21. In three or four lines each, explain *any five* of the following :

(a) Hollandaise

(b) Sorbet

(c) EPNS

(d) Garnish

(e) Canape

(f) K.O.T.

(g) Gueridon

(h) Baize. [BHM]

Q. 22. Give reasons in about 4 or 5-lines for each situation as to what the waiter should say and do in the following :

(a) A male guest arrives at your dinning area wearing no jacket. His dress therefore does not meet the standards laid down by your establishment.

(b) The guest is in a hurry and wishes to order this meal be served, eat and leave within 20-minutes.

(c) You suspect that a prospective guest asking for a table has too much to drink. [BHM]

Q. 23. Make a chart of 10 different types of food and beverage services. List the type of service down the left margin. Across the top of the chart label the vertical columns with the following heads :

(a) Distinguishing features

(b) Server's responsibilities

(c) Advantages

(d) Disadvantages. Complete the chart.

Q. 24. Invite a local doctor to come to your training session and discuss first aid in emerging situations.

Q. 25. Invite a health officer to discuss the trainees the sanitation laws in your city and state as they apply to serving.

Q. 26. Make a visit to restaurants of various sizes and types and ask for food and beverage service personnel how they place and pick up orders in the kitchen. Bring this information to the class and discuss it with other trainees.

Q. 27. Do a role-play exercise of seating the guests. Include :

(a) Conversation with the guests.

(b) Placement of parties in the dinning room

(c) Removal of extra service ware

(d) Provision of water and

(e) Other services to make the guest comfortable.

Q. 28. Have a brain storming session to find out ways to save time and effort in the serving process.

Q. 29. Distinguished between Russian service and French service.

Q. 30. Draw an organizational chart of a food and beverage establishment of your choice. Indicate who would be your immediate superior if you were working as a server.

Q. 31. Make a comparative statement showing the job of a sales person in retail store with the job of a waiter/ress. In what ways are their jobs alike? In what ways do they differ?

Q. 32. How will you identify the host ? Explain methods to remember the food each guest ordered.

Q. 33. The waiter/ress written order on a pad of paper is most popular for dinning rooms with *table d' hote* elections on the menu'. Explain.

Q. 34. Explain some of the topics that are appropriate for conversation with guests.

Q. 35. What suggestions would you make in the following instance :

(a) A couple is celebrating their anniversary

(b) A guest orders apple pie

(c) The guests have finished their dessert

Q. 36. Define the following terms :

(a) Crumbling

(b) Appetizer.

Q. 37. Differentiate between serving food and serving beverages.

Q. 38. Why should the waiter/ress avoid scraping and stacking dishes at the table in front of the guest?

Q. 39. Give reason, about 5-lines for each situation, as to what the waiter should say and do in the following :

(a) A guest suggests the the fish dish served is off'; and

(b) A waiter finds a wallet under a chair recently vacated by one of the clients. [BHM]

Q. 40. Illustrate with the help of a flow chart, the triplicate checking system of restaurant sales control. [BHM]

Q. 41. Explain the importance of a Dumb Waiter in a restaurant. Illustrate it with a neat diagram.

Q. 42. 'A proper briefing before the service plays a very important role for the success of any service operation'. Elaborate. [BHM]

Q. 43. How does a supervisor plan his job for supervising a mean service ? [BHM]

Q. 44. Every category of room service personnel have an imporant role to play in providing personalized service, bringing about guest satisfaction and achieving sales targets. Discuss in about 250-words.

Q. 45. Give your assessment of the view that in food service establishments too little time and attention is given towards effective supervision. How do you see the role of the supervisor in the food service situation? [HCIMA (London)]

Q. 46. List down the attributes of a good waiter. [BHM]

Q. 47. As a *maitre d'hotel* of a first class restaurant (international), what responsibilities do you have during the bench *mise-en-place* operation? BBM(M)(MTA]

Q. 48. W*rite short notes on :

(a) Service Charge

(b) K.O.T. (Kitchen Order Ticket)

(c) City ledger.

Q. 49. When a hotel/restaurant is for sale what are some of the questions that should be asked ?

Q. 50. Examine current trends in food productiona nd service. To what extent do you feel technology will influence the catering industry in the future ? (HCIMA (London)]

Q. 51. What is 'Door knob' style of ordering? Give a sample of an ideal room service door knob menu format. [BHM]

3 Service of Breakfast and Afternoon Tea

After learning this lesson, you should be able :

1. *Understand and practice the procedures of breakfast preparations*
2. *Practice the sercies of brakfast, afternon tea reception tea Lounge service floor service minibar bospital tary service and air line tray service*
3. *Demonstate.*

In hotels breakfast is an important meal because it is one that a customer invariably takes in the establishment itself.

At breakfast it is usual to serve any dish from number 1 & 2 (fruit and cereal) followed by 5 to 7 (eggs, fish, meat-hot or cold). Finally a guest completes his meal with, say, toast and marmalade. The beverages although appearing on the menus at number 3 are served directly after the first course but this is the only case where service does not follow the printed sequence. A dish need not be chosen from every heading. As few, as many, or none at all can be chosen to suit the menu's requirement. For example, a continental breakfast comprises only one course, usually headed by 4 (bread items), followed by 9 (preserves) and ending with 3 (beverages). Some breakfast menus revert to this sequence.

Table 2.10 indicates the breakfast sequence but it is rare for any guest to take more than one preliminary course, fruit/fruit juice or cereals and one cooked course followed by rolls, toast and preserves.

Pre-preparation

For the two types of breakfast served in hotels — plain or continental breakfast, and full or English breakfast — pre-preparation varies. A plain breakfast consists of tea or coffee, rolls, toast (perhaps also croissants and rolls) butter and marmalade, requires only a modest *'mise-en-place'*

1. Mise en place

A full English breakfast is most elaborate meal and requires preparation in the dinning room before service. Grape fruits and oranges should be arranged. The various juices, cereals, jugs of cream and cold milk are arranged on a table in the dinning room. Services of jam, honey and marmalade are to be prepared but in many operations. These (and butter) are pre-packaged in individual portions. In order to be ready on time for breakfast, services as much as possible *mise en place* is done the previous night.

2. *Table and Cover : Previous evening preparations*

The evening before, a clean tablecloth is laid on the table then the cover is set. A full breakfast cover consisted of :

(i) One of a medium sized plate
(ii) A joint knife and a fish knife to the right
(iii) A joint fork and a fish fork to the left
(iv) In front, a sweet fork is placed, handle to the left and a dessertspoon, and handle to the right
(v) On the left side of this, a side plate is placed with a side knife on the right edge of the plate, in line with the other cutlery
(vi) Butter cups and sauces, if set the night before, are placed to the right beside the tip of the meat knife (for fish knife if laid) and with the cup upside down and a covering with cloth cover
(vii) A slop basin, a cruet set and an astray are positioned symmetrically on the table.

3. *Morning Preparation*

Next morning, complete setting with :

(i) Breakfast-size cups and saucers.
(ii) Tea spoons.
(iii) Table napkins (placed square on the medium sized plate).
(iv) A bowl of soft sugar and one of lump sugar are then placed on the table, together with a jug of cold cream and a service of preservers (marmalade, honey and jam usually in miniature jars or individual packs).

4. *Check the Covers*

Check that the full breakfast table consists of :

(i) Breakfast cups (tea cups) to the right of the covers leaving space for beverage pots to be placed later. Sugar basin (tilted with tongs or spoon). Slop basin and tea strainer near the place earmarked for beverage pots.
(ii) Cruet (salt, pepper) centrally placed.
(iii) Preserve dish (marmalade/jam) within reach.
(iv) Space near Alamo marked for toast rack and butter dish.
(v) The cover itself (side plate, napkin and a knife with cereal spoon, large knife and fork or fish knife and fork) should, with other items, all be neatly arranged.

5. Sideboard Requirements

During the *mise en place* time, the waiters attend to sideboards, staking cutlery, plates, cups, saucers, napkins, large and small tablecloths and anything that may be required during service. Preparations of grapefruit, orange juices, grapefruit juices, tomato juices, etc. and jug of iced water. Assembly of condiments t iclude fresh mustard. Worcestershire sauce, and bottles of vinegar, etc. floral decorations are seldom used for breakfast.

Summary of Morning Breakfast and Mise en Place

Kitchen

Porridge made
Bacon, sausages; batch grilling starts
Eggs available : prepare to order.

Stillroom

Coffee made in batches in advance (but cona or similar services be provided in the room)
Tea to order
Toast to order
...lls warmed.

Restaurant

For Tables :

Milk on table
Preserves
Butters
Menu
Flowers.

For sideboards :

Iced water (American guests)
Rolls/butter.
Cream.
Mustards, sauces.
Extra covers.

Breakfast Service

Breakfast meals have been modified in recent years. In hotels, breakfast is an important meal because it is one that a customer invariably takes in the establishment itself. People in Britain eat less traditional breakfast food such as egg and bacon and have turned to more healthy or high fibre foods such as cereals, together with increases in consumption of yoghurt. In cities like London, the current trends are for hotels to have a continental breakfast inclusive in room rate and to serve the full English breakfast at an 'a *la carte*' charge.

Breakfast may be served in the hotel restaurant or dinning room in a breakfast room set aside for this one meal, or in the guest's bedroom or suite. *'Cafe complete'* is widely used on the continental and means, a continental breakfast with coffee as the beverage. On the other hand, a guest may order a 'cafe' simple or the 'simple' in which case she/he requires on beverage (coffee/tea) with nothing to eat.

Breakfast menus are presented to each guest by the headwaiter/waiter and the order taken in the usual manner. For coffee service there are two methods. The traditional method is to place coffee, milk and sugar on the table in a coffeepot, milk jug and sugar bale. Customer help themselves when several people in one party occupy a table, coffee is placed on the right of the senior or eldest lady present. The other method is the coffee is brewed on a sideboard in a cona/machine. The waiter carries this with an accompanying jug of hot milk from table to table.

Typical Service of Breakfast — Sequence

Continental Breakfast

1. Presentation of menu
2. Taking order
3. Adjusting covers
4. Serving starters (*e.g.* fruit juices)
5. Serving hot beverages: For tea checking of strainer, slop basin, cold milk or dish or lemon slices and fork on side plate
6. At the last minute serving of hot rolls (leave on table) and/or toast, butter and jam (or doilies on side plates).

FIG. 3.1. An example of continental breakfast

Full Breakfast Service Procedure

1. Presentation of menus
2. Take order noting of guest order, separate check for stillroom
3. Adjusting order
4. Collections of starters
5. Placing of hot beverages, roll, etc. unless customer indicate otherwise
6. Cleaning starter
7. Serving of main course
8. Removing unwanted items (*e.g.* sugar shaker)
9. Clearing main course plate: adjustment of covers (morning side plate to centre) placing jam etc. conveniently near the guest
10. Checking toast etc. for replenishment.

FIG. 3.2. Full breakfast cover

English Breakfast Menu

It may consist of two to eight courses. The extent and variety of the menu will depend on the type of establishment in which it is being served. Today's full table d'hote breakfast menu of three courses is usually presented. There are four sections but only three courses as beverages and breads are served earlier in the meal, Table 2.11 is an example of such a breakfast menu.

FIG. 3.3. A Typical English breakfast table setting for one person.

TABLE 3.1.
A Typical Breakfast Menu

Breakfast Menu

1.	*Fruit Juices*	Orange Pineapple Lemon Grapefruit etc.
2.	Tomato Juice	Tomato Juice
3.	Stewed Fruits	Plums Prunes Apples Figs Pears etc.
4.	Cereals	Porridge or other cereals.
5.	Fish	Steamed fillet of hadlock Fried Fillet of Sole Grilled herring Kedgeree

(Contd...)

6.	Eggs	Fried egg Poached egg on toast Grilled fried egg Fried, boiled, scrambled plain or savery omelet.
7.	Meat	Fried or grilled bacon Grilled kidneys and bacon Fried or grilled sauces.
8.	Cold Buffet	York Ham Calves Tongue Breakfast sausages
9.	Breads	Toast Rolls Croissants Brioches Ryvitta Hovis and Procea Brown bread
10.	Fresh Fruits	Orange Apples Pears Banana
11.	Preserves	Marmalade Hor ey Plum Cherry
12.	Beverages	Tea Coffee Milk Chocolate Tisanes.

The fish knife and fork are positioned outside, the meat knife and fork inside. A dessert spoon for porridge or cereals is laid at the top of the cover. A small knife is placed on the side plate to the right. The teapot, milking and hot water jug are positioned to the right. Note the angle of the handles for the guest's convenience.

FIG. 3.4. A Typical Continental Breakfast table Setting for One Person

FIG. 3.5. A Tray Typically Laid for Breakfast with White Coffee Menu

1. Small napkin
2. Dessert plate
3. Small knife
4. Saucer
5. Coffee cup
6. Coffee spoon
7. Bread or toast plate
8. Butter dish
9. Jam dish
10. Sugar bowl
11. Milk jug
12. Coffee pot

Continental breakfast originated in France. The current trend in this breakfast is towards offering a wider variety of choices. Figure 3.6 is a specimen of a continental breakfast.

Continental Breakfast

1. Fruit Juice	– Orange
	– Grapefruit or Tomato
	– Fresh grapefruits or orange segments.
2. Stewed Fruits	– Prunes
	– Figs or Apricots.
3. Fresh Fruits	– Fresh fruit salad.
4. Yoghurt	– Choice of cereals, porridge, etc.
5. Baker Selection	– Croissant
	– White and whole-meal rolls.
	– Continental Pastry
	– White/Brown Toast.
	– Marmalade, preserve, honey, country butter or flor-a-margarine.
6. Cold Buffet	– Cold ham and cheese.
7. Beverages	– English breakfast tea with milk or lemon.
	– Coffee - freshly brewed or decaffeinated with milk or
	– Cream.
	– Hot chocolate.
	– Cold milk.
	– Chilled water.

FIG. 3.6. A Typical Continental Breakfast Menu

English Breakfast Cover	*Continental Breakfast Cover*
(Table D'Hote)	
1. Joint knife and fork.	1. Side plate.
2. English knife and fork.	2. Side knife.
3. Sweet spoon and fork.	3. Serviette, normally placed on the side plate and under the side knife.
4. Side knife.	4. Bread boat containing the croissant or brioche in a serviette to keep them hot or a toast rack on an under plate.
5. Side plate.	5. Butter dish on a doily on a side plate with a butter knife.
6. Breakfast cup, saucer and teaspoon.	6. Preserve dish on a doily on a side plate with preserves spoon.
7. Slop basin.	7. Breakfast cup and saucer and a teaspoon
8. Tea strainer.	8. Stands or under plates for coffee/tea pot with preserve spoon.

9. Jug of cold milk.
10. Sugar basin and tongs.
11. Stand or under plates for teapot/coffee Pot and hot water jug/hot milk jug.
12. Butter dish on a doily on an under plate
13. Preserve dish on a doily on an under plate and hot milk/hot water jug.
14. Cruet: salt, pepper, mustard and mustard spoon.
15. Sugar and Castor.
16. Serviette: either laid flat between the joint knife and fork or placed on the side Plate under the side knife.
17. Astray,
18. Toast rack on an under plate.
19. Table number.
20. Bread boat containing the croissant or brioche In a serviette to keep them warm.

9. Ashtray.
10. Table Number.
11. Sugar basin and tongs.

Note: If tea is served then following additional items will be needed.

(i) Slop basin.
(ii) Tea strainer.
(iii) Jug of cold milk.

Note: Most of these items should be placed on the table as a part *of mise en place,* before the guest is seated. Items Placed on table after the guest is seated are :

(i) Butter dish and butter.
(ii) Preserve dish with preserve.
(iii) Jug of cold milk.
(iv) Toast rack with toast and/or breadbasket with hot rolls.

FIG. 3.7. Cover for a Breakfast — English and Continental

Morning Preparations

Kitchen	*Still Room*	*Restaurant*	
		For Tables	*For Sideboard*
1. Porridge made	1. Coffee made in	1. Milk on table.	1. Iced water (American
2. Bacon,sausages:	batches in advance	2. Preserve.	guests)
2. Bacon, sausages:	(put cona or similar,	3. Butters.	2. Rolls/butter
Batches grilling starts	serves in the room)	4. Menu.	3. Cream.
3. Eggs available:	2. Tea to order.	5. Flowers.	4. Mustard sauces
prepare to order.	3. Toast to order.		5. Mustard sauces.
	4. Rolls warmed.		

FIG. 3.8. A Typical Mise en Place (Morning Preparation)

Breakfast Service Sequence

English Breakfast	*Continental Breakfast*
1. Present menu	1. Present menu
2. Take order (Note guests wishes)	2. Take order (Note guest's wishes)
3. Adjust covers	3. Adjust covers as per customer's order
4. Collect starters	4. Serve first course; starter, *e.g.* fruit juice
5. Place hot beverages, rolls etc. unless customer indicates otherwise	5. Serve hot beverages: Tea
6. Clear starter	6. At the last minute serve hot rolls (have on table) and/or toast, butter and Jam (on doilies or side plates)
7. Service main course	
8. Remove any unwanted items *e.g.* sugar shakers.	
9. Clear main course plate : adjust cover (move side plate to centre), place jam, etc. conveniently near the guest.	
10. Check toast, etc. for replenishment.	

FIG. 3.9. A Typical Breakfast Service Sequence

Buffet Breakfast

Some hotels have introduced a self-service breakfast buffet. For the service of this style of breakfast meal, guests are presented with the breakfast menu when they sit down and from that they make their choice of either the buffet or other type of breakfast. All items are self-served from the buffet with perhaps the exception of an egg dish or other cooked item and the beverage required. The waiter should serve these.

AFTERNOON TEA

The old English tradition of taking afternoon tea at 4 o'clock is being replaced by teas and pastries only and the venue changing from hotel lounge to the coffee bars or shops and tea gardens found in the modern day shopping precincts. However, there are many hotels where afternoon tea is still served which may be classified into three main types:

1. Full afternoon tea – served in first class hotels.
2. High tea as served in a popular prices restaurant/cafe.
3. Reception or buffet tea.

Service Sequence for Afternoon Tea

1. Beverages
2. Hot smokes – bread and butter sometimes salads
3. Hot toasted items
4. Sandwiches
5. Buttered scones
6. Bread and butler
7. Preserves
8. Cake and pastries:
   (i) Toast, teacakes and crumpets from stillroom.
   (ii) Sandwiches from larder.
   (iii) Scones and assorted buttered bread from stillroom.
   (iv) Gateaux and pastries from Patisserie

Note :

(i) High tea only : The beverage should be served first, followed by hot snacks ordered with its accompaniments of bread and butters. When this is consumed and cleared, the service then follows that of afternoon tea.

(ii) Ice creams are served last.

(iii) Checking is usually the duplicate method.

FIG. 3.10. Given a Typical Service Sequence for Afternoon Tea

Afternoon Tea

1. Beverages : Tea/Coffee (Indian, Ceylon, China, Russia, Iced, etc.).
2. Hot Buttered Toast or Toasted Teacake or Crumpets
3. Assorted Sandwiches :
   (i) Smoked Salmon.
   (ii) Cucumber - Tomato sandwich.
   (iii) Egg.
   (iv) Gentleman's Relish.
4. Bread and Butter
   (i) White, Brown, White meal fruit.
   (ii) Buttered Scones.
   Jam, Lemon, Curd, Honey.
5. Conserves
6. Pastries and Gateaux

FIG. 3.11. A Typical menu for Afternoon Tea

Menu for high tea

A high tea may be available in addition to the full afternoon tea. It is usually in a modified a *la carte* form and the menu will offer, in addition to the normal full afternoon tea menu, such items as grills. toasted snacks, fish and meat dishes, salads, cold sweets and ices. The meat dishes normally consists in the main of pics and pastries, whereas the fish dishes are usually fried or grilled.

The following accompaniments (proprietary sauces) may often be offered with high tea :

- Tomato ketchup
- Worcestershire sauce
- Brown sauce (e.g. 'HP')
- Vinegar
- Mustard

Departmental stores and popular-price restaurants offer high tea in addition to the full afternoon tea.

Menu for High Tea

Normal full after tea menu

Meat dishes: fried and pastries.
Fish dishes: fried or grilled.
Accompaniments: (Proprietary sauces):

Tomato ketchup
Worcester Sauce
Vinegar
Mustard

FIG. 3.12. A Typical Menu for High Tea

Afternoon Tea Covers

The afternoon tea cover may be divided into two types :

- Full afternoon tea cover
- High tea cover

FIG. 3.13. Cover for full afternoon tea

The following cover should normally be laid for a full afternoon tea :

1. Sideplate
2. Napkin
3. Side or tea knife
4. Pastry fork
5. Tea cup and saucer and a teaspoon
6. Slop basin and tea stainer
7. Sugar basin and tongs
8. Teapot and hot water jug stands or underplates
9. Jug of cold milk
10. Preserve dish on an underplate with a preserve spoon
11. Ashtray (depending on smoking policy)

Note : The Jug of cold milk and preserve dish should only be brought to the table when the guests are seated, and are not part of the *mise-en-place.*

Cover for High Tea

The cover for high tea may include :

1. Napkin
2. Joint knife and fork
3. Side plate
4. Side knife
5. Cruet : salt, pepper, mustard and mustard spoon
6. Teacup, saucer and teaspoon
7. Sugar basin and tongs
8. Slop basin and tea strainer
9. Teapot and hot water jug stands or underplates
10. Jug of cold milk
11. Preserve dish on an underplate with a preserve spoon
12. Ashtray (depending on smoking policy)

*Note :*As for the full afternoon tea cover, the jug of cold milk and the preserve dish should only be brought to the table when the guests are seated and are not part of the *mise-en-place.* Any other items of tableware that may be required are brought to the table as for a la carte service.

1. Teacup and saucer and a teaspoon
2. Slop basin and rea strainer
3. Sugar basin and tongs
4. Teapot and hot water jug stands of underplates
5. Jug of cold milk
6. Preserve dish on an underplate with a preserve spoon

7. Ashtray (depending on smoking policy)
8. Table number

Note : The beverage, jug of cold milk, preerve dish and butter dish should only be brought to the table when the guests are seated, and are not part of the *mise-en-place.*

FIG. 3.14. Cover for full afternoon tea (after the order has been taken)

As for the full afternoon tea cover, the jug of cold milk, butter dish and the preserve dish should only be brought to the table when the guests are seated and are not part of the *mise-en-place.* Any other items of tableware that may be required are brought to the table as for a la carte service.

FIG. 3.15. Cover for high tea (prior to the guest's order being taken)

COVER FOR AFTERNOON AND HIGH TEA

Full Afternoon Tea	*High Tea*
1. Side plates.	1. Serviette
2. Paper serviette	2. Joint knife and fork.
3. Side or ta knief	3. Side plates
4. Pastry form	4. Side knife
5. Tea cup and a saucer & a teaspoon	5. Cruet set : salt, pepper, mustard & mustard spoon.
6. Slop basin and tea strainer	6. Tea cup, Saucer and tea spoons.
7. Sugar basin and tongs	7. Sugar basin and tongs.
8. Tea pot and hot water jug stands or under plates	8. Slop basin and tea strainer.
9. Jug of cold milk	9. Tea pot and hot water jug stand or under plates.
10. Preserve dish on a doily or an under plate with preserve spoon	10. Jug of cold milk
11. Ashtray	11. Preserve dish on a doily or an under plate with preserve spoon.

Note: Item no. 9 & 10 should only be brought to the Table when the guests are seated and are not part of the 'mise-en-place'.

RECEPTION TEA

The food and beverages are served from the buffet table and not at individual tables. The buffet should be in a prominent position and easy access of the stillroom and wash up.

The normal afternoon tea cutlery, china and serviette are laid along the front of the buffet in groups with the teacups, saucers and teaspoons. Sugar basins and tongs are placed on the buffet or on the occasional tables that are spread around the room. The tea is served at the separate tea service points along the buffet from silver urns, which should be kept hot with mythelated spirit burners. Milk is served separately from silver milk jugs. A raised floral centre-piece should be the focal point around which dishes of food would be placed. Cake stands may also be used for presentation and display purposes.

Source of the staff is positioned behind the buffet for service and replenishment of dishes of food and the beverage. Others should circulate the room with the food and also clear away dirties as they accumulate.

Floor Service/Room Service

Guests summon a floor waiter by push button/lamp signal or by telephoning room service or reception, according to house custom. Floor/room service of the day's meal is offered under the supervision of a head floor waiter with waiters working shifts. There must be good cooperation with housekeeping and kitchen to ensure smooth service.

Guest summons a floor waiter by push button/lamp signal or by telephone room service or reception, according to the house custom. Floor/room service varies from basic 'in room' tea and coffee making facilities, as well as possibly mini - bars, to vending machines on floors, or to the service of variety of meals in rooms. The pantry from which the floor service staff operates may be linked to a mini stillroom and holds the following equipment required for the preparation and service of any meal :

1. Sink unit
2. Saucers
3. Preserves
4. Worcester Sauce, etc.
5. Sugar
6. Linen
7. Trays
8. Salvers
9. Trolleys
10. Chaffing lamps
11. Suzette pans
12. Wine serving equipment, wine buckets, stands, baskets, etc.
13. Internal telephone
14. Cruets
15. Hot plate
16. Refrigerator
17. Lift to main kitchen
18. Salamander
19. Open Gas ring
20. Small Still set/coffee making machine
21. Cutting boards
22. Knives
23. Storage space for china
24. Silverware
25. Cutlery, Flatware
26. Glassware, Gueridon Trolley
27. Lift to Central Kitchen.

Floor service crockery, cutlery and other equipment may be of different design and/or colour or marked distinctly from that used in restaurant and other department. A floor waiter should arrange his entire *'mise en place'* before the service of meals.

Breakfast only Service

In some hotels, only breakfast service is available, which is often provided by the housekeeping staff. The menu acts as an order, which completed is hung on the outside of the guest's bedroom. The bottom portion of the card is detachable and sends to the billing office for charging to the guest's account. The remaining portion goes to the central kitchen.

Trays are made up and delivered to the room within the appropriate time range. With standing orders for breakfast in the apartments the tray should be laid up the night before, placed in the pantry and covered with a clean cloth. The beverage, toast and first course, together with the preserves and other accompaniments that may be acquired according to the order given and prepared by the floor service staff in the service or floor pantry. The main course is sent up already plated from the kitchen by the service lift.

Mini Bar

In mini bars a mini card is placed. This card acts as a guest self completion bill. These bars are restocked each day and the consumption reconciled with the billing office. The contents of mini bar are :

1. Number of items in the bar
2. Name of item
3. Quantity consumed
4. Unit price
5. Total
6. Name of the guest
7. Date
8. Room number.

The items generally included are, such as, whiskey, malt whiskey, gin, white rum, vodka, martini dry, cognac, baileys, beer, champagne, white wine, mineral water, coke/diet coke, spirit/dry spirit, mixers each, orange juice, tomato juice, aqua Libra, peanuts, pistachios, mixed nuts, cashew nuts, chocolate, short bread tin, Edinburg Rock.

Lounge Service

Many hotels and restaurants encourage guests to take coffee in the lounge after lunch or dinner in order to free restaurant tables for new seating. This type of service of continental breakfast, morning coffee, luncheon snacks, ice creams and sundaes, alcoholic and other cold drinks before, between or after meals.

The lounge staff generally has small service cupboards, which holds a basic stock of items such as :

1. Small linen stock
2. Astray
3. Salvers
4. Glass : assorted
5. Cups saucers for the service of hot beverages
6. Alcoholic drinks such as:
   (a) Spirits
   (b) Aperitifs
   (c) Brandies

(d) Liqueurs
(e) Minerals

7. Cocktail snacks, such as:
   (a) Cocktail onions
   (b) Cocktail cherries
   (c) Salted peanut
   (d) Olives
   (e) Gherkins
   (f) Cheese sticks, etc.
8. Beverages:
   (a) Horlicks
   (b) Ovaltine
   (c) Bovril
   (d) Coffee
   (e) Cocoa
   (f) Chocolate.
9. Dry goods : Coffee, tea, sugar, check-pads, bill pads, stock seat for alcoholic drinks. The staff must be prepared for the service, of the items as per list, in the lounge.

TABLE 3.2
Items Generally Served in a Lounge

S.No.	*Items Generally Served in a Lounge*
1.	Morning coffee.
2.	Aperitifs and cocktail before lunch.
3.	Coffee, liqueurs and brandy after luncheon.
4.	Afternoon tea.
5.	Aperitifs and cocktail before dinner.
6.	Coffee, liqueur and brandy after dinner.
7.	Serving of late night beverages - both alcoholic and non-alcoholic.
8.	Other snacks throughout the day depending upon the type of establishment.

The lounge service may involve:

1. Morning coffee, which may include other beverages hot and cold, includes tea and chocolate. Biscuits are normally served with morning tea.
2. Afternoon teas - It includes:
   (i) Assorted sandwiches - brown/white bread well buttered, filled with eggs, cress tomato, lettuce, cucumber, fish and meat pastes, chicken ham, foie gras, smoked salmon.
   (ii) Hot plate and yeast good — Buttered or toasted, scones, buns, tea cakes, salt, sally luann, scott pancakes, muffins, crumpets, and toast.
   (iii) Bread and butter: white, brown, whitemeal, fruits, etc.

(iv) Conserves.

(v) Pastries.

(vi) Tea - Indian, Ceylon, China, Russian, iced tea/ green tea, etc.

3. Ice creams, sundaes, etc.
4. Afternoon coffee.
5. Alcoholic and other drinks before, between and after meals.

Hospital Tray Service

Hospital patients may be grouped under the following categories :

1. Medical
2. Surgical
3. Geriatric
4. Orthopedic
5. Maternity
6. Pediatric.

Generally the meal timings are :

Breakfast	:	7.30 - 8.00 AM
Lunch	:	12 Noon
Tea	:	3.00-3.30 PM
Supper	:	6.00 - 6.30 PM
Late hot drink	:	Anytime between 8.00 - 10.00 PM

The Ganymede System

The Ganymede system is a tray service method used in hospital catering. Under this system individual patient trays are made upon a conveyor system according to patient's pre-ordered requirements. Trays are transported to the wards in ambient cabinets. Beverages are added at ward sites before presentation to the patient.

Airline Tray Service

A commissary is the term used to cover catering, cabin requirements, bounded stores, cleaning and other passenger requirements in airline catering. In short distances snack type meals or sandwiches and beverages are offered, whereas for longer distances, an extensive service of food and beverages is given. When the aircraft is in the air it is the well-trained cabin crew who provide service to the passengers. The required quantities of each dish are placed in trays either into the cupboards and kept hot until being transported into plane or alternatively chilled and stored in the catering unit until required. When necessary it is reheated on tableware, china, glassware and so on.

Rail Service

The rail catering is moving towards the operation of a tray system similar to airlines. The food and drink is served on trays to passengers at any seat.

Home Delivery

The 'meal on wheels' service is the most well-known home delivery method of service of food. Service range from Indian and Chinese takeaway deliveries, to restaurant providing full meals *i.e.* hot or cold or customer to heat. The pizza home delivery system is most popular. In this system thick cardboard with intern corrugation are utilized to provide a form of insulation to keep the pizza hot.

QUESTIONS AND ASSIGNMENTS

Q. 52. There are various forms of food service. What factors would influence the different patterns of services for a coffee shop as opposed to a continental specialty restaurant. [BHM]

Q. 53. As a restaurant manager emphasize in 10-sentences the importance of briefing and debriefing function to your maitre d' hotel and in another 10-sentences discuss some of the points that must be considered in a briefing of F&B waiters in an Indian specialty restaurant. [BHM]

Q. 54. The 'Dummy waiter' is very important piece of restaurant equipment. Explain its uses briefly and make a diagram of what you think would be the perfect working design. [BHM]

Q. 55. Profit is the main motive of commercial establishments. In about 250-words describe how a waiter contributes in achieving this objective. [BHM]

Q. 56. As a trainee group, select a familiar restaurant and discuss its order taking methods.

Q. 57. Do a thorough practice taking orders from fellow trainees posing as guests. Be sure to include suggestion selling.

Q. 58. As a guest in a restaurant, observe waiter/ress and note down the errors made by the service personnel. Discuss points with other trainees.

Q. 59. Do a role-play exercise serving and clearing dishes from the table. Take terms beings the guest and the waiter/ress.

Q. 60. Have a brain storming session to find out ways to save time and effort in the serving process.

Q. 61. Observe different types of service in various restaurants located in hotels and discuss with other trainees what you have learned.

Q. 62. Using proper service ware set up the American breakfast and lunch cover and the American dinner cover.

Q. 63. In a training session, point out some similarities and differentiate between the settings. Identify the purpose of each service piece and show the placement of various foods as they are served.

Q. 64. For an efficient service, Breakfast Buffet is a necessity in hotels. Plan a Breakfast Buffet menu for Rs. 150.00 and also explain the layout of the buffet table in right sequence.

Q. 65. Interview a restaurant manager whose serving staff uses a computer. Find out what dinning room hardware they use. Write a short paper discussing the step-by-step procedure they follow for using the computer from taking the order to settling the guest account.

Q. 66. Breakfast buffet is becoming increasingly popular in hotels-justify the statement.

Q. 67. How do you tackle a guest who is too much talkative? [BHM]

Q. 68. Discuss the functioning of a flight kitchen, catering to international airlines. [BHM]

Q. 69. Discuss the various purchase systems adopted in the catering industry [BHM]

Q. 70. What is "Door-knob" style of ordering? Give a sample of an idea; room service doorknob menu format [BHM]

Q 71. How does impulse buying react for increasing the sales in a restaurant? Explain. [BHM]

4 Display Cooking or Gueridon Service

After learning this lesson you should be able to :

1. Know the significance of display cooking and gueridon service;

2. Understand the system and procedure of guerdion service;

3. Explain the technique of carving and joining; and

4. Practice the display of flambe sweet dishes.

Flambe dishes first became popular in the Edwardian era. The first claimed flambe dish was Crepe Suzette, which was supposedly invented by Henri Charpentier when working as *commis* at the cafe de Paris in Monte Carlo (1894).

Gueridon is a movable service table or trolley (see fig. 4.1) from which food may be carved, filleted, flambeed or prepared and served. It is in other words movable sideboard carrying out sufficient equipment for the immediate operation in hand, together with surplus equipment. The gueridon come in various forms *i.e.*, a Calor gas trolley, or a Plain trolley or even a Small table.

Special Equipment Required

1. Flare lamps
2. Hot plates
3. Gueridon (Calor gas)
4. Chaffing dish or Suzette pans
5. Gueridon

As with the gueridon, the flambe trolley may be set up in a certain basic format, observe the following safety points :

1. Always know when the flambe damper is for the fare lamp.
2. Have an empty joint plate beside the lamp for the hot pan.
3. Place the flammable spirit away from the lamp.
4. Never move the trolley near to curtains or hangings.In many first class restaurants with an a *'la carte'* menu, a Gueridon service may be employed to a greater or lesser extent depending upon the menu/being served, the dishes ordered by the guest and the cost of the meal. Basically guerdon is a movable service table or trolley from which food may be carved, filleted, flambeed or prepared and served.

(a)

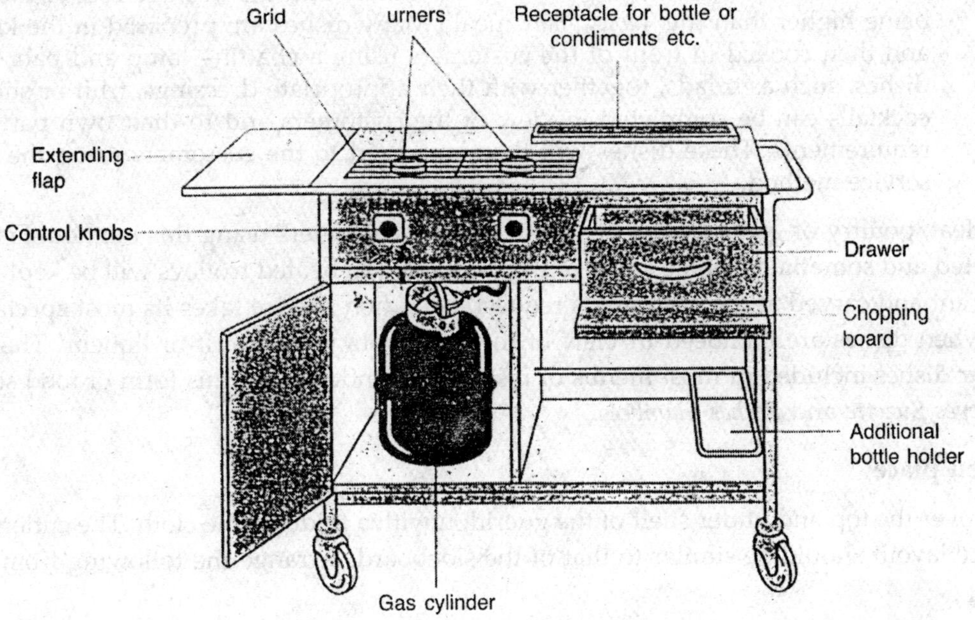

FIG. 4.1. Gas-fuelled flambe trolley flare lamp

(b)

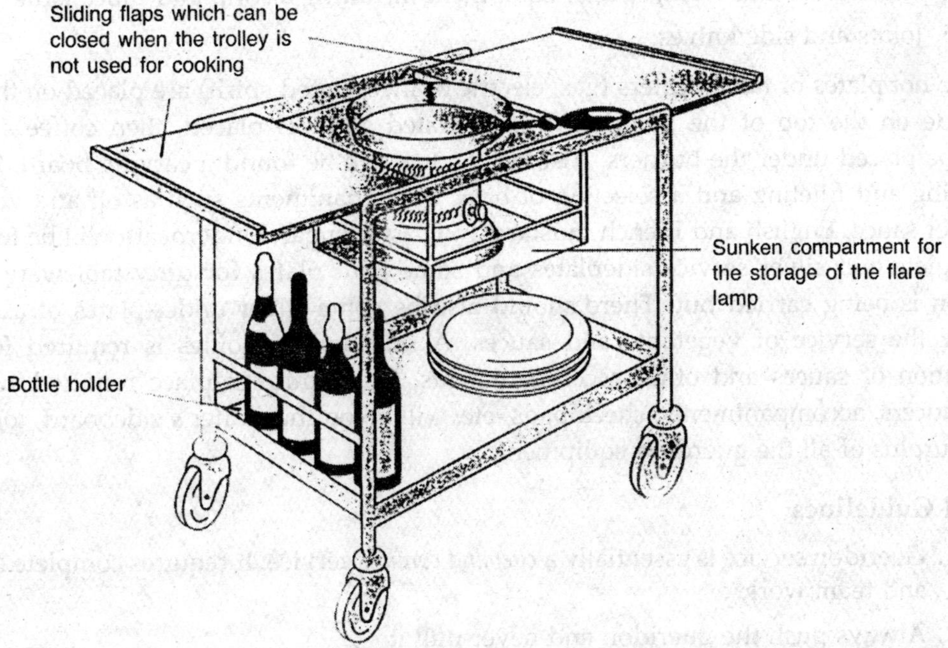

FIG. 4.2. Flambe trolley with

The cost of the dishes being priced individually and the average cost of the meal being higher than the *'table d'hote* meal'. Many dishes are prepared in the kitchen and then cooked in front of the customers using a chaffing lamp and pan. Other dishes, such as salads, together with their appropriate dressings, fruit or shellfish cocktails can be completed in view of the customers and to their own particular requirements. These dishes will then be served to the customers using the silver service method.

Meat, poultry or game can be carved in front of customers using this method. Fish can be filleted and sometimes-whole joints of the meat, held in heated trolleys will be kept in the restaurant and carved at the customer's request. Guerdion service takes its most spectacular form when dishes are flambeed in view of the customers using spirit or liqueur. The most popular dishes included in most menus of restaurants undertaking this form of food service are *Crepes Suzette* and *Peches Flambees.*

Mise en place

Cover the top and under shelf of the gueridon with a folded table cloth. The cutlery and flatware layout should be similar to that of the sideboard. Arrange the following from right to left :

1. Service spoons and forks (joint)
2. Sweet spoons and forks
3. Soup, tea and coffee spoons
4. Fish knives and forks, special equipment including a soup and sauce ladle
5. Joints and side knives.

The hot plates or table heaters (gas, electric or methylated spirit) are placed on the left-hand side on the top of the guerdon. If methylated spirit is placed, then coffee saucers should be placed under the burners. Also on the top will be found a carving board, knives for carving and filleting and a selection of basic accompaniments such as oil and vinegar, Worcester sauce, English and French mustard and castor sugar. Underneath will be found a service plate and silver service sideplates and some joint plates for dirty tableware when operation is being carried out. There should also be some silver under-plates of assorted sizes for the service of vegetable and sauces. A selection of doilies is required for the presentation of sauces and other accompaniments. Other mise-en-place required such as coffee saucers, accompaniments, check pads, etc. will be on the waiter's sideboard, together with a surplus of all the guerdion equipment.

General Guidelines

1. Gueridon service is essentially a *chef and commis* service. It requires complete liaison and team work.
2. Always push the gueridon and never pull it.
3. When the service is finished at one table, move the gueridon on to the next immediately.

4. The gueridon should be kept in one position for the service of a complete course and not moved from guest to guest.
5. Serve only the main dish of each course from the gueridon.
6. For good control when handling the food for service hold the spoon in one hand and the fork on the other.
7. When transferring goods and liquids from the silver to the plate, always run the fork along the underside of the spoon to avoid drips marking the plate.
8. Never fillet or carve on a silver dish.
9. Use either a carving board or a hot joint plate.
10. When using a fork in carving, always work with the curved side downward; otherwise the prongs will puncture the meat.
11. Always keep the gueridons clear of dirties.
12. Never leave any spirit near a heated appliance or naked flame.
13. Handle carefully when adding spirits to a finished dish for flame purposes.
14. Safety and showmanship is of prime importance in guerdion service.

TABLE 4.1
Different Types of Liquors used in Lamp Cookery and Flame Work

S.No.	*Types of Liquors*	*Purpose*
1.	Spirits	To Flambe
2.	Fortified Wines	To Sweeten
3.	Sparkling Wines	To Colour
4.	Still Wines	To Balance flavours
5.	Beer	To Determine correct consistency
6.	Cider	To Remove excessive fat/grease
7.	Syrups	To sweeten

Check List

1. Gas Lamps :
   (i) Check that all moving parts move freely.
   (ii) Ensure both the jet and burners are free from soot and dirt.
   (iii) Clean by appropriate method — silvo or goddard's plate powder — but remember : do not ever immerse in water.
2. *Gas Bottles* : When changing a gas bottle, consider the following factors :
   (i) Ensure that in all items there is no heated equipment or necked flames near the lamp
   (ii) Follow the manufacturer's instructions and directions and use the correct spanner
   (iii) Check all taps are in the off-position.
   (iv) During storage all gas bottles should be kept cool.

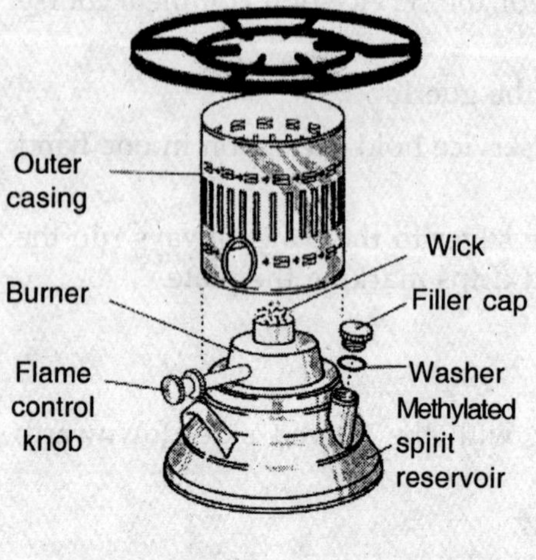

(a) Traditional methylated spirit lamp

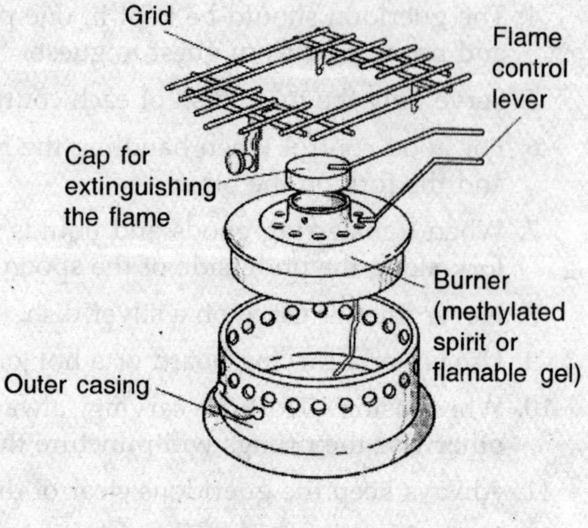

(b) Modern methylated spirit or flamable gel lamp

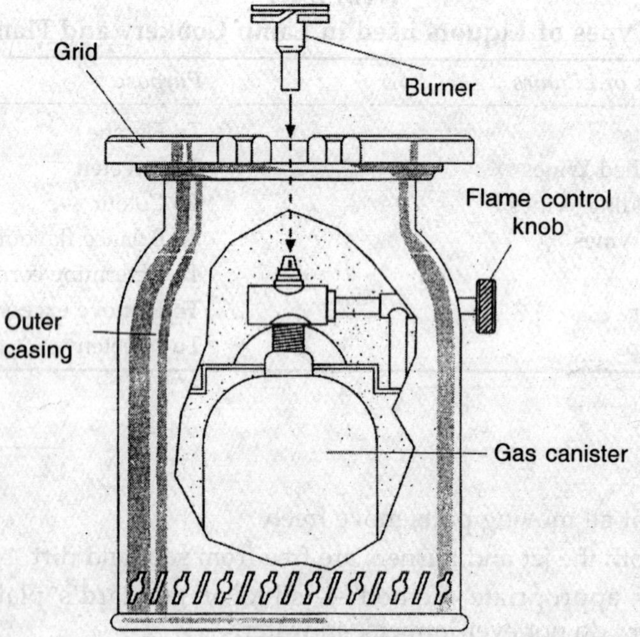

(c) Gas lamp

FIG. 4.3. Specimen of Three Types of Geridon lamps

3. Spirit Lamps

(i) Check the amount of methylated spirit

(ii) See that the air hole is free

(iii) Train the wick and check it for length

(iv) Clean off any excessive dirt and spint matches

(v) Ensure all moving parts move freely

(vi) Clean by the appropriate method–but remember : do not immerse in water

(vii) Any direction on equipment should be checked carefully and, if necessary, cleaned with toothbrush.

Sequence of Gueridon Service

Presentation of all dishes is very important in gueridon service. When filleting and carving proper presentation be done before the actual service commences and placing the meals on the plate. The usual sequence is as given below :

1. ***Hors d'oeuvre or Substitutes.*** Serve in normal way except speciality dishes such as *pate de foie gras,* which may have to be cut into slices. Accompaniments passed in the normal manner.
2. ***Soup.*** Always serve from the gueridon. All accompaniments passed.
3. ***Fish.*** Filleted when necessary and serve from gueridon.
4. ***Meat.*** Carved where necessary and serve from gueridon.
5. ***Potatoes and Vegetables.*** Served as usually together with sauces and accompaniments.
6. ***Sweet.*** Serve from the gueridon if a flambe type of dish.

   or

   Serve from the cold sweet trolley. All accompaniments passed.
7. ***Savoury.*** Serve from the gueridon.
8. **Coffee.** Normal silver service unless speciality coffee are required.

Service Method

1. Taking the order :

(i) Stand to the left of the host. Each guest should have a menu including the host. Have one yourself for reference purposes.

(ii) Size up your host and guest according to age, dress and nature of the party business lunch/eating at celebration and so on).

(iii) Take all orders through the host. Warn customers of waiting times.

(iv) Take note as whether the party is all male, female or male/female.

(v) Always take the order as soon as possible.

2. Method of service at the table :
   (i) Present the dish to the customer
   (ii) Return to the gueridon
   (iii) Place the hot plates on the side of the trolley, with the food for service standing on the hotplates
   (iv) The food for service is then carved or filleted if necessary, and is placed into the plate of the guest
   (v) In this service, the spoon and fork are used one in each hand
   (vi) Place the vegetables and potato onto the plate while the plates are still on the gueridon
   (vii) Plate the sauces onto the plates
   (viii) Place the plate in front of the guest.

When there are more than two people at one table, the main dish is served as described but the vegetables and potato dishes are served as for normal silver service and keep hot in readiness for service on the hot plate on the sideboard. The *commas* or *debarrasseur* will keep the gueridon clear of dishes and equipment.

It is a policy to standardize the basic layout of the gueridon. There are many designs of gueridon in use; the main object is to ensure that the required standards of service are met and that safety is a prime consideration of all the service staff. The increased circulation area, which would be needed, must be assessed and it must be borne in mind that however delightful the ritual or preparation may be to the client who has ordered the dish, it may well be somewhat less pleasant for another client.

Carving and Joining

The carving of a joint is a skilled art only perfected by continual practice. The carving of all hot food should be performed quickly so that no heat is allowed to escape. The carving trolley may be a very expensive item of equipment depending on style and design. The correct *mise-en-place* must be placed on the carving trolley (see fig. 4.4) *e.g.*,

1. Carving board
2. Carving knives/forks
3. Sauce ladles
4. Service spoons and forks
5. Joint plates for dirty cutlery and tableware
6. Spare serviette and service cloth.

The trencher must always ensure that the carving trolley is correctly laid up before it is taken to the table. The correct preparation of joints before cooking is very important. Any bone, which makes carving difficult, should be removed prior to cooking. The carver should be able to :

1. Recognize the joint, poultry or game to be carved.

2. Be ware of the bone structure and muscle fibre of the product being carved.
3. Recognize the correct carving implements for the task in hand.
4. Handle the carving implemer .s correctly and safely.
5. Steel a knife correctly.

Carving trolley

The carving trolley is a very expensive item of equipment. Because of this, great care must always be taken with the maintenance and use of the carving trolley to ensure that it functions correctly.

The function of the carving trolley is to act as an aid to selling. At all times the waiting staffmust be salespeople and sell the dishes on the menu by brief and accurate description. The carving trolley supplements this by being a visual aid to selling and should be at the table as the waiter takes order so that he may suggest and show particular items to the customer. Always remember to push the trolley and not pull it. This enables the trolleyto be steered and moved safely and helps to avoid accidents.

The carving trolley should be cleaned at regular intervals with the aid of plate powder, ensuring that all the powder is finally polished off so that none comes into contact with any foodstuffs. A toothbrush may be used for cleaning any intricate design work.

FIG. 4.4. Carving trolley

Safety factors

There are certain safety factors to observe in the handling of the carving trolley and these must be carefully adhered to.

- The container on which the carving board rests contains hot water. Ensure the base is filled with hot water before the burners are lit.

- Make sure the safety valve on the base is set on correctly and screwed down tight. There is a small hole set in the safety valve which allows the surplus steam to escape. This value must be placed so it is on the opposite side of the trolley from where the trancheur works, to avoid the hands being scalded by the escaping steam. The safety valve must never escaping steam. The safety valve must never be blocked or covered over. If it is, pressure will build up within the base, which can buckle the trolley and may cause an accident.
- Two methylated spirit or flammable gel lamps heat the carving trolley. Ensure the lamps are functioning properly, with trimmed wicks and the spirit holders filled with methylated spirit or the gel holders filled. There must be sufficient fuel to last throughout the service period.
- The lower shelf should be used for carrying the service plate, spare service cutlery and a clean joint plate.
- Handle the carving implements correctly and safely and sharpen a knife using a steel safely.

Mise en place

For its satisfactory operation in the restaurant, the correct equipment must be placed on the carving trolley before service. This includes:

- carving board
- service spoons and forks
- carving knives/forks
- joint plates for dirty cutlery
- sauce ladles
- spare napkin and service cloth.

Preparation of joints

The correct preparation of joints before cooking is very important and any bones which may make carving difficult should be removed prior to cooking. At the same time, the person carving must have knowledge of the bone structure of a joint in order to carve correctly and thus acquire the maximum number of porions. Therefore the carver must be able to:

- recognise the joint, poultry or game to be carved
- be aware of the bone structure and muscle fibre of the product being carved
- recognise the correct implements required.

Presentation of the trolley

- The trancheur must always ensure that the carving trolley is correctly laid up before it is

- The plate rest for the hot joint plates should be extended and two containers for gravy and sauces should be already filled. These two containers should always be placed at the end nearest the plate rest. This is fore ease of service and also provides the shortest distance between the containers and the plates.
- When being used the carving trolley should be placed next to the customer's table, in between the customer and the trancheur. This ensures that the customer can see every operation performed by the trancheur and appreciate the skills involved.
- The trolley should be positioned to ensure that the safety valve is on the side away from the trancheur. This is to ensure that the transcheur will not be scalded when using the trolley.
- The trolley should be positioned in such a way that the lid is drawn back from the trolley towards the transcheur so as to reveal the foods to the customer.

Techniques of Carving

The carving of all hot food must be performed quickly. This way heat is not allowed to escape. The carving techniques are :

1. ***Beef and ham :*** Cut thinly.
2. ***Lamb. mutton, pork, tongue and veal :*** Carved at double the thickness of beef and ham.
3. ***Boiled beef and pressed meats :*** cut a shade thicker than roasts and each portion of the former will include some fat.
4. ***Saddle of Lamb :*** Carved along the loin in long, thickish slices.
5. ***Shoulder of Lamb :*** Starting from the top, cut down to the bone, then work from top to bottom the turn the piece over and work gradually round.
6. ***Cold ham :*** Carved onto the bone from top to bottom in very thin slices.
7. ***Whole chicken :*** Medium-size bird is dissected into six portions.
8. ***Broilers :*** Dissected into four portions.
9. ***Poussin :*** Offered whole or split into two portions.
10. ***Duckling :*** Carve into four/six portions, two legs two wings and the breast cut into long strips.
11. ***Turkey :*** Slice the breast into nice even portions and give each guest a slice of brown meat off the leg as well as space of the stuffing.
12. ***Salmon :*** First skin whether it is hot or cold. Then slice in fillets, one from each side of the bone. Cut slices up to 10 cm (4 in.) long and 2.5 cm (1 in.) thick.
13. ***Lobster and Crayfish :*** Hold firmly. Pierce vertically with a strong knife and cut with a levering motion towards tail and head. Hold shell down with a spoon on a dish, slowly lifting out the meat with a fork. Slice the meat diagonally.
14. ***Sole :*** Remove the bones along either edge. Then the fillets are drawn apart with the aid of two large forks. Serve a top and bottom fillet per portion.

TABLE 4.2
Selected Dishes Involving Work on the Gueridon

1. Hors d'oeuvre or Substitutes

Smoked Eel (Anguille Fumee)
Smoked Trout (Truite Fumee)
Smoke Salmon (Saumon Fumee)
Caviare (Roe of the Sturgeon)
Whole Memon (Melon Frapee)
Globe Artichokel (Artichaut)
Pate de Foie Gras
Shellfish cocktail (Cocktail de Crevettes).

2. Soup

Real Turtle soup (Tortue Vraile Aux Xeres.

Fish

Sole (Sole Grittee ou Meuniere)
Poached Sole (Sole Pochee)
Deep fried Sole (Sole Frite)
Poached or grilled Salmon (Saumon Poche ou Grille) (Cutlet or Darne of Salmon).
Blue Trout (Fruite au Blen).
Scampi (Scampi a 'la Creme Flambe, 'a L'ainisette, Au Pernod, etc.),

3. Steaks

Double Entrecote Steak (Entrecote Double)
Double Fillet Steak (Chateau briand)
'T Bone Steak (Porterhouse Steak)
Steak Tartare
Steak Diane
Monkey Gland Steak
Fillet Steak (Fillet de Boeuf Strongnoff)
Veal Escalope (Escalope de Veau Suedoise).

4. Salads

Salad (Salade Verte) Dressing: French Dressing
English Dressing
Sauce Dressing
Sauce Vinaigrette
Roquefort Dressing
Acidulated Cream dressing
Mustard Cream
Lemon Dressing.

5. **Poultry**

Chicken (Poulet Roti)
Young chicken (six week old) Poussin
Duck (Canard Roti)
Pressed wild duck (Canard Saurage a la Presse)
Turkey (Dindonneau Roti)
Chicken Breast Flambed (Supreme de Volaille Flambe).

6. **Game**

Grouse (Grouse)
Partridge (Perdeau)
Woodcock (Becausse)
Snipe (Becassine)]
Pheasant (Faisan)
Wood Pigeon (Pigeon)
Saddle of Hare (Sadle de Lievre).

7. **Joints**

Boned sirloin of Beef (Centre filet de Boeuf)
Sirloin of Beef on the bone (A loyan de Boeuf)
Best end of lamb (Carre d'agneau)
Saddle of lamb (Selle d'agneau)
Leg of lamb (Gigot d'agneau)
Leg of Pork (Cuissot de porc)
Ham (Jambon).

8. **Flambe Sweet Dishes**

The Flambe trolley
Peach Flambe (Peche Flambee)
Pears Flambe (Poire Flambee)
Bananas Flambe (Banane Flambee)
Cherries Flambe (Cerise's Flambees au Kirsch)
Cerise's Flambees au Glace Vanille
Cerise's Jubilees (Conelette Souffle aux Cerises Jubuilees)
Rum Omelet (Omelette au Rhum)
Strawberry Roman off (Fraises Roman Off)
Pineapple Flambe (Ananas Rafraiche au kirsch Flambe)
Crepes Suzette.

9. **Dessert**

Fresh fruit and Nuts (Dessert)
Orange Salad (Salade 'd' orange)
Pears (Poire)

Chafing dish or Suzette pans

A *chafing dish* is deep, has a lid and is made to fir onto its own individual heating unit. langer versions of these are now found *on* buffers. The shallower pans which are used for lamp cookery are called *Suzette pans.* They resemble frying pans in shape and size and have diameter of 23 30 cm (9-12 in.) with or without a lip. The lip is usually found on the left hand side. The pans are generally made of silver-plated copper as this gives an even distribution of heat.

Hotplates

The hotplate's main function is to keep food hot before it is served to the guest. They are always positioned on the sideboard, but may often be found on both the sideboard and the gueridon. They come in a vast range of sizes and may be heated by gas, electricity or merhv-lated spirits, flammable gel and there are even infra-red ones available.

Gueridon (calor gas)

A gueridon may use a gas lamp connected to a Calor gas cylinder. The service top is flat as the gas lamp has been lowered into the upper casing. This makes it much safer when cooking dishes or carrying out any form of flambe work at the table. The top of the trolley is stainless steel which allows for, easy cleaning. The gueridon will normally also have/a control switch for the gas lamp, a drawer for surplus service equipment; a cutting board for use when cooking dishes at the table a bracket on the lower tray used for holding bottles of spirit and liqueurs; and the indentation on top of the trolley for holding accompanliments.

Care and maintenance of equipment

There are various factors which make hygiene and safety so important in gueridon service. From a legal perspective various acts and regulations apply which hold you personally responsible for hygiene and safety incidents which arise, and these include the Food Safety Acts, Food Safety (general food hygiene), Regulations and the Health and Safety at Work Act.

When preparing food at the table it is a visual display that will attract many observers so all your actions should be of the highest hygiene and safety standards. This can be achieved by good planning and organisation.

The following quideline should be observed when carrying out work at the gueridon :

1. Hygiene and appearance should be of the highest standard (see Section 1.8)
2. All equipment should be spotlessly clean and polished daily
3. Do not handle food with bare hands
4. Ensure trolleys are wiped down between each use
5. Never place hotplate or lamp outside the trolley legs

Nothing should be placed on the upper shelf of the trolley. The reason for this is that when the cover of the carving trolley is in the lowered position it would come into contact with. anything placed on the upper shelf, knocking them over and thus causing delays and may be accidents during the service. The lower shelf should be used for carrying the service plate, spare service cutlery and flatware and a clean joint plate.

Safety Guidelines

There are certain safety factors to observe in the handling of the carving trolley and these must be carefully adhered to :

1. Ensure the lamps are functioning properly, with trimmed wicks and holders filled with methylated spirits. There must be sufficient to last over the service period
2. Ensure the base is filled with hot water before the lamps are lit

FIG. 4.4. A Specimen of Carving trolley

3. Ensure the safety valve is set on correctly and screwed down tight. There is a small hole set in the safety valve which allows the surplus steam to escape. This must never be covered over. If it is, the pressure builds up within the base which can buckle the trolley and may cause an accident.

Salad Dressings

When a guest requests salads, an appropriate dressing should always be on hand. The traditional method is to prepare an appro ate dressing selected by the guest and blended to match the dish. These are several popular dressings, which can be made simply, the best known being referred to as vinaigrette. These dressings are prepared at the table. The utensils needed are a cold soup plate, a fork and a dessertspoon. The ingredients are as with other preparations produced in a ready-to-use form in the kitchen.

Service of salad

1. Place the dressed salad onto the salad crescents.
2. Serve the salad crescent to the top left of the customer's cover.
3. Place a sweet fork with the pongs facing down on the left hand edge of the salad crescent with the handle at an angle of 45° to the cover for service.
4. Now serve the course that the salad is to accompany (for example, hot roast poultry, game) as quickly as possible.

Note : If salad is to be served alone the cover is a small knief and fork, with the salad served onto a plate (rather than a salad crescent) or into a bowl or a soup plate.

Caesar salad

Equipment

- salad bowl
- service spoon and form
- plates or bowls for numbers of covers to be served
- garlic press.

Ingredients

- fresh clean, dry cos (or Romaine) salad leaves on separate joint plate
- croutons
- grated or shaved Parmesan cheese.

Dressing

- olive oil
- white wine vinegar
- Dijon mustard
- raw egg yolk
- Worcestershire sauce
- salt and pepper mill
- peeled garlic cloves
- chopped anchovy filets.

*Some establishments may substitute pasteurised egg for fresh egg yolk.

Accompaniments

- none.

Cover

- small
- cold plates or bowls with underplates.

Method

1. Ensure all ingredients and equipment are organised before commencing.
2. Present the gueridon at the table.
3. Mix the ingredients for the dressing in the salad mixing bowl using a service fork: crushed garlic (depending on the customer's requirements) mustard, dash of Worcestershire sauce; vinegar and raw egg yolk.
4. Blend in the oil using the service fork as a whisk.
5. Add chopped anchovies.
6. Add seasonings to taste (according to the customer's requirements) and stir.
7. Put the lettuce leaves into the mixing bowl and break into smaller pieces (largish fragments) using a spoon and fork (one in each hand).
8. Add the croutons and fold in.
9. Move the salad in the bowl with the service spoon and fork to ensure that it is fully covered by the dressing.
10. Present the salad onto the cold plates for service.
11. Sprinkle with grated (or shaved) parmesan.
12. Serve.

There are many variations to this salad. One specific variation replaces the egg that is incorporated into the dressing with a one-minute boiled egg broken over the salad just before serving. Other variants include making the dressing by incorporating two or three chopped anchovy fillets into a basic vinaigrette that has been seasoned with garlic and some horseradish cream. Some recipes substitute English mustard for Dijon. Garlic is usually used but some variants involve rubbing this over the wooden bowl before making the salad, while others use chapons (garlic croutons). Other ingredients that might be used include Roquefort cheese and seasonings such as Tabasco. Some recipes keep the anchovy fillets separate and then decorate the salad with them rather than incorporating them, chopped, into the dressing. As well as finishing with the sprinkling of grated Parmesan, some variations also sprinkle with ground pepper and lemon juice.

Salad dressings

Standard equipment

The standard equipment required on the gueridon when preparing a salad dressing is :

- soup plate in which to mix the dressing
- service cloth

- service spoons and forks on a service plate
- teaspoons in a small jug of water (for tasting the dressing as it is being made)
- spare plate for dirty cutlery.

The ingredients are dependant upon the type of dressing required. Examples of seven different dressings are given below :

French dressing

Ingredients

- French or Dijon mustard
- service cloth

- service spoons and forks on a service plate
- teaspoons in a small jug of water (for tasting the dressing as it is being made)
- spare plate for dirty cutlery.

The ingredients are dependant upon the type of dressing required. Examples of seven different dressings are given below :

French dressing

Ingredients

- French or Dijon mustard

- seasonings of salt, pepper, cayenne pepper (sometimes caster sugar)
- four to six parts olive oil to one part vinegar.

Method

1. Place the mustard and seasonings in a soup plate which is resting on the folded service cloth at an angle, thus retaining the mixture in one part of the soup plate to make mixing easier.
2. Blend the seasonings together with a service fork.
3. Add the measure of vinegar to the seasonings and mix well to form a smooth mixture.
4. Now add the oil and blend together with the service fork.
5. Taste and adjust seasonings if required.

English dressing

As for French dressing with the exception that English mustard replaces the French mustard, the proportions of oil to vinegar are one to two, and one teaspoon of caster sugar is added to the seasonings.

Sauce vinaigrette

Ingredients

- one teaspoonful French, Dijon or English mustard

- seasoning of salt and peppermill
- one tablespoon of vinegar
- two tablespoons of oil.

Method

1. Place the mustard, seasoning and vinegar in a soup plate and mix together using a fork.
2. Add the oill, mixing slowly.
3. The proportions of vinegar and oil used are according to individual taste.

Roquefort dressing

Ingredients

- Roquefort cheese
- wine vinegar (see Method A)
- olive oil (see Method A)
- sauce mayonnaise (see Method B)
- seasoning (salt)
- jug of single cream
- lemon juice.

Method A

1. Break down the Roquefort cheese into small lumps or cream it right down by mixing in a soup plate with a little wine vinegar or lemon juice.
2. Add the olive oil and season with salt. This will help to bring out the full flavour of the cheese. A little single cream may be added.

Method B

1. Break down the Roquefort cheese into small pieces in a soup plate.
2. With the aid of a large fork, fold the pieces of Roquefort cheese into some sauce mayonnaise.
3. Season with salt to help bring out the flavour.

Acidulated cream dressing

This from of dressing is mainly offered with salads containing fruit, such as orange salad (*salade d'orange*).

Ingredients

- lemon juice
- seasoning (salt)

- jug of single cream
- paprika.

Method

1. Break down the Roquefort cheese into small pieces in a soup plate.
2. With the aid of a large fork, fold the pieces of Roquefort cheese into some sauce mayonnaise.
3. Season with salt to help bring out the flavour.

Acidulated cream dressing

This form of dressing is mainly offered with salads containing fruit, such as orange salad (*salade d'orange).*

Ingredients

- lemon juice
- seasoning (salt)
- jug of single cream
- paprika

Method

1. Mix the lemon juice with the seasoning.
2. Add the single cream.
3. Check the taste.

Note : For the preparation of a fresh orange for orange salad, see Fresh Fruit.

Mustard cream

Ingredients

- 1/3 litre (1/2 pt) single cream
- tablespoon of mustard
- juice of a lemon
- seasonings.

Method

1. Place the dry ingredients into the soup plate and blend together.
2. Mix the single cream in slowly and thoroughly to avoid lumps.
3. Add juice of the lemon to taste.
4. Adjust seasoning if necessary.

Lemon dressing

Ingredients

- two tablespoons of oil
- fresh lemon juice to taste
- seasonings.

Method

1. Place the dry ingredients into the soup plate and blend together.
2. Mix the single cream in slowly and thoroughly to avoid lumps.
3. Add juice of the lemon to taste.
4. Adjust seasoning if necessary.

Lemon dressing

Ingredients

- two tablespoons of oil
- fresh lemon juice to taste
- seasonings.

Method

1. Blend the oil and seasonings well together in a soup plate.
2. Add the fresh lemon juice sparingly.
3. Taste as the dressing is made; the dressing should produce a 'bite' at the back of the throat.

Soups

Clear soup with sherry (consomme aux xeres)

Equipment

1. lamp
2. sauce ladle (but more often a soup ladle as this has more visual appea).

Ingredients

- portion of soup in a soup tureen
- measure of warm sherry (or Madeira etc.)

Accompaniments

- Segments of lemon in a lemon press, placed on a side plate at the head of the cover.
- cheese straws are offered and traditionally brown bread and butter.

Cover

- sweet spoon (this is traditional when eating consomme — see Chapter 3, page 88)
- hot consomme cup on consomme saucer on an underplate.

Method

1. Ensure all the mise-en-place is completed before commencing.
2. Present the gueridon at the table and serve from the gueridon.
3. Keep the soup hot on a lamp or hotplate and then ladle/pour into the consomme cups which will be sitting on the consomme saucer on an underplate.
4. The measure of sherry may be warmed and added to the soup at the last moment in the kitchen, or it may be heated in a sauce (or soup) ladle over the lamp, flambed and then poured over the soup.
5. Serve immediately.

Fish dishes

Grilled or shallow fried sole (sole grillee on meuniere)

Equipment

- lamp
- service spoons and forks on a service plate
- hot joint plate for filleting
- spare plate for dirty cutlery
- spare plate for fish debris.

Ingredients

- silver flat with the sole together with lemon wedges.

Accompaniments

- lemon wedge.

Cover

- fish knief and fork
- hot joint plate.

Method A

1. Ensure all the mise-en-place is completed before commencing.
2. Present the dish to the customer then return to the hot plate or lamp on the gueridon.
3. Remove the fish from the silver flat on to the hot joint plate.
4. With the aid of a service spoon and fork remove the side bones (Figure 8.5a).
5. Run the tip of the spoon down the backbone.

6. Place two large forks back to back at the head of the fish and on the backbone. Press the forks down so that the tips of the forks pierce the flesh on either side of the backbone (Figure 8.5b). Nc v ease the fillets slowly away from the backbone.
7. Continue to do this working .ne forks gradually down the backbone towards the tail.
8. Lift out the bone (Figure 4.3(c))
9. Place the fillets back together in their original shape on the silver flat. Re-heat as necessary
10. Coat the fondue or replace garnish and serve.

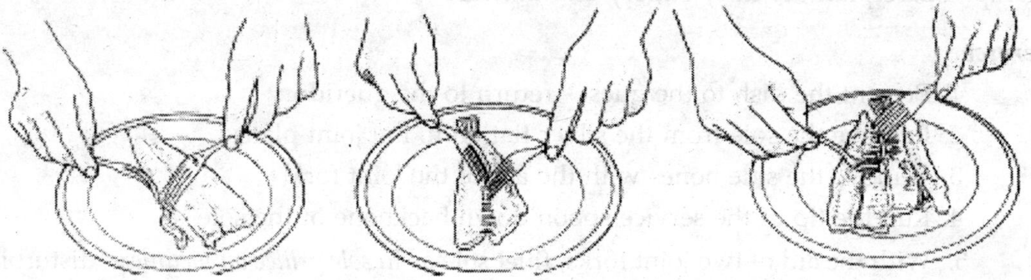

FIG. 4.5. Technique of preparation of a dover sale.

Equipment

- lamp
- spare plate for debris
- service spoons and forks on a service plate
- spare plate for dirty cutlery.

Ingredients

- poached or grilled salmon in an earthenware dish plus garnishes.

Method' B

1. 1-4 as in A above
2. Start at head of fish and, with the aid of a service spoon and fork, loosen the two top fillets
3. Hold the fish firmly with the spoon and run the fork down from head to tail between the two top fillets and the backbone
4. Repeat this with the other two fillets, placing fork between the bottom fillets and the backbone
5. Lift out the backbone
6. 8/9 as in A, above

Poached sole (sole-pochee)

Cover

Fish knife and fork – hot fish plate or hot joint plate if to be served as a main course.

Accompaniments

According to garnish

Equipment for gueridon

Sole on silver flat - hot joint plate for filleting - service spoon and fork - two joint forks - lamp - spare plate for dirty cutlery and flatware

Service

1. Present the dish to the guest - return to the gueridon
2. Remove the sole from the silver flat on to hot joint plate
3. Remove the side bones with the aid of the joint fork
4. Run the tip of the service spoon down backbone of the sole
5. With the aid of two joint forks, fillet sole as in *sole grillee ou meuniere,* disturbing the glazed sauce, coating the fillets as little as possible.

Double fillet steak (Chateaubriand)

Although the Chateaubriand is commonly termed a *double fillet steak* it may be large enough to serve a party of two, three, four or five guests as required.

The *cover, accompaniments, equipment* required for gueridon and *service* are as for *Entrecote double;* with the following exception :

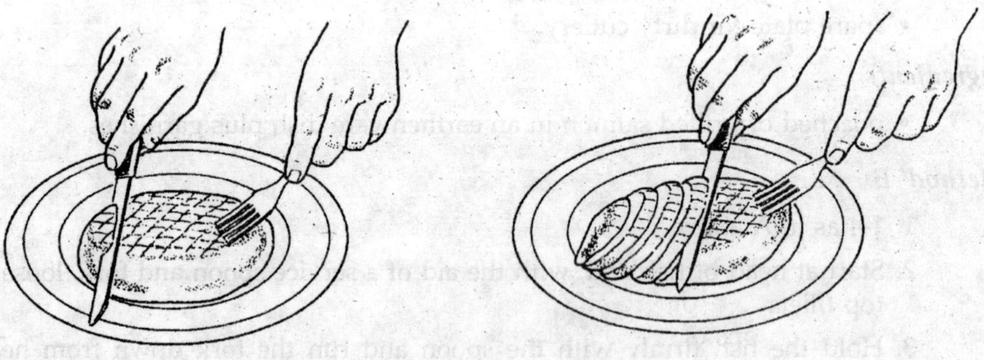

FIG. 4.6. Carving of Chateaubriand

When the *Chateaubriand* is being carved each portion will be carved into approximately two or three slices, each 13 mm (½ in.) thick, rather than being left in one whole piece as is the case with an *Entrecote double.*

Service Technique

1. Present the dish to the customer-return to the gueridon
2. Remove from the silver flat or to the carving board
3. Cue out the "T' bone to give two separate pieces of meat: one of sirloin and one of Fillet
4. Return the two pieces of meat to the silver flat: re-heat quickly
5. Dress attractively on to the hot joint plate with the garnish
6. If the Porterhouse steak is for more than one person then carve the fillets as for a *Chateaubriand.*

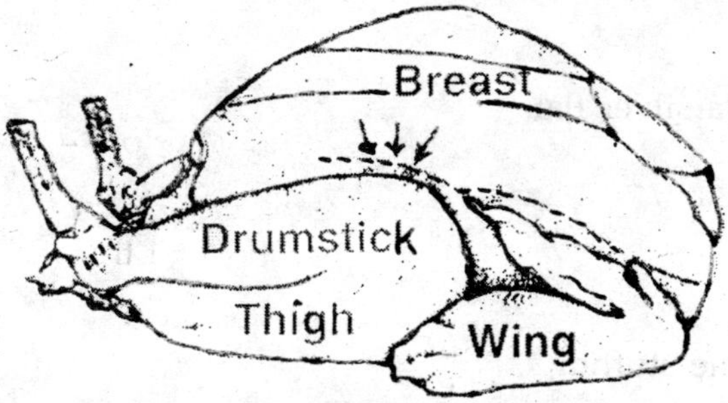

FIG. 4.7. Carving a roast chicken

7. Proceed in the same manner with the other wing
8. Position the bird on its back. Cut down one side of the breastbone and lever off half the breast
9. Proceed in the same manner with the other side of the breast
10. An alternative method of removing the breast is by turning the chicken on its side and cutting through the wishbone joints
11. Turn the chicken on to its breast, holding it firmly in place with the service fork
12. Insert the knife between the flesh and the wishbone. Holding the whole breast on the board with the knife lever the carcass away with the aid of the service fork
13. Cue the whole breast into two portions lengthways
14. Replace the carved chicken on the lamp. If necessary whilst the carving operation is being carried out add a little liquid (gravy) to the silver flat to prevent the carved portions of chicken from burning
15. Serve the chicken giving some brown and some white meat per portion. Remember to add some game chips, bacon rolls and watercress if these make up the garnish

Note : Having completed the carving of the chicken,.the carcass should be turned over. The 'oyster' piece is found on the underside of the carcass and is a small brown portion of meat found on either side of the back.

Poultry

Roast chicken (poulet roti)

Equipment

- lamp
- carving board
- sharp carving knife (a filleting knife can also be used)
- service spoons and forks on a service plate
- spare plate for dirty cutlery
- spare plate for debris

Ingredients

- roast chicken on a silver flat.

Accompaniments

- bread sauce
- roast gravy
- parsley and thyme stuffing
- bacon rolls
- game chips
- watercress.

Cover

- joint knife and fork
- hot joint plate.

Method

1. Ensure all the mise-en-place is completed before commencing.
2. Present the whole chicken to the host at the table, then return to the lamp or hotplate on the gueridon.
3. With the service spoon and fork lift the chicken from the silver flat onto the carving board, draning off any liquid that may be inside.
4. Lay the chicken on its side on the board from right to left in front of you, with a leg uppermost.
5. Holdisng the bird firmly on the board with the flat of the knife, insert the service fork beneath the leg joint and raise the leg until the skin surrounding it is taut.
6. Cut round the taut skin surrounding the leg with the tip of the knife, at the same time pulling the leg away from the joint and cutting the flesh where necessary.
7. Cut the leg into two pieces through the joint, also removing the claw end.
8. Place the two pieces of leg onto the silver flat.

9. Proceed in the same manner with the other leg.
10. Turn the chicken onto the base of the carcass to hold it firmly.
11. Carve part f the breast and down through the wing joint, giving one piece made up of the wing and a little breast.
12. If necessary turn the chicken on its side and, with the aid of the service fork, lever the wing away from the carcass, at the same time holding the chicken firmly with the flat of the knife.
13. Proceed in the same manner with the other wing.
14. Position the bird on its back. Cut down one side of the breastbone and lever off half the breast.
15. Proceed in the same manner with the other side of the breast.
16. An alternative method of removing the breast is by turning the chicken on its side and cutting through the wishbone joints.
17. Turn the chicken onto its breast, holding it firmly in place with the service fork.
18. Insert the knife between the flesh and the wishbone. Holding the whole breast on the board with the nife, lever the carcass away with the aid of the service fork.
19. Cut the whole breast into two portions lengthways.
20. Replace the carved chicken on the lamp. If necessary, while the carving operation is being carried out add a little liquid (gravy) to the silver flat to prevent the carved portions of chiecken from burning.
21. Serve the chicken giving some brown and some white meat per portion. Remember to add some game chips, bacon rolls and watercress if these make up the garnish.

    Note : Having completed the arving of the chicken, the carcass should be turned over. The 'oyster' piece is found on the underside of the carcass and is a small brown portion of meat found on either side of the back.

Roast duck (canard roti)

Equipment

- lamp
- carving board
- sharp carving knief
- service spoons and forks on a service plate
- spare plate for dirty cutlery
- spare plate for debris.

Ingredients

- roast duck on a silver flat

Accompaniments

- apple sauce

- sage and onion stuffing
- roast gravy.

Cover

- joint knief and fork
- hot joint plate.

Note : Before beginning to carve a duck, remember that the joints are much tighter and more compact than those of a chicken and are therefore more difficult to find and cut through when carving. Also, the wing joints lie a little further under the base of the carcass than those on a chicken.

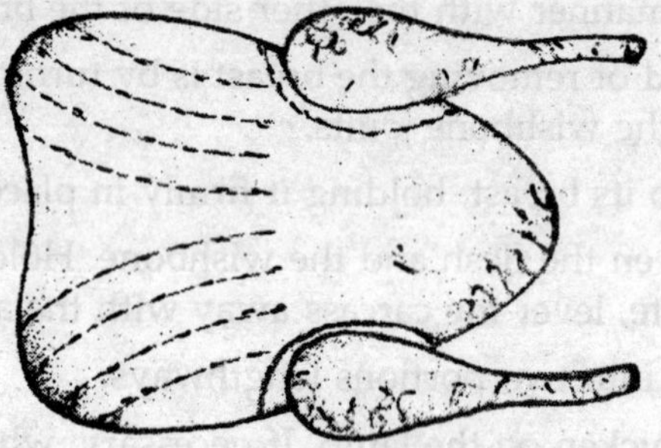

FIG. 4.9. Carving a duck

The initial stages in carving a duck are the same as for a chicken until the legs and wings have been removed.

Method

1. Ensure all the mise-en-place is completed before commencing.
2. Present the dish to the customer then return to the gueridon.
3. transfer the duck to the carving board using a service spoon and fork.
4. Hold the duck firmly on the carving board with the aid of a joint fork in the base of the carcass.
5. The breastbone on a duck is wide and flat in comparison with that of the chicken. It is therefore easier to remove the complete half breast from the breastbone.
6. Now cut into long thin slices (aiguillettes) on the carving board.
7. Repeat with the other half breast.
8. Dress back onto the silver flat. Reheat if necessary. Serve with the appropriate accompaniments.

Note : Before beginning to carve a duck, remember that the joints are much tighter and more compact than those of a chicken and are therefore more difficult to find and cut through when carving. Also, the wing joints lie a little further under the base of the carcass than those on a chicken.

The initial stages in carving a duck are the same as for a chicken until the legs and wings have been removed.

Note :

- In the case of a duckling, very often the wing and breast are carved all in one portion.
- When carving the breast, a cut on an angle should be made with the carving knife along the length of the breast. This is because the meat is shallow and to carve straight down onto the flat breastbone would take the edge of the carving knife. This method allows aiguillettes to be carved with the breast still on the carcass.

Roast turkey (dindonneau roti)

Equipment

- lamp
- carving board
- sharp carving knife
- service spoons and forks on a service plate
- spare plate for dirty equipment
- spare plate for debris.

Ingredients

- Roast turkey on a silver flat.

Accompaniments

- cranberry sauce
- bread sauce
- chestnut stuffing
- chipolatas
- gravy
- game chips
- watercress.

Cover

- joint knife and fork
- hot joint plate.

Method

1. Ensure all the mise-en-place is completed before commencing.
2. Larger birds are normally served from a carving trolley. The trolley is presented at the table before carving. For smaller birds, which are served on a flat, present the whole turkey to the host at the table then return to the lamp or hotplate on

the gueridon. Using the service spoon and fork lift the turkey from the silver flat onto the carving board, draining off any liquid that may be insuide.

3. The legs and wings should be separated but not entirely removed from the carcass (i.e. pulled to one side). This is to allow the trancheur to carve thin slices the full length of the body on either side.
4. If possible, carve and serve the stuffing with slices.
5. As with roast chicken, the dark meat from the legs should be carved and a portion made up of both white and dark meat.
6. Serve with accompaniments.

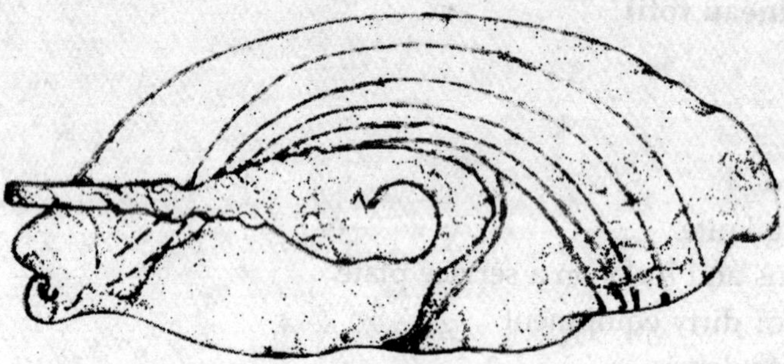

FIG. 4.10. Carving a turkey

Service Technique

1. The legs and wings should be separated, but not entirely removed from the carcass (*i.e.* pulled to one side). This is to allow the trancheur to carve thin slices the full length of the body on either side
2. If possible, carve and serve the stuffing with the slices
3. As with roast chicken, the dark meat from the legs should be carved and a portion made up of both white and dark meat. Serve with accompaniments.

Flambeed chicken breast (supreme de volaille flambee)

Cover

Joint knife and fork-hot joint plate

Accompaniments

None or possibly a side salad

Equipment for gueridon

- flare lamp
- pan on an underplate

- service spoons and forks on a service plate
- spare plate for dirty equipment
- butter knife
- sauce ladle

Ingredients

Prepared supremes on a silver flat (if required the supremes may be marinaded in wine or liqueur before hand)

- glass of red or white wine
- Drambuie Double cream in a sance boat
- butter–oil
- tomato concasse (in a small glass bowl)
- sliced mushrooms (in a small glass bowl)
- onions finely chopped (in a small glass bowl)
- seasonings of salt, pepper, cayenne pepper-double cream in a sauceboat

Method Service technique

1. Place pan on a low heat to melt the butter, add a little oil
2. Season the supremes
3. Saute off the onions to pearl stage without colouring and add the mushrooms
4. Add the supremes and cook as quickly as possible without browning too much
5. Add the wine and reduce the liquor
6. Flambe with Drambuie and add the double cream
7. Reduce the cream as quickly as possible and finish by combining tomato concasse into the cream sauce
8. Serve on to the hot joint plate and offer to the guest

Note :

1. During cooking time a salad dressing could be prepared, adding to the salad once the main course is served.
2. There are many variations : by adding ingredients such as curry powder and other seasonings, and by altering the wines and flambe spirit.

GAME

Grouse (grouse)

Season 12 August to 12 December. Grouse is regarded as a particularly choice dish. If small it is generally served whole. Otherwise it should be split into two portions by carving down through the middle of the breastbone.

1. A larger bird may be carved into three portions as indicated - from either side of the bird remove a leg and wing in one piece. This gives two portions. The

third portion is made up of the remainder of the breast separated from the carcass.

2. Partridge may be carved in exactly the same fashion as (see Fig. 3).

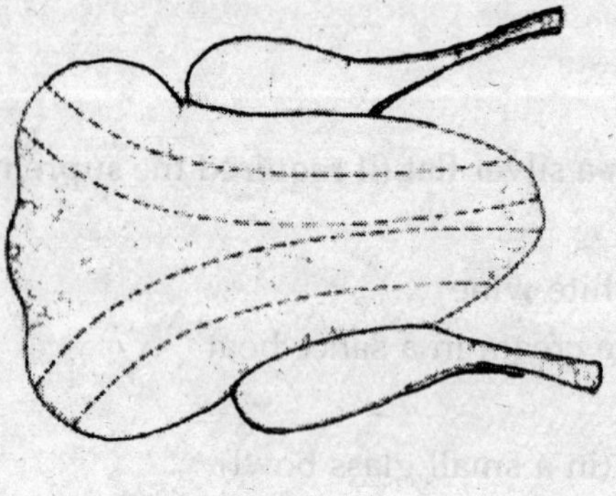

FIG. 4.12. Carving a partridge or grouse

Partridge (perdeau)

Season : 1 September to 1 February. Depending on its size the partridge may be carved into two or three portions. If large, the three portions would consist of :

1. One leg and one wing with a little of the breast attached
2. As in Fig. 4.13.
3. The breast, left on the bone.

If small it would be split into two portions by carving down through the breastbone.

Joints

All the descriptions for joints are for carving from a carving trolley. Before commencing carving the trolley must be checked to ensure all the mise-en-place has been completed. The trolley is then presented at the table.

For all the joints listed the cover is a joint knife and fork and a joint plate.

Boned sirloin of beet (contrefilet de boeuf)

Accompaniments

- roast gravy (from the trolley)
- Yorkshire pudding (from the trolley)
- English and French mustard and horseradish sauce (placed on the table by the waiteer or offered to the customer and served as required).

Note :

- The beef is normally cooked to be a little underdone.
- Beef is carved in thin slices giving mainly lean meat and a little fat per portion.

Sirloin of beet of the bone (aloyau de boeuf)

The accompaniments offered are as for a boned sirloin of beef. The sirloin is comprised of two parts:

- The undercut, which can be removed from the sirloin and may be served separately, either as fillets or tournedos, or larded anc oasted. If it is to be carved then this should be done across the joint and not par...el to the side with the grain. A piece of fat should be served with each portion.
- The uppercut, where the portions should be carved in thin slices down towards the ribs. On reaching a rib-bone the water must releast the meat attached to the bone by running the knife along and between the bone and the sirloin. This then allows the slices of meat carved to fall free.

Note :

- Boiled beef is carved with the grain as this prevents shredding. A little cooking liquor should accompany each portion.
- Ribs of beef are carved in a similar fashion to the uppercut of the sirloin.

With the upper-cut the portions should be carved in thin slices down towards the ribs. On reac'ing a rib-bone the waiter must release the meat attached to the bone by running the knife along and between the bone and the sirloin. This then allows the slices of meat carved to fall free.

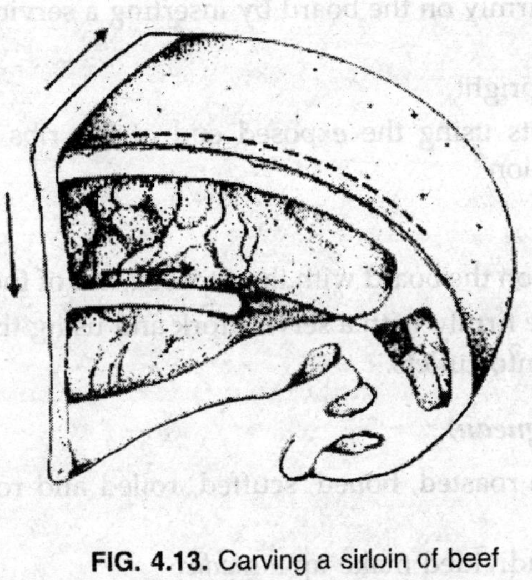

FIG. 4.13. Carving a sirloin of beef

Note:

1. Boiled beef will be carved with the grain as this prevents shredding. A little cooking liquor should accompany each portion.
2. Ribs of beef are carved in a similar fashion to the uppercut of the sirloin.

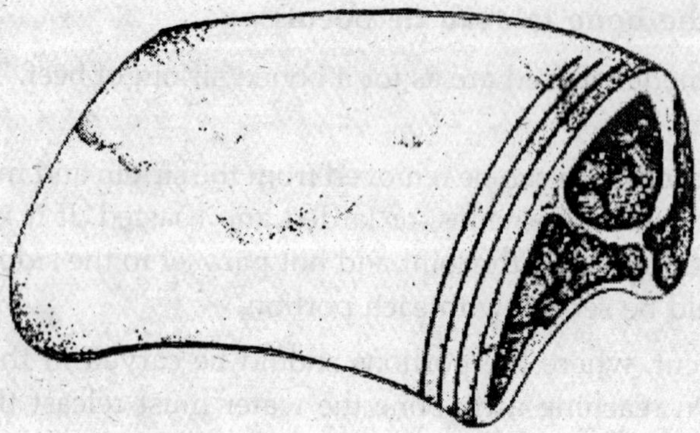

FIG. 4.14. Carving a saddle of lamb (method A)

Best end of lamb (carre d'agneau)

Accompaniments

- Roast gravy
- mint sauce
- redcurrant jelly
- Carve two cutlets per portion.

Method A

1. Hold the *carre* firmly on the board by inserting a service fork into the base at one end
2. Turn the *carre* upright
3. Carve into cutlets using the exposed end of the ribs as a guide to the correct amount per portion

Method B

1. Lay the *carre* flat on the board with the exposed end of the ribs pointing downwards
2. Holding the *carre* firmly with a service fork and using the exposed ends of the ribs as guide, carve into cutlets.

Saddle of lamb (selle d'agneau)

Note: 1. The loin may be roasted, boned, scuffed, rolled and roasted, or may be cut into chops.
2. The two loins undivided make up a *saddle.*

Accompaniments

Roast gravy - mint sauce - redcurrant jelly

There are two alternative methods of carving the saddle :

Method A

1. Remove the whole side loin from the saddle
2. Carve into slices parallel with the ribs and approximately 6 mm thick (½ in.)
3. Serve time lean meat and some fat per portion

Method B

1. Cut down one side of the backbone reaching approximately halfway along the length of the saddle
2. Cut right down the side of the backbone to the short ribs
3. Where you finished cutting halfway along the backbone, turn the knife at right angles and cut down through the meat and fat
4. Cut out lengths of meat from the saddle, commencing at the backbone, parallel to the backbone where the initial incision was made
5. Work outwards to the edge of the saddle
6. Each wedge of meat should then be carved into thin slices lengthwise

Note:

1. With Method A each customer is given a porrion of some lean meat and a little fat.
2. With Method B if the waiter is not careful it is possible for one customer to have a portion of all lean meat and another to receive nearly all fat and very little lean meat.

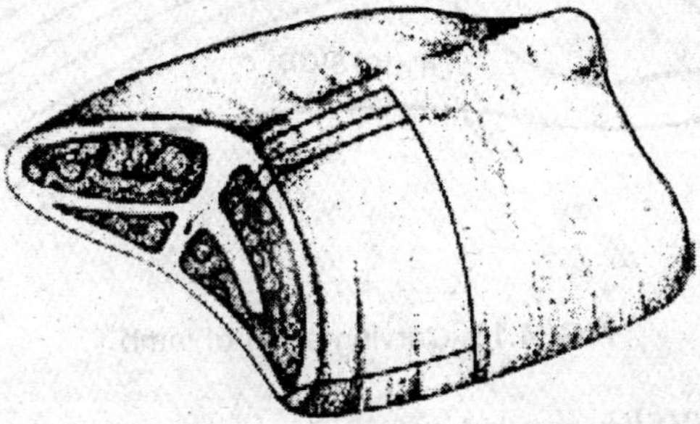

FIG. 4.15. Carving a saddle of lamb (Method B)

Leg of lamb (gigot d'agneau)

Accompaniments

- Rroast gravy
- mint sauce
- redcurrant jelly

Service

1. The waiter should remember chat initially he/she should carve on to the bone
2. Take out a small V-shaped portion of meat just above the knuckle
3. Proceed to carve che portions of meat by carving on to the bone from the V-shaped cut. This part of the joint is known as the *nut* and is the most choice part
4. After the initial portions have been carved from the nut of meat, the succeeding portions should be carved : a slice from the nut and a slice from the underside

Note:

1. When carving a leg of lamb, to keep it steady on the board, the waiter should hold che knuckle in a clean serviette.
2. The flesh of lamb should be cooked evenly arid be rose (pink) in colour.
3. Always cut generously.

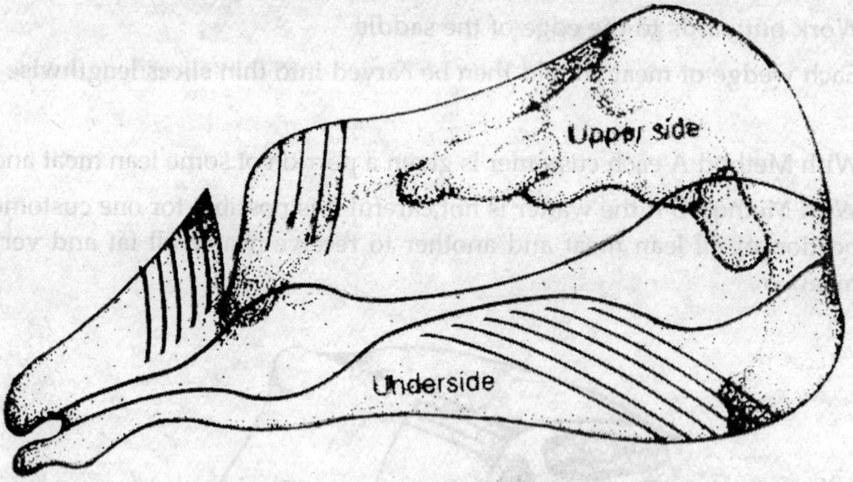

FIG. 4.16. Carving a leg of lamb

Leg of pork (cuissot de porc)

Accompaniments

- Roast gravy
- apple sauce
- sage and
- onion stuffing

Service

Carved in a similar fashion to a leg of lamb, but the slices carved here should be thin.

Ham (jambon)

There are two methods of carving hams, namely :

1. *French* : the ham is cut into very thin slices down the length of the ham.
2. *English:* the ham is carved at the thick end where' the meat is at its most tender.

Note: If the ham is boned and rolled it will then be carved in slices across the fibre of the meat.

FLAMBE SWEET DISHES

As with the gueridon, the flambe trolley may be set up following a certain basic format. The ideal fresh fruits to use for this purpose are peaches, pineapple or bananas. The choice of a particular fruit will indicate the choice of spirits used. For fresh peaches, brandy is to be recommended, for bananas use rum and with fresh pineapples choose rum or Kirsch. The different flavour will enhance and complement each other. As usual for flambe work, one needs butter and sugar to produce the syrup-sauce. A sprinkling of ground almonds is also a part of the dish and serves to thicken the sauce. The procedure is fairly standardized, as given below :

1. Melt the butter in the pan,
2. Heat the prepared fruit,
3. At this stage put in the castor sugar and ground almonds,
4. Flambe with the spirit, and
5. Serve at once.

Fresh cream may be offered with the dish. There are many variations of flambe dishes, the ingredients differ but the basic procedure remains the same.

The main flambe sweet dishes are :

1. Peach flambe.
2. Pears flambe.
3. Bananas flambe.
4. Cherries flambe.
5. Cerise's flambe au glace vanill.
6. Cerise's jubilees.
7. Rum omelets.
8. Strawberry Rammanoff.
9. Pineapples flambe.
10. Crepes Suzette.

FLAMBE DISHES

1. Crepes Suzette

Cover : Sweet spoon and fork hot sweet plate.

Accompaniment : None.

Ingredients : (two portions)

Ingredients		*Quantity*
1. Castor sugar	:	85 gms (3 oz.)
2. Salmons	:	2
3. Lemon	:	1/2
4. Zest Salmons	:	2
5. Butter	:	85 gms (3 oz.)
6. Orange Curacao	:	1 measure
7. Brandy	:	1 measure
8. Pancakes	:	4

Equipment for Flambe Trolley

1. Lamp
2. Pan on an under-plate
3. Service spoons and forks on a service plate
4. 2 teaspoons on a side plate
5. 2 sweet forks on a side plate
6. Oval flat with a doily for a portion of pancakes
7. Oval flat with plus 3 small sauceboats for the creamed mixture, orange juice and leme juice
8. Brandy and liqueur glass on an under plate
9. 1 bottle of orange Curacao and 1 of brandy
10. 2 hot sweet plates.

Service Technique

1. Pour out the required measure of liqueur.
2. Place the creamed mixture of castor sugar, butter and zest into the pan and melt. Allow to colour slightly to a light golden shade.
3. Add three sauce ladles of orange juice and blend well.
4. Add the juice of half a lemon if required-according to taste.
5. Add one measure of orange Curacao.
6. Mix well, stirring with a large fork-taste.
7. Place in the pancakes, one at a time; heat well, turnover and then fold.

8. During this process, the sauce should be reducing all the time and thickening.
9. When the sauce is reduced-sufficiently, add the measure of brandy and flambe.
10. Serve on to the hot sweet plates .rom the pan, at the table.

Orange salad (salade d'orange)

Accompaniment

Caster sugar

Equipment for gueridon

Small very sharp knife-sweet fork-two oranges on plate—fruit plate-spare plate for dirty cutlery and flatware-small glass dish-board

Orange (orange)

Service Technique

1. Cut a slice from one end of the orange with the aid of the sharp knife
2. Pierce the cut slice with the fork to act as a guard when sectioning the whole orange
3. Now pierce the whole orange with the fork from the uncut end, so that it is firmly held on the fork
4. Make an incision around the uncut end of the whole orange through the skin to the flesh — (through the rind and pith)
5. Remove the peel and pith by cutting strips from the cut end co the incision made around the orange (Figure 8.15 a&b)
6. At this stage you should now have a whole orange on your fork with the peel and pith removed
7. Holding the orange over the glass bowl cut out each section of the orange leaving the pith on the fork. Let the sections of orange fall into the glass bowl (Figure 3.12c)
8. With the aid of a second fork squeeze the pith over the glass bowl to remove all the juice
9. Sprinkle with caster sugar
10. Dress on to the fruit plate and serve (Figure 3.12d).

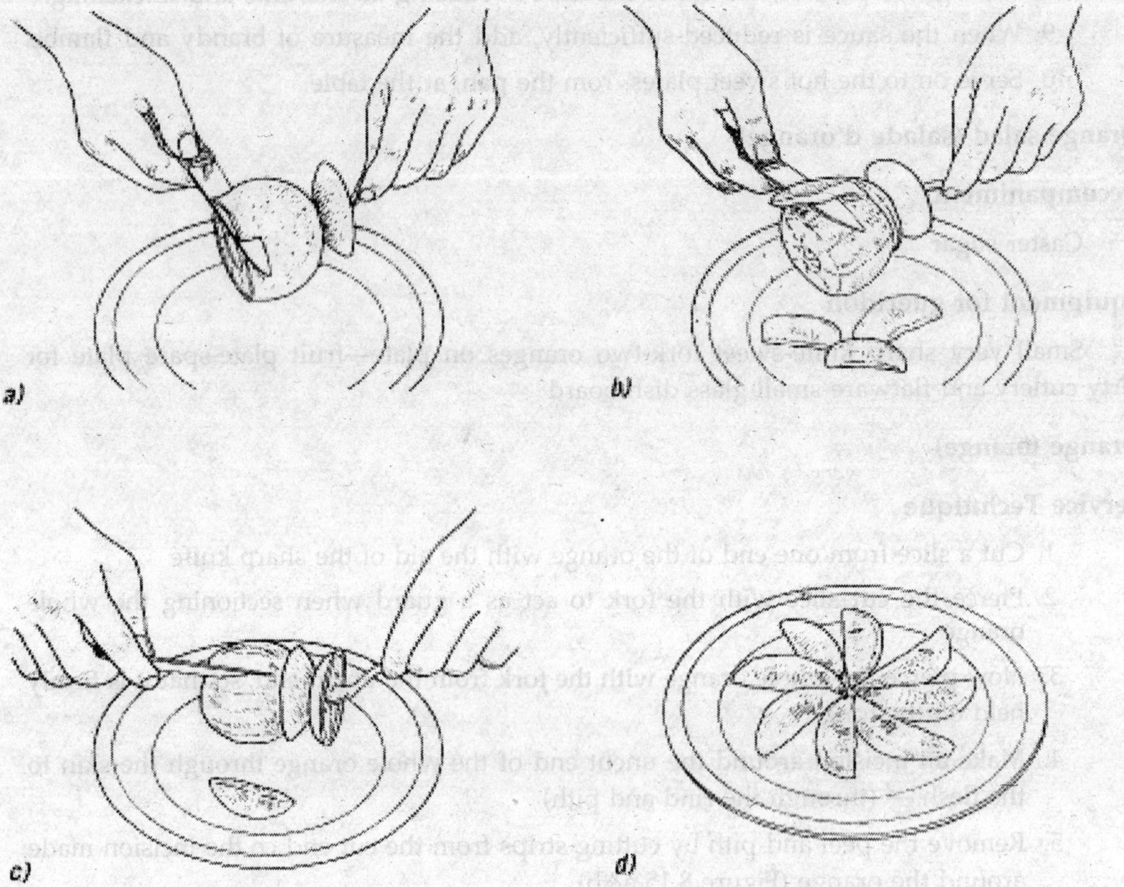

FIG. 4.17. Preparation of an orange

Apple or pear (pomme au poire)

1. Cut a cone from the top of the apple or pear around the stalk approximately 2.5 cm in diameter and put aside for later use (Figure 3.14a)
2. Cut the base of the apple or pear
3. Place a fork into the top of the apple or pear where the stalk cone was removed from
4. Peel the apple in strips from top to bottom or in a spiral from top to bottom (Figure 3.13b or c)
5. Cut the apple into two then into quarters (Figure 3.14d)
6. Remove the core from each quarter (Figure 3.14e)
7. Decorate on the plate using the stalk cone to garnish (Figure 3.14f)
8. Dress with spirit on liquir should be customer request etc.

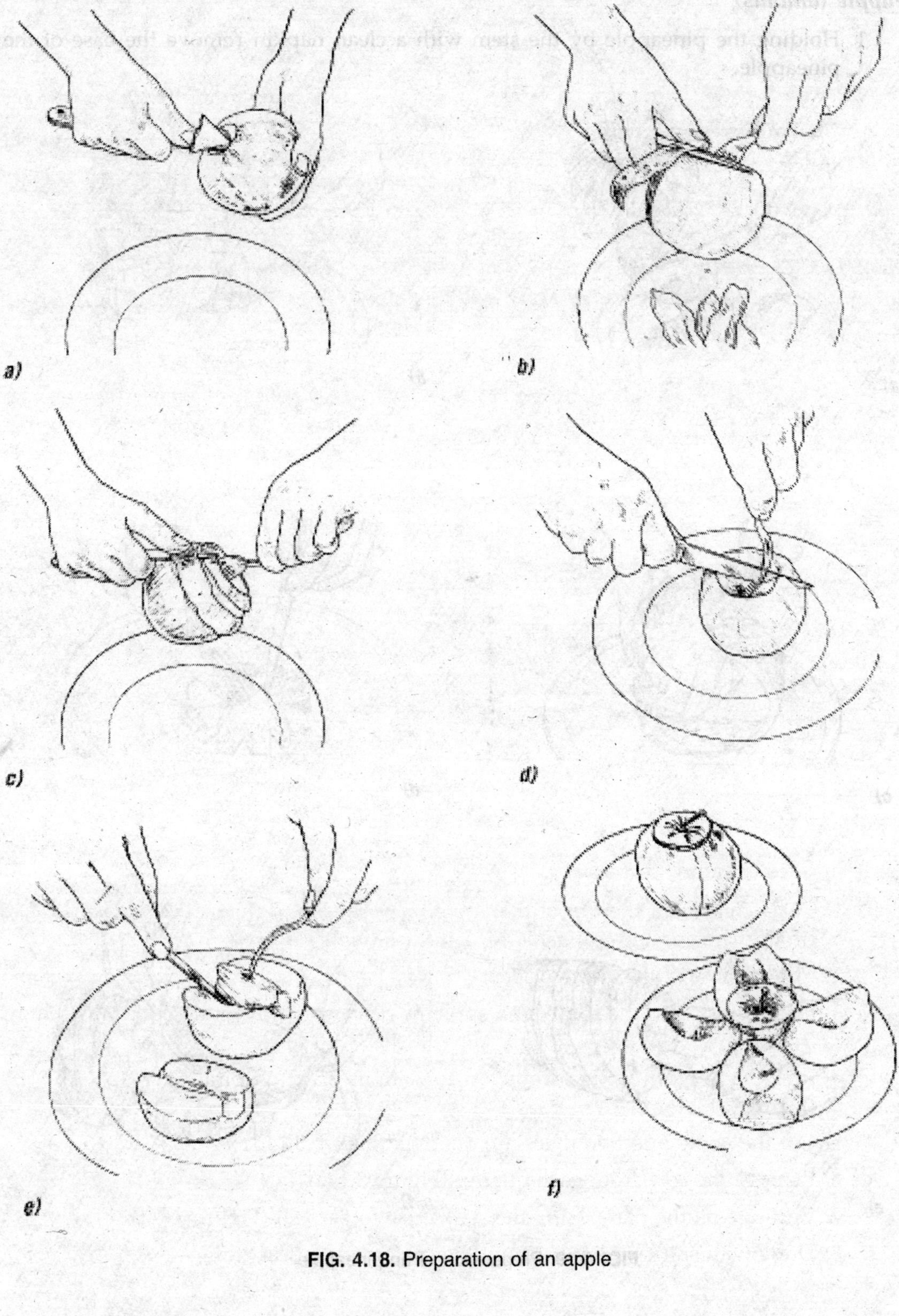

FIG. 4.18. Preparation of an apple

Pineapple (ananas)

1. Holding the pineapple by the stem with a clean napkin remove the base of the pineapple

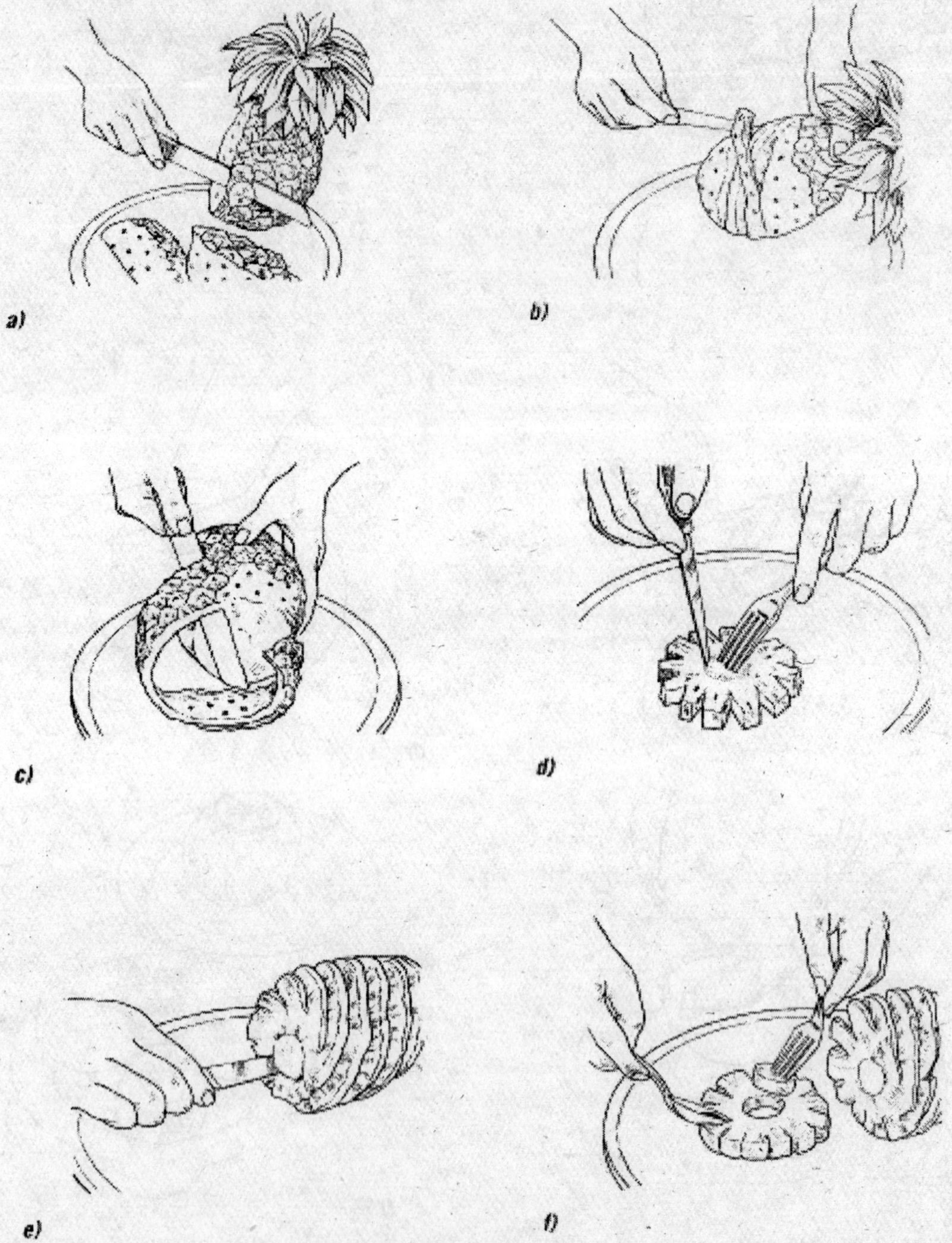

FIG. 4.19. Preparation of an pineapple

2. Peel the pineapple in strips from top to bottom or Cut the pineapple in a spiral from bottom to top (Figure 4.19a or c)
3. Remove the eyes by cutting a V shaped channel. Note that each channel should, go from left to right as this will give a less complex spiral that does not all run into one (Figure 4.19b)
4. Slice the pineapple
5. Remove the core using the point of a paring knife or an apple corer
6. Dress cash Kcrsch, if requested.
7. Present nearly on to the cold fruit plat.

Banana (banane)

1. Remove the end of the banana (fig. 4.20)
2. Slice through the banana and through the stalk lengthways to give two even slices. Your knuckles may rest against the board to keep the knife straight (fig. 4.20)
3. Insert a fruit fork into the end of the stalk and peel the skin back using your knife on the outside of the skin to fold it away from the flesh, using year knife on the outside of the skin to keep the half banana fruity head on the board (fig. 4.20)
4. Dress with dark rum of requested.
5. Present neatly a cold fruit plate.

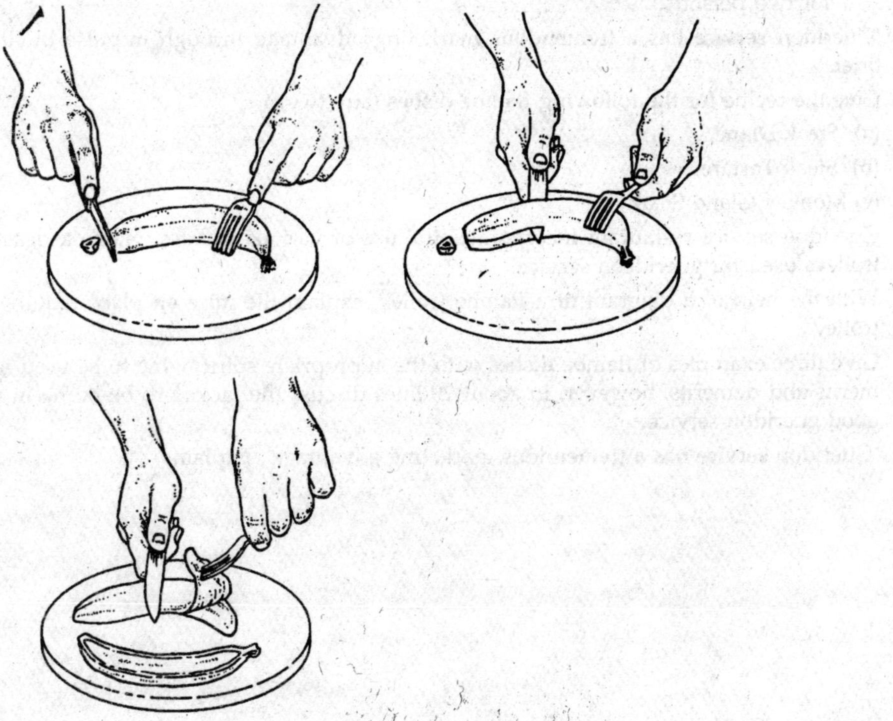

FIG. 4.20. Preparation of a banana

QUESTIONS AND ASSIGNMENTS

Objective Type

Q. 1. Match 'B' with column 'A':

Column 'A'	**Column 'B'**
(a) Cream of tomato	(i) Worcestershire
(b) Entremet	(ii) Yorkshire pudding
(c) Gueridon	(iii) USA.
(d) Reachaud candles	(iv) Crepe suzette
(e) Tomato Juice	(v) Sommelier
	(vi) Buffet
	(vii) Black forest.

Essay Type

Q. 2. Give the recipe *of any two* of the following :

(i) Steak Diane,

(ii) Banana Flambe,

(iii) Crepe Suzette (BHM)

Q. 3. (a) Draw a neat Gueridon Top diagram indicating therein-different types of equipment required for the preparation of 'CREPE SUZETTE' for two persons.

(b) Name the ingredients and quantities required for two persons.

(c) "Explain in detail step by step method you would adopt for the preparation of CREPE SUZETTE for two person". [BHM]

Q. 4. 'Gueridon service has a tremendous marketing advantage through impulse buying'. Elucidate in brief.

Q. 5. Give the recipe for the following flambe dishes (any two):

(a) Steak Diane,

(b) Steak Tartare,

(c) Monkey Gland Steak [BHM]

Q. 6. Gueridon service restaurant incorporates the use of various trolleys. Name at least four important trolleys used for guerideon service. [BHM]

Q. 7. With the help of a diagram of a flambe trolley, explain the mise en place required for the flambe trolley.

Q. 8. Give three examples of flambe dishes with the appropriate spirit/wine to be used for service has its merits and demerits, however, in about 20-lines discuss the factors to be borne in mind to provide good gueridon service. [BHM]

Q. 9. 'Gueridon service has a tremendous marketing advantage'. Explain. [BHM]

5 Functions Banquets Conferences : Conventions and Exhibitions

After learning this lesson you should be able to :

1. *Explain the term 'functions ', 'banquets', 'conferences', 'conventions ', and 'exhibitions';*
2. *Estimate the service staff requirement for a banquet, such as kitchen equipment, light equipment etc;*
3. *Understand the service techniques, communication, arrangement for drinks, briefing system, Junction etiquette, toast and speeches, service methods etc;*
4. *Explain the booking procedure, menus and banquet spacing;*
5. *Discuss with the client, room set up, table set up, floor plans, seating arrangements and banquet planning;*
6. *Maintain the Function Book, draw a suitable banquet policy, fill up the Banquet Report Form, Function Prospect and Banquet Form;*
7. *Understand the procedure for wedding functions, outdoor catering, conferences and conventions and exhibitions;*
8. *Study and analyze and banquet menus of different hotels.*

The term 'function' in relation to food and beverage includes occasions such as luncheon parties, conferences, cocktail parties, buffets, weddings, dinner dances, birthday parties, supper balls, business conferences, and so on. Thus, 'functional catering' is the term used to cover the service of special function for specific group of people at specific time, the food and beverages provided being predetermined. Banquets and other functions are today offered not only in hotels, conference establishments and function rooms but also in pub cafes, banquet hotels and restaurants.

Some Guidelines for Regularizing Banquet Halls

1. A detailed policy should be laid down for banquet halls. The banquet halls have been in the eye of a storm for the last few years. A survey conducted had revealed that nearly 97 percent of them were running from the premises, which were dangerous, and in gross violation of building by-laws.
2. All the existing and new banquet halls should now be 'regularized as per the new policy for regularization of banquet halls. Ever since banquet halls came

into existence, all of them continue to operate illegally as the government did not have any policy to regularize them nor was there any provision for them in the plan.

3. The rules and regulations are constituted for banquet halls should have been framed largely on the recommendations given by a multi-agency committee constituted for the purpose. The Land Development's principal commissioner headed this important committee,
4. Among its members should be Land Development Commissioner (planning), Commissioner (land and management), Additional Commissioner (planning), Chief Fire Officer, DCP-licensing, Municipal Corporation and local town planners and joint secretary in State government's urban development ministry.
5. According to the new proposal, banquet halls will have to apply to the Municipal Corporation for a trade license and pay annual charges to the civic body. But the owners will first have to obtain a no objection certificate from the city police licensing wing as well as the fire department. For serving liquor, a separate license will be required from the excise department.
6. Stringent guidelines should be laid down for obtaining NOCs from the fire department and no banquet hall will be allowed to operate without this clearance. The guidelines should state that no banquet halls will be allowed to operate in a basement and there should be at least two entries and exits for fire safety. The basement to be used for parking and for installation of water tanks and other needs. The new rules, however, disallow the basement of the halls to be used either for storage or office facilities.
7. In order to obtain a license, banquet halls should also be required to ensure regular availability of electricity with back up facilities like generators. A separate set of rules and guidelines should be laid down for existing and new banquet halls.
8. Some of the recommendations for existing banquet halls include: -
   (i) The minimum plot size should be 333 square meters. The banquet hall owners association, however, wants this to be reduced to 250 square meters.
   (ii) The minimum right of way (width of the road) in front of the existing banquet halls should be 13.5 meters.
9. Recommendations for new halls include:-
   (i) The minimum plot size should be 800 square meters.
   (ii) Maximum ground coverage to be allowed - 33.33 percent.
   (iii) Maximum height of the structure will be 15 meters.
   (iv) Minimum right of way should be 18 meters.
   (v) Nearly 100 square meters of the floor area is to be reserved for parking.
10. According to the police, banquet halls will have to maintain proper hygiene, provide sufficient parking, water for cooking, washing and drinking as well as ensure proper disposal of garbage.
11. All existing and new banquet halls will have to ensure that vehicles are not parked

on the road in front in order to allow easy access to fire tenders in the event of fire.

Types of Functions

All functions may be classified under the following heads: -

1. ***Formal Meals (Banquets)***
   (i) Lunch
   (ii) Dinner
   (iii) Weddings.
2. ***Buffet - Receptions***
   (i) Wedding Receptions
   (ii) Cocktail parties
   (iii) Buffet teas
   (iv) Dances
   (v) Anniversary parties
   (vi) Conferences and conventions.
3. ***Another way of classifying the function is: -***
   I Social functions: -
      (a) Wedding receptions
      b) Luncheons
      (c) Receptions
      (d) Cocktail parties
      (e) Cocktail parties
   II. Conferences: -
      (a) Political Conferences
      (b) Trade Unions
      (c) National and International Conferences.
   III. Public Relations: -
      (a) Press party to launch a new product
      (b) Fashion parade
      (c) Dealers' meetings
      (d) Seminars
      (e) Exhibitions.

BANQUET STAFF

In large and luxurious hotels, all functions take place in the banquet halls/suits and are under the administrative control of the Banquet Manager/Conference Manager. In small hotels, these functions normally take place in a room set aside for the purpose and come under the jurisdiction of the hotel manager. In addition, there are specialist-banqueting centres; most of the staff for banqueting is employed on a casual basis. Depending upon the size of the functions, the banqueting staff may include:-

1. Sales Administration Manager

2. Banquet Manager/Conference Manager
3. Secretary
4. Banquet Headwaiter
5. Dispense Bar Staff
6. Banquet Head Wine waiter
7. Permanent Waiting Staff
8. Casual Staff
9. Porters.

The number of people and the capacity in which they work-in depends on the size of the facility and the type of service being offered. In some hotels, banquet staff consists of the following:

1. Chef and First Cook
2. Assistant Cook(s)
3. Caterer's Assistant
4. Waiters (Waitresses)
5. Bartender
6. Bas boys
7. Pantry or Salad man
8. Kitchen man
9. Dishwashers
10. Additional staff:
    (i) Taking tickets
    (ii) Check room
    (iii) Musicians
    (iv) Photographers.

Once the menu and type of service is decided upon, then the staff required and the responsibilities of each staff member can be determined. Table 5.1 can be used as a guide for the staff needed under normal conditions to serve the number of guest indicated at each of me different types of affairs. The number of persons should be sufficient to set up the room, to serve and clear tables with a reasonable amount of time. The chart does not indicate the staff needed to cook the meal in advance, or in the case of off-premise caterer, the staff needed to transport food to the kitchen.

Staff required for Service

The number of waiters and waitresses required both for the service of drinks and food will have to be decided well in advance on the basis of forecast numbers.

In a silver service a waiter usually serves 10-12 covers. The springs should be made up to seat guest in multiples of 10 or 12 or whatever figure each waiter is to serve. Waiters may serve more guests up to sixteen or even more, when simpler services are introduced. One wine waiter is associated for each twenty five to forty guests, if wine is preordered inclusive in the function.

TABLE 5.1

Service Staff Requirements for a Function For 300 in a Highclass Hotel

Service/staff Requirements : Basic Information

1. Hotel	: High-class category.	
2. Menu	: Four-course dinner menu plus coffee.	
3. Beverage	: Table wines	
	(i) Sherry with consomme.	
	(ii) A white wine with fish.	
	(iii) A red wine with the main course.	
	(iv) Brandy/liqueurs with coffee.	
4. Service staff	(i) Banquet Headwaiter	: One
	(ii) Assistant Banquet Headwaiter	: One
	(iii) Waiters/waitresses	: 20
	(iv) Wine waiters	: 6

Control

There are different methods of controlling the number of main courses, taken by the waiters to the function room, for example, issuing 'roast slips' to the waiters. These slips can be made out by the captain in charge or by a control person in the kitchen. Every waiter reports his table number and the number of guests seated. A pre-printed slip is quickly filled out with this information. 'This waiter then hands the slip to the chef or steward in-charge for food. The beverages must be controlled in the same way. The closing captain should fill out a captain's report. After the function, the banquet sales person should fill out a Banquet Follow up form, which will go in the file for future reference. This provides yet another means of banquet cost control.

Safety and Legal Liabilities

Fire training to employees, legal counsel, storage of chairs and tables, dance permits, exhibition requirements, tax exemptions, insurance claims etc. need careful attention.

Kitchen Equipments

Heavy Equipment

It is expensive and is intended to last for a long time. Some of the equipment is given in the Table 5.2.

TABLE 5.2.
Heavy Kitchen Equipment for Banquets

1. Steam Cooking	:	(i) Kettles
		(ii) Steamers
		(iii) Large Steam Tables
		(iv) Compartment Steamers.
2. Tilting Frying Pans		
3. Bain Marie/stainless steel pan/basin		
4. Holding cabinets and food carts		
5. Broilers		
6. Ranges		
7. Ovens		
8. Microwave ovens		
9. Other kitchen equipment		(i) Stoves
		(ii) Heaters
		(iii) Deep flat fryers
		(iv) Table space
		(v) Electric heat lamps
		(vi) Slicing machines/slicers
		(vii) Vertical cutter/mixers
		(viii) Meat grinders
		(ix) Buffalo choppers
		(x) Menu Board
		(xi) Coffee urns
		(xii) Dishwashing machine
		(xiii) Scrapping table
		(xiv) Grinders
		(xv) Refrigerators
		(xvi) Freezers
		(xvii) Walk in boxes
		(xviii) Pots and pans.

Light Equipment

It refers to all equipment for the guest service, as well as other portable equipment. It also includes linen, paper goods and novelties. The equipment required for guest service is given in the Table 5.3

TABLE 5.3
Light equipment in a Banquet for the Guest Service

Dishes

(i) Service plates
ii) Cups and saucers
(iii) Dinner plates
(iv) Relish trays
(v) Luncheon plates
(vi) Platters
(vii) Salad plates
(viii) Ramekins
(ix) Soup bowls
(x) Sherbet cups
(xi) Soup bowls
(xii) Ash trays
(xiii) Bouillon cups.
(xiv) Fish Plates

Silver Service

(i) Chaffing Dish
(ii) Creamer and sugar sets
(iii) Champagne ice bucket and stand
(iv) Candelabra
(v) Champagne or punch fountain
(vi) Display trays.

Gold Service

All dishes and flatware are of good and the glasses are very fine crystal with gold rims.

Flatware

(i) Binner fork
(ii) Luncheon knife
(iii) Entree fork
(iv) Bread spreader
(v) Salad fork
(vi) Soup spoon
(vii) Fish fork
(viii) Creamed soup spoon
(ix) Dessert fork
(x) Tea spoon
(xi) Dinner knife
(xii) Ice spoon.

Glasses

(i) Fruit juice glass	— 5 oz
(ii) Water Tumbler or goblet	— 8-10 oz
(iii) General Beverage glass	— 9 oz
(iv) Ice tea glass	— 12 oz
(v) Wine glass	— 2-4 oz

(vi) Champagne glass — 4-5 1/4 oz
(vii) Supreme glass and liner (used for meal service).
(viii) Parfait glass (used for meal service)

Coffee Urns (Coffee Makers)

(i) Coffee serving urns — 35 - 100 cups
(ii) Pitchers — 2 qt.

Tea Service/sanover

(i) Tea pourer
(ii) Pot with boiling water
(iii) A cream and sugar set.

Trays

(i) Display trays (as given under silver)
(ii) Utility trays
(iii) Waiters trays (28 × 22 in. oral)
(iv) Kitchen trays (12 × 20 in.)
(v) Bar trays (12- 14in. round, cork lined)

Box/Boxes (Utility boxes)

For carrying dirty dishes and flatware from the dinning room to the kitchen. Metal or plastic boxes - 12" × 18"- 18" × 24", 5 – $\frac{1}{2}$ in. deep.

Portable Equipment

(i) Carrying cases
(ii) Glass boxes
(iii) Tray boxes
(iv) Candelabra boxes
(v) Chaffing dish boxes
(vi) Heavy-duty cardboxes: These are used for:
(i) Flatware
(ii) Lenin
(iii) Kitchen utensils
(iv) Pots and pans
(v) Pitchers
(vi) Coffee urns
(vii) All other equipment.

(v) Portable eqpment for cooking and carrying food:
(a) Electric frying pans and roasters
(b) Insulated food carriers
(c) Ice chests
(d) Heated units

Lenin (Banquet Hall)

Specialty linen :
(a) Buffet cloths- 80 × 120 in.
(b) Lace covers for buffet 54 × 120 in.
(c) Over skirts
(d) Coloured table linen.

TABLE 5.4.
Standard Size of Table Linen, Linen Napkins

The colour of linen on buffet tables could be :

1. White
2. Pale yellow
3. Pale Pink
4. Blue-light, medium or electric
5. Red-bright or vibrant for valentine day and Christmas
6. Fiesta shades - bright yellow or angel green for special informal occasions.

Kitchen Linen

1. Potholders: large, heavy duty.
2. Dish towels for wiping pots and pans.
3. Hand towels or clean rags for general clean up and for wiping silver trays and chaffing dishes.
4. Bar rags: small, clean hand towels.
5. Mop up rags: clean rags for general use.

Paper Goods

(1) Silver Service Units	(I) Paper plates	: (a) Plastic coated.
	(II) Cups – imprinted	: (b) Stew bowls
		(c) Sandwich wrappers or bags
		(d) Napkins
		(e) Glassine or plastic bags
		(f) Cold cups
		(g) Salad cups with covers
		(h) Printed sandwich labels
		(i) Straws
		(j) Plastic or wooden forks and spoons.
	(III) Paper Napkins	: (a) Breakfast or luncheon- 18 × 18 in.
		(b) Dinner - 20 x 20 in.
		(c) Cocktail-from 9x9 to 12xl2in.
	(IV) Paper Table covers	(a) Solid colours or imprinted
	(V) Paper mats	(a) Designed with name and address of the restaurant, menus etc.
	(VI) Paper doilies	(a) Gold or silver colour liner 5-6 in.; placed under the fruit cocktail or sherb glass on the serving plate.
	(VII) Paper (cardboard) boxes	: (a) Flat (pizza) box: for storage *ofhors d'oeuve* in freezer and for delivery of the same — 12 × 12 × 1 - !/2 in. to 16 × l6 × 1- ½ in.
		(b) Pie Box: For assorted food items - 9 x 9 x Sin
		(c) Cake Box: 12 × 12 × 6 in.

(d) Leaf Box: 9 × 5 × 5 in.
  (i) Candles
  (ii) Gifts for departing guests
  (iii) Jordan Almonds (packed in tinny ceramic)
  (iv) Sugar coated nuts or plastic shoes or wrapped in small squares of coloured net.
  (v) Cake: Groom's cake. Bride's cake, etc.
  (vi) Rice: Wrapped in fine net and tied with a ribbon.
  (vii) Other gifts: Cigarettes, Lighters, holders, Small compacts, Rain bonnets, Key chains, etc.

Equipment and maintenance

The condition of the banquet space and the condition of the *'big four'* (China, silver, glasses and linen) are among the most important points on the banquet manager's agenda. Keeping the chairs in good repair, maintaining walls and carpets in good order and having a room arranged in a neat and orderly manner be important factors in the impression made on a prospective client.

Menu Coordination

The menu coordination is essential to making the work in the kitchen as efficient as possible. Attractively printed menu, proper accompaniment etc. needs to be properly planned.

Styles of Service

The various types of services are :

1. French Service
2. Russian Service *(a la Russe)*
3. Plate Service
4. Family style service
5. Buffet Service
6. Pre-set Service
7. Butler service etc.

The type of service offered depends on physical exigencies such as the equipment, the staff available, the layout of the rooms, the layout of the kitchen and the distance from the kitchen to the dinning halVrooms. Of course, it should reflect the wishes of the guests.

The Trainees

Good training costs money. Many training aids are available. A good training programme can be established. It takes pleasant, well-trained employees to have a successful banquet hall business.

Communicating

Communicating information is vital to the success of the banquet. Information be recorded on the Function Order Forms (Fig. 4.' note customer's requirements and a banquet or function prospects. The following departments require prior notification of a function :

1. Kitchen
2. Restaurant (banqueting/function manager)
3. Cellar
4. Housekeeper
5. Hall porter
6. Stillroom
7. Plate room.

Apart from the usual "Special Business Sheet" sent to all departments each week, further forms giving all the necessary information to departments concerned are to be sent to all those concerned departments from the manager's office of the function.

The kitchen staff requires the following information:

1. Date and time of the function
2. Number of services required
3. Number of covers per service
4. Any other information.

The waiting staff, i.e. the banquet manager or function headwaiter, requires the following information:

1. Date and time of the function
2. Number to be served
3. Where to assemble
4. Where to serve
5. Menu detail
6. Plans of table
7. List of guests
8. Drinks, aperitifs, wines, liqueurs, spirits and whether pre-ordered or cash.
9. Cigars, cigarettes, etc.
10. Any other information.

The plate-room must be notified in advance of the date, time and place and total numbers attending the function. They have to attend not only to the supply of the silver for the kitchen but also to plates, cutlery and glasses. They will, therefore, require to know:

1. Details of menu, number of services required
2. How many on each service ?
3. Size and types of each course
4. Requirements of finger bowls

5. Requirements of special glasses
6. Any other particular information.

The stillroom requires information to provide adequately for rolls, butter, toast, Melba, coffee and milk. They need to know the date, time, place and total number. On certain occasions, tea, sandwiches and cakes or breakfast may be served during the evenings or early hours of the morning, in such cases, the stillroom will need advance notification.

Arrangements for Drinks and Tobacco

A special reception bar is provided for a function of any size so as to.facilitate service. It is set up in or near the room where reception is being held, with a barman or a wine waiter in charge. Stock for this bar is drawn directly from cellars. As for the aperitifs, organizers of function may decide that a limited number of glasses will be paid for by them and rest to be on the cash basis (cash drinks).

Liqueurs and spirits can also be obtained from the cellars and these again can be paid for by the organizers or by the individual customer.

The function headwaiter must be informed as to what time a special license, if any has been obtained for this function. He is responsible for seeing that no drinks are served after the time limit has expired.

The organizers sometimes provide cigars and cigarettes themselves. These should be handed over to the headwaiter at the time of the function. The organizers can also order these when the function is first booked. In this case, the function headwaiter will have to be notified. He may then draw his requirements from the store on the morning of the function. Cigars are passed round in boxes by the wine waiter at a large function or by the function headwaiter at a small one. Cigarettes in glasses or boxes (a dozen or so in each) are placed at intervals on tables after the royal toast (of the queen).

Briefing

Each member of the staff must be quite clear as to what is expected of him/her. All should be '*briefed* either by the caterer or by their immediate superior. The kitchen staff should be briefed well in advance and receipts and quantities should be provided in writing. It is best of the menu, the individual duties, the time of service and the number of services written up. The extent to which the caterer will be involved in the briefing of the kitchen staff and the amount of extra supervision, which he may be required to give, will obviously depend upon the competence of the head chef in the field of function work.

The person responsible for the dinning room-the headwaiter, dinning room supervisor or plate-room incharge must be given a list of everything well in advance, and also told about where the different items are to be put in readiness. This list is useful for checking that everything is returned after the function. The food and beverage staff needs careful briefing on several important points :

1. All waiting staff must know their station.
2. If a function is large enough to require two services or two strips, it is essential that the staff know which to use. Colouring coding could be useful here.

3. The staff should have the menus explained to them in terms, which they will understand and remember so that they can give a (brief) translation to the guest who enquires. The menu and ' ιe translation are best displayed prominently in the servery.
4. Wine waiter should be similarly briefed.
5. Food service staff should know where they could obtain the items ordered by the guests; to whom they should refer any other requests and where that person is to be found.
6. The order of serving and clearing must be stated in details and this can also be displayed in the servery. Such things as glasses, condiments and butter dishes can be cleared at one specific time, so the briefing should include something like 'Clear the condiments, to this table place, before serving the sweet'.
7. Finally, any casual staff should be told if and when they will receive a meal, when and where they will be paid, and if there are any conditions attached to payment such as the return of coffee spoons and or waiter's clothes.

Function Etiquette

You must be familiar with the normal procedure at formal occasions,, as explained below :

1. On Arrival

At a formal meal there is always a reception area and guests are announced when they join the company i.e. after they have checked in their coats and hats under no circumstances should anyone other than a toast master attempt to do this. Usually the host will receive the guest on arrival.

2. Announcing the Meal

As usual form of announcement is:

'Ladies and Gentlemen, kindly take your place at table. Dinner (or luncheon) is about to be served'.

At small, relatively informal/formal meals, it quite often falls to the caterer to make this announcement and under these circumstances, it is the responsibility of the client and the host to make sure that the guest do drink up and move in.

Once the meals have been announced, it is often necessary for the toast masters (sometimes assisted by the waiter) to shepherd the guests discreetly into the dinning-room because invariably there are a few groups which are reluctant to break their conversation since they may not be at the same table for the meal. A second and occasionally tried announcement is sometimes needed at large functions, particularly, if the reception has been fairly long and the drinks have been served.

It is customary for the top table guests to enter the dinning room last, after everyone else has taken their place and this may be announced to the company by the toastmaster in such terms as :

'Ladies and Gentlemen, kindly be up standing to receive your Chairman and distinguished guests'

At a dinner dance, the band often plays a suitable march as the top table enters.

3. Grace

Occasionally, grace before meals is omitted which is pity. It is usually said by the Chairman or host, unless someone in holy orders is on the top table, in which case they are normally asked to say grace. There is no set form for grace, unless the function is either a Bums evening or Masonic event.

4. Taking Wine with

At large dinners, it is quite usual for the toastmaster to announce:

'Ladies and Gentlemen, your Chairman would like to take wine with you'.

(The ladies or the guests or the prize winners or any other group within the general company).

The Chairman and the particular group stand up, take a drink of wine, bow and sit down again. A good toast master will ascertain from the Chairman, how many times this little ceremony is to take place, and then liaise closely and the headwaiter to ensure that the service is not delayed.

Toasts and Speeches

These vary in number, length and importance, therefore, find out from the client, as much as possible, about the length of the speeches in order to plan the staffing arrangements.

There must be no noise in the dinning-room during the speeches. Usually only the headwaiter remains in the dinning room during the speeches to ensure that the Chairman and top table has all that they require. Therefore, the coffee and the liqueurs must all be served before the speeches begin.

It is often possible to serve the staff their meals during the speeches and if they are likely to be prolonged, it is also often possible to pay off some temporary staff, remaining only enough to clear up once the function has *'broken'*.

An awkward situation can arise when the wines are inclusive but limited in quantity, there is no cash sale of liqueurs and there are two or more toasts. The problem is that the guests may have nothing left in their glasses when asked:

"Be upstanding for the Toast of............. ".

You should bring it to the attention of your client when discussing the function and be prepared to instruct the wine waiter to say:

'For the Toasts' to each guest as they pour the last glass of wine.

The first toast is always the Loyal Toast or Her Majesty the Queen. This may appear on the toast list as :

"The *Loyal Toast*", *"The Queen"*, or *"Her Majesty the Queen"*,

and if there is no toastmaster, you should be able to announce this toast. The announcement in these circumstances would be :

'Ladies and Gentlemen please see that your glasses are charged and be upstanding for the Loyal Toast '.

Once everyone is standing, the proposer say:

The Queen ' and *the guests reply, ' The Queen'.*

It frequently happens that the guests will 'respond' by saying, *' The Queen'* as they stand up before the toast has been proposed but this cannot be prevented nor rectified.

If the Chairman is to propose 'Loyal Toast', the announcement would be:

'Pray silence for your Chairman, who will propose the Loyal Toast,

but in these circumstances, a toastmaster would be present.

It is traditional that no one smokes beyond the Loyal Toast and for this reason it is kindness to many guests if the toast is given as soon as possible. When a sherbet is served halfway through a meal, the Royal Toast is often given, then so that the guest can smoke with the sherbet. The toast is sometimes followed by the announcement:

'Ladies and Gentlemen, you may smoke',

but in general, this is not to be recommended. If no one, has lit a cigarette before the Loyal Toast it is safe to assume that everyone knows the normal etiquette and if people have begin to smoke, the statement sound too much like a reprimand. However, some hosts even to the extent of requesting anyone who has begin to smoke extinguish their cigarettes until after the Loyal Toast. It is a good idea to have a five minutes break between the Loyal Roast and subsequent toasts and speeches. (In coach-tour terminology, this would be known as *'comfort stop')*.

Service Methods

The service methods in function may take any of the following forms :

1. Silver
2. Family
3. Plate
4. Assisted Service
5. Self service.

The food may be eaten in a variety of ways :

Normal :

1. Guest being served the food on to plates by waiters.
2. Guest helping themselves from a 'buffet' by staff, then sitting down to eat.
3. Guest helping themselves from a 'buffet (or cafeteria) prior to sitting down.
4. Guest keeping themselves from dishes on the table at which they are eating.

Guest Being Served from a Buffet, then:

1. Standing whilst eating with or without cutlery.

2. Sitting on upright or low early chairs with no easy access to a place on which to rest the plate or dish from which they are eating (with or without cutlery).
3. Food being passed round or served by waiters whilst the guests are standing or sitting in a semi- reclining position (with or without cutlery).

The type of service method chosen must be determined by standing the ergonomics of every item on the menu so as the food can be served competently and that the guest can eat it with as little difficulty as possible without embarrassment. Following factors also require due consideration :

1. Host's wishes
2. Time factor
3. Skills of the service staff available
4. Equipment available
5. Type of function - formal, less formal or buffet type.

Booking of Functions

The following procedure could be adopted :

1. At the initial meeting with the client, open a file recording all points mentioned and concerning the function. If the inquiry is not firm booking, the provisional details should be noted only in pencil and on confirmation could be written in ink.

   The guest must be given a clear picture of the facilities available in the price range he can afford. Show him the specimen luncheon and dinner menus with the cost per head and photographs of the various table layouts for different members.
2. On confirmation, the following basic points should be noted:
   (i) Type of function;
   (ii) Date;
   (iii) Time;
   (iv) Number of covers;
   (v) Price per head;
   (vi) Menu and method of service;
   (vii) Wines-inclusive or cash;
   (viii) Types of organization; and
   (ix) Table plan.
3. Decide the following :
   (i) Toast master;
   (ii) Band, cabaret, dancing;
   (iii) Place cards;
   (iv) Seating plan;

(v) Type of menu for printing-formal; harmonious etc.

(vi) Specialist information: Vegetarian, Vegas, ethnic.

4. Consider the following points :

(i) List of toast-who is proposing and who is replying

(ii) Floral decor for the tables, rooms, reception area and possibly button holes

(iii) Audio-visual equipment required

(iv) Special license-occasional license and number

(v) Friar dishes

(vi) Car parking

(vii) Cloak room

(viii) Changing rooms

(ix) Cigars and cigarettes

(x) Accommodations

(xi) Telephones

(xii) Special light arrangements

(xiii) Lectern

(xiv) Secretarial facilities

(xv) Syndicate rooms

(xvi) Photographers

(xvii) Sign-posting

(xviii) Private bar facilities

(xix) Function cancellation fee-amount and deadline date

(xx) Date for final inspection by the client

(xxi) Security

(xxii) Marketing-press briefing and release.

Banquet Menus

There should be a variety choice of menu within an aide price range; with special menus available for different occasions. Special care is called for with regard to food in season. The minimum number of courses is usually four plus coffee. These are made up of: -

1. *Hors d' oeuvre* or substitute
2. Fish
3. Meat with selection of seasonal vegetables
4. Sweet
5. Coffee-with selection of petite fours.

Extra dishes such as entrees and savories may be added. A combination of these courses could be made to suit the guests' requirements. Each dish should be selected, not only for all the culinary, aesthetic and cost reasons, heat also for servablity. Following points required to be considered :

1. Are there enough service dishes, china cutlery available for simultaneous use ?
2. Is the kitchen equipped for simultaneous cooking and assembly of dishes and is the hot plate etc. enough to cope ?
3. Will each dish be easy to serve quickly ?
4. Are the dishes of such a nature as to withstand heating and standing at serving temperature for as long as may be necessary, without determination (drying, discolouring etc.).

Alcoholic Beverages

The banqueting wine-list should be small. Wines may be inclusive with the meal or on a cash basis, the money being payable to the sommeliers who work on float system. Very often the aperitifs served before the function is also inclusive with the meal but if not, there is generally a 'cash bar" set up in the reception area.

Banquet Checklist

Every banquet party is different; therefore, additional information must be collected. There is much more to be discussed than food and beverages. The following check list outlines the subjects that the sales person and a client should discuss: -

1. Time
2. Control
3. Signs
4. Checkroom
5. Beverages
6. Decorations
7. Gifts, door prizes
8. Music
9. Amplification
10. Photographer
11. Room setup
12. Flags
13. Programs
14. Sales Tax
15. Seating list
16. Master of Ceremonies/announcer
17. Mechanical

18. National Anthem
19. Permits
20. Arrival-entrance.

Banquet Layout

Decide about whether the room should be ꞁ pared reception, buffet, or butler style. Should there be bars in the room or will liquor be passed on trays? A number of different sizes and shapes of tables are available.

Table 5.5 Specing for Seating etc.

TABLE 5.5
List of Typical Banquet Folding Table

1. Round Tables :	(a) 2 ½ ft. Cocktails	54 by 54 in. table cloth.
	(b) 3 ft. Cocktails	64 by 64 in. table cloth.
	(c) 4 ½ ft. Cocktails	64 by 64 in. table cloth.
	(d) 5ft. l0 peisons	84 by 84 in. table cloth.
	(e) 5 ½ ft.. 10 persons	90 by 90 in. table cloth.
	(f) 6 ft. 12 persons	90 by 90 in. table cloth.
2. Rectangular Tables:		
	(a) 6 by 1 Vi ft.	used for buffet with spirits.
	(b) 6 by 2 ft.	used for buffet with spirits.
	(c) 6 by 2½ ft.	Seats 3 persons on one side for head tables and dais
	(d) 6 by 3 ft.	used for buffet with skirts.
	(e) 5 by 2½ ft.	used for buffet with skirts.
	(f) 4 by 2½ ft.	used for buffet with skirts.
3. Square Table	2½ by 216ft.	used for buffet with skirts.
4. Half Round Table :	5 by 30 in.	used for buffet with skirts.
5. Quarter Round Table :	30 by 30 in.	used for buffet with skirts.
6. Cresent Table :	6 ft. by 36 in.	used for buffet with skirts.
7. Large oval Table : (for 16 guests)	half rounds – 5 ft. by 36 in. Four rectangular – 6 ft. by 2½ ft.	
8. Hollow Buffet Table :	Combination of four crescent tables and a sufficient number of 6 by 3 ft. or 5 by 3 ft. tables.	
9. Cover Leaf Table	Four half-round tables 5 ft. by 36 in. Sixteen rectangular tables — 6 ft. by 2-*Vi* ft. One square table- 2 *V-i* by 2 *Vi* ft. 90 by 90 in. table clothes are normally used for draping under lace.	

TABLE 5.6
Banquet layouts for the covers

Top table and sprigs

Function for 110 covers: 15 guests on top table; 3 springs required.

Dimension of room = 18 m (60ft) long by 11 m (36 ft) wide.

Working

1. Length of table required for top table :

   15 guests × 60 cm (2ft) cover width = 9 m (30 ft) or 5 × 2m (6 ft) tables.

2. Number of covers on each spring :

   110 Covers – 15 covers on top table = 95 covers

   95 covers ¸ 3 sprigs = sprigs of 32, 32 and 31 covers

   Therefore, each side of a sprig will have 16 covers, except one, which will have 15 covers.

3. Length of sprig :

   16 covers × 60 cm (2 ft) cover width ¾ 9.7 m (32 ft) or 5 × 2m (6 ft) tables.

4. To check if three sprigs may be fitted on top table :

3 spring × 75 cm (2ft 6 in) (width)	= 2.25m (7 ft 6 in)
2 gangways × 1 m (3 ft) (width)	= 2m (6 ft)
4 chair depths 46 cm (18 in)	= 2m (6 ft)
Total	= 6.25m (19 ft 6 in)

   Thus, there is plenty of room (see Figure 5.1)

This layout also allows for five extra covers in case of emergency. These are located :

1 either end of the top table	= 2
1 either end of the springs	= 3
Total	= 5

If the host had so wished, could a similar plan be developed making the layout more compact, for use in a slightly smaller room? In other words would it be possible to get four sprigs on a 10 m (30 ft) long top table? The answer is yes.

4 sprigs × 75 cm (2 ft 6 in) width	= 3 m (10 ft)
3 gangways × 1m (3 ft) width	= 3m (9 ft)
6 chair depths = 46 cm (1 ft 6 in)	= 3m (9 ft)
Total	= 9m (approx. 30 ft)

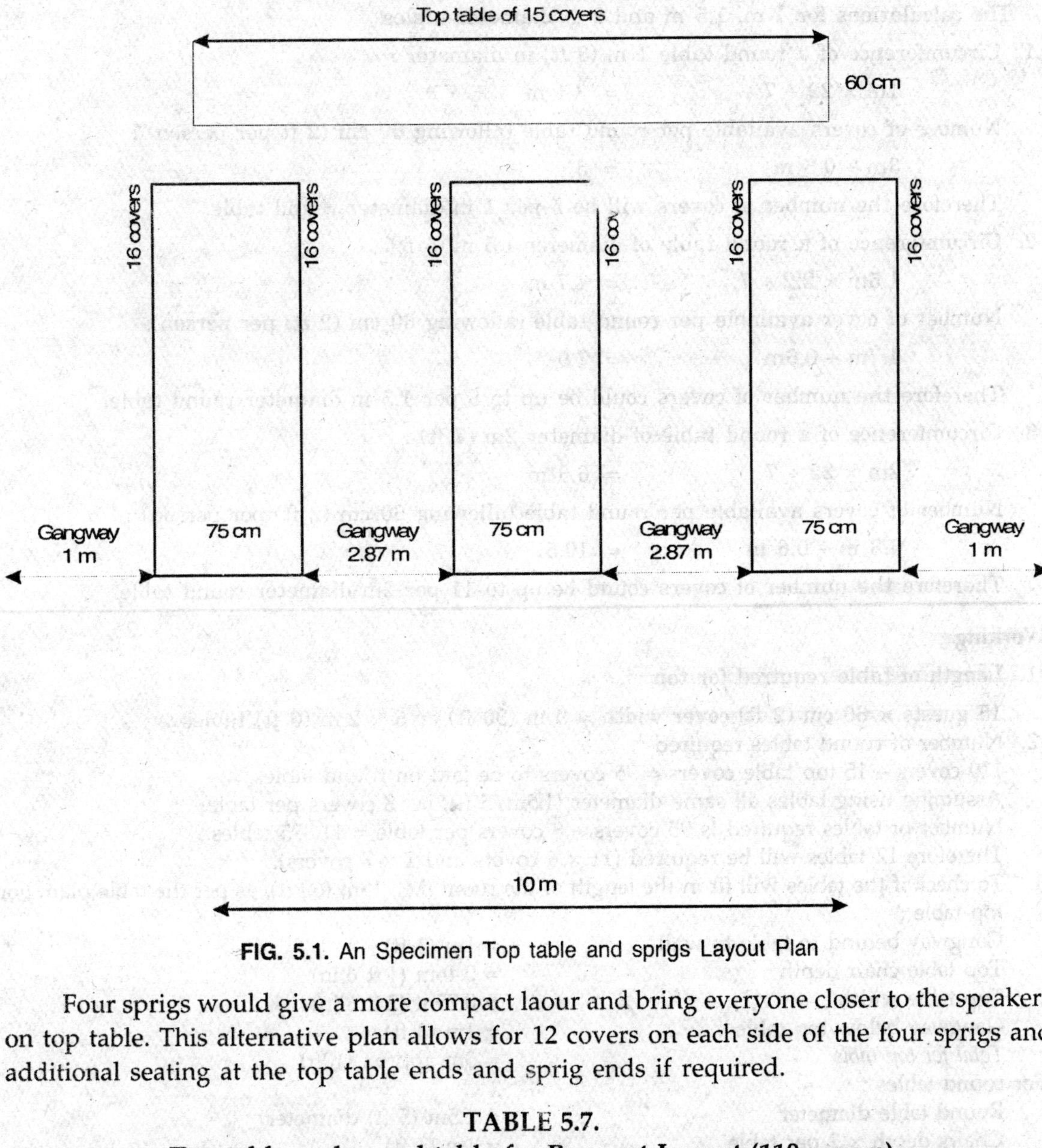

FIG. 5.1. An Specimen Top table and sprigs Layout Plan

Four sprigs would give a more compact laour and bring everyone closer to the speakers on top table. This alternative plan allows for 12 covers on each side of the four sprigs and additional seating at the top table ends and sprig ends if required.

TABLE 5.7.

Top table and round table for Banquet Layout (110 covers)

When using round tables it is first necessary to calculate the number of covers that could be seated at round tables of different diameters. In all cases it is necessary first to calculate the circumference of the round table. This is done by multiplying the diameter of the table by pi (p) (where p = 22 ÷ 7). Therefore, circumference is the diameter of the table × 22 ÷ 7. A cover would normally require 60 cm (2 ft) width on the circumference of a round table.

Function for 110 covers:	15 guests on top table
	95 covers on round tables.
Dimension of room	= 18m (60 ft) long by 12m (36 ft) wide.

The calculations for 1 m, 1.5 m and 2 m diameter tables

1. Circumference of a round table 1 m (3 ft) in diameter :

   1m × 22 ÷ 7 = 3.1 m

   Number of covers available per round table (allowing 60 cm (2 ft per person) :

   3m ÷ 0.6 m = 5

   Therefore the number of covers will be 5 per 1 m diameter round table.

2. Circumference of a round table of diameter 1.5 m (5 ft):

   1.5m × 2.2 ÷ 7 = 4.7 m

   Number of cover available per round table (allowing 60 cm (2 ft) per person):

   4.7m ÷ 0.6m = 7.9

   Therefore the number of covers could be up to 8 per 1.5 m diameter round table.

3. Circumference of a round table of diameter 2m (7 ft) :

   2m × 22 ÷ 7 = 6.3 m

   Number of covers available per round table (allowing 60 cm (2 ft) per person) :

   6.3 m ÷ 0.6 m = 10.5

   Therefore the number of covers cound be up to 11 per 2m diameter round table.

Working

1. Length of table required for top :

   15 guests × 60 cm (2 ft) cover width = 9 m (30 ft) or 5 × 2 m (6 ft) tables.

2. Number of round tables required :
   110 covers – 15 top table covers = 95 covers to be laid on round tables.
   Assuming using tables all same diameter (1.5m/5 ft), i.e. 8 covers per table.
   Number of tables required is 95 covers ÷ 8 covers per table = 11.875 tables.
   Therefore 12 tables will be required (11 × 8 covers and 1 × 7 covers).

3. To check if the tables will fit in the length of the room (i.e., 18m (60 ft), as per the table plan: For top table :
   Gangway behind to table to wall = 1m (3 ft)
   Top table chair depth = 0.46m (1 ft 6 in)
   Top table width = 0.75m (2 ft 6 in)
   Gangway below top table = 1m (3 ft)
   Total for top table = 3m approx (10ft)

For round tables :
   Round table diameter = 1.5m (5 ft) diameter
   Chairs depth × 2 per table = 1m (3 ft)
   Gangways (allow below each table) = 1m (3 ft)
   Total = 3.5m (11 ft)
   Total for round tables × 4 = 14m (46 ft)
   Total length required = 3m (10ft) for top table plus 14m (46 ft) for four round tables. 17m (56 ft)

   The length of the room is 18m (60ft) so the proposed table plan fits.

4. To check if the tables, as per the table plan, will fit in the 12m width of the room :
   3 round tables each 1.5m (5ft) diameter = 4.5m (15 ft)
   6 chair widths each 0.46m (1 ft 6 in) = 3m (9 ft)
   4 gangways each at 1m (3 ft) = 4m (12 ft)
   Total = 11.5m (36 ft)

Thus the table plan will fit within the 12m width of the room (see Figure 5.2).

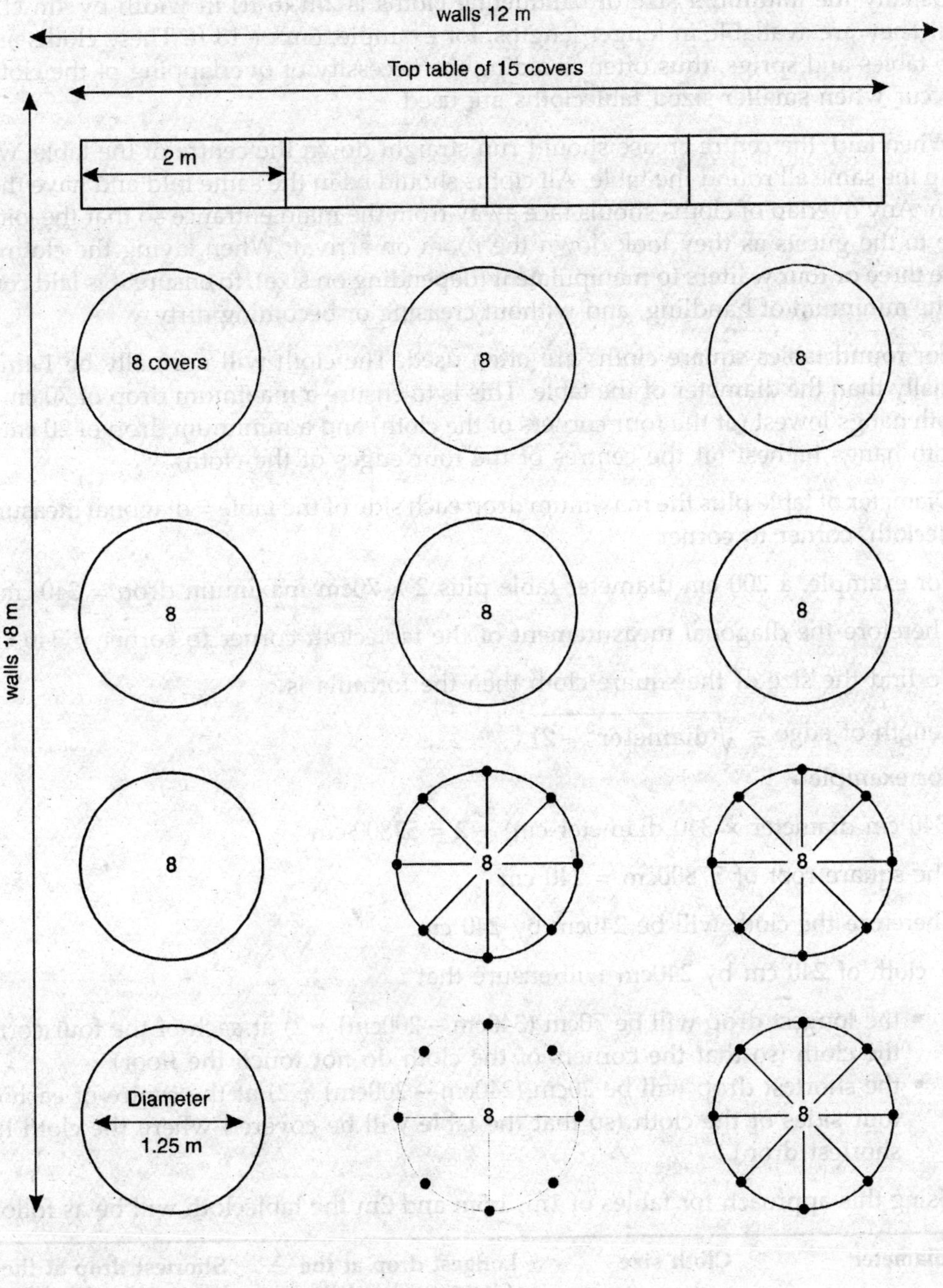

FIG. 5.2. Top table and round tables

Clothing up

Usually the minimum size of banqueting cloths is 2m (6 ft) in width by 4m (12 ft) in length. They are available in longer lengths, for example, 6m or 18 ft. These cloths are used on top tables and sprigs, thus often avoiding the necessity of overlapping of the cloths that will occur when smaller-sized tablecloths are used.

When laid, the centre crease should run straight down the centre of the table, with the overlap the same all round the table. All cloths should be in the same fold and have the same pattern. Any overlap of cloths shouls face away from the main entrance so that the join is not visible to the guests as they look down the room on arrival. When laying the cloth it may require three or four waiters to manipulate it (depending on size), to ensure it is laid correctly, with the minimum of handling, and without creasing or becoming dirty.

For round tables square cloths are often used. The cloth will normally be 1.4m larger diagonally than the diameter of the table. This is to ensure a maximum drop of 70 cm where the cloth hangs lowest (at the four corners of the cloth) and a minimum drop of 20 cm where the cloth hangs highest (at the centres of the four edges of the cloth).

Diameter of table plus the maximum drop each side of the table = diagonal measurement of tablecloth, corner to corner.

For example, a 200 cm diameter table plus 2 × 70cm maximum drop = 340 cm.

Therefore the diagonal measurement of the tablecloth corner to corner = 340 cm.

To find the size of the square cloth then the formula is :

Length of edge = $\sqrt{(\text{diameter}^2 \div 2)}$

For example :

(340 cm diameter × 340 diameter cm) ÷ 2 = 57800 cm

The square root of 57800cm = 240 cm

Therefore the cloth will be 240cm by 240 cm.

A cloth of 240 cm by 240cm will ensure that :

- the longest drop will be 70cm (340cm – 200cm) ÷ 2) at each of the four corners of the cloth (so that the corners of the cloth do not touch the floor)
- the shortest drop will be 20cm (240cm – 200cm) ÷ 2) at the centre of each of the four sides of the cloth (so that the table will be covered where the cloth has the shortest drop).

Using this approach for tables of 1m, 1.5m and 2m the tablecloth will be as follows:

Table diameter	Cloth size	Longest drop at the four corners of the cloth	Shortest drop at the centre of the four sides of the cloth
1m	170 × 170 cm	70 cm	35 cm
1.5m	205 × 205 cm	70 cm	27 cm
2m	240 × 240 cm	70 cm	20 cm

TABLE 5.8

ROOM SETUPS FOR BANQUETING STYLE

Theatre Style	:	Rows of hairs facing the speaker's table or lectern.
School Room Style	:	Rows of 6 ft. by 2½ ft. or 6 ft. by 2 ft. rectangular tables with chairs placed behind them facing the speaker.
Vander Bilt Style	:	Round cocktail tables scattered informally around the room.

Table Plans

Usually there are three or four different standard seating plans. The type of plan will depend upon :

1. Organizer's wish
2. Nature of function
3. Size and shape of room where function is to be held
4. Number of covers.

The most common recommended table plans are:

1. 'U' or 'T'shaped tables for smaller functions
2. Top table and separate table for formal luncheon or dinner parties
3. Round or Rectangular table for various parties of guests.

Floor Plans

Table arrangements are usually the decision of a committee. A certain amount of table space must be reserved for each guest. The following gives some idea of the space required:

1. *Buffet*: Allow 10 ft. of buffet table to serve each 60-75 guests. A heavy menu, such as dinner, might require additional table space. For table space settings, allow 18-20 in. between covers. Ten guests can be seated at an 8 ft. table, four each side, and one at each end.
2. *Dinner Served* : Allow 20-24 in. per guest.
3. *Formal French Service* : Allow 24-30 in. per guest. Additional space is required, because the food is served on trays to the seated guests.

The floor plans adequate space to be provided for guests › be seated comfortably for waiters to pass between the tables and for waiters' stands. These stands can be set up immediately after the guests are seated. The floor plan should be so arranged that none of the guests are seated with their backs to the head table. The plan should be expanded or reduced depending on the number of guests and the size and shape of the room.

FLOOR PLAN I *(for 100 Guests)*

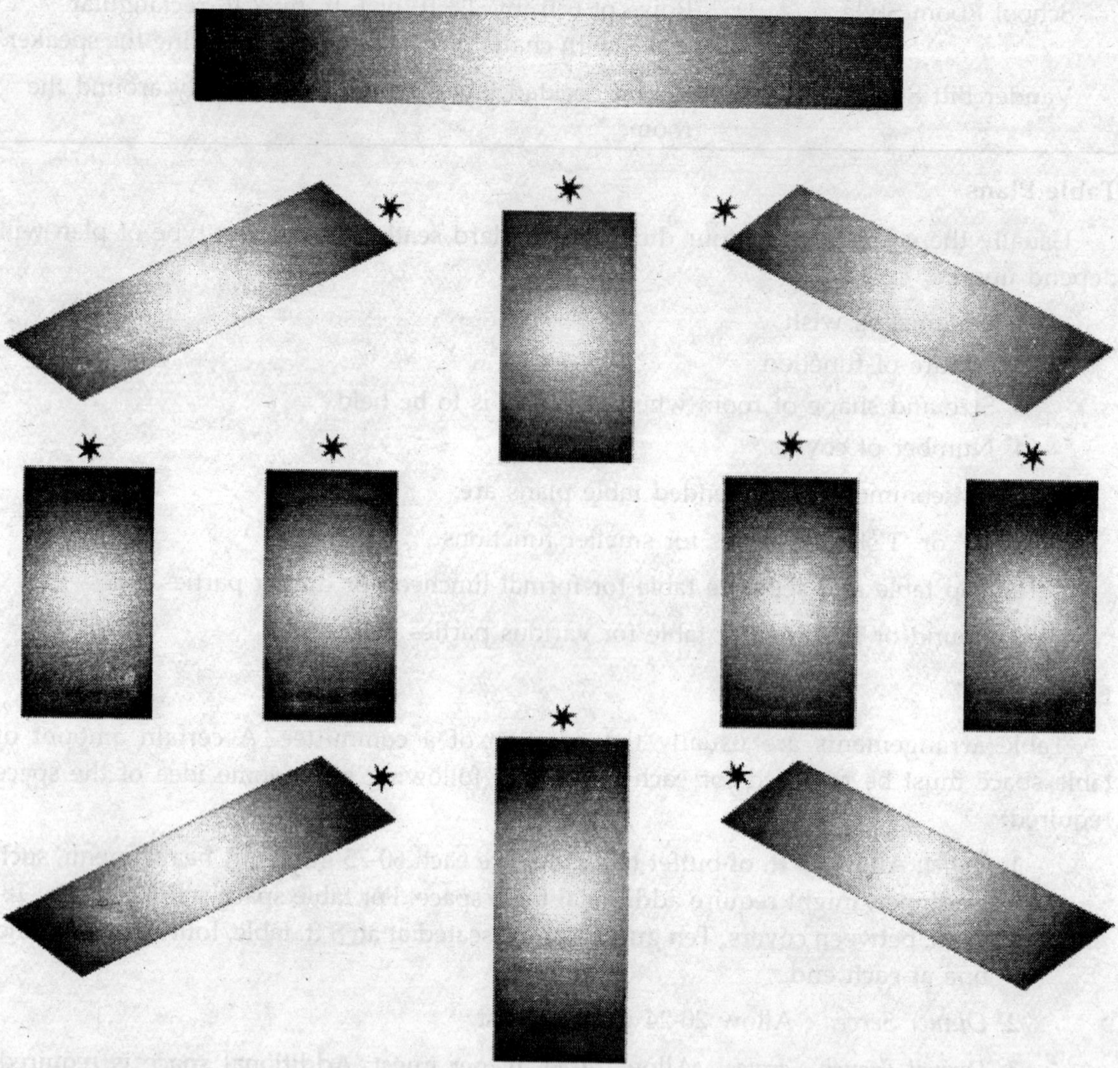

FIG. 5.3. A typical Floor Plan to seat 100 quests (No Bar and No Dancing)
10 Tables of 9, Plus 12 At Head Table (102 Actual Seats).
No seating where marked * So that no geuests sits with his back to head table.

FLOOR PLAN II *(For 100 Guests)*

FIG. 5.4. A Typical Basic Floor Plan, Bar and Room For Dancing
10 Tables of 9, Plus 12 At Head Table (102 Actual Seats).
No Seating where Marked * So that No Geuest sits with his back to head table.

FLOOR PLAN III : Horse Shoe or 'U' Floor Plan

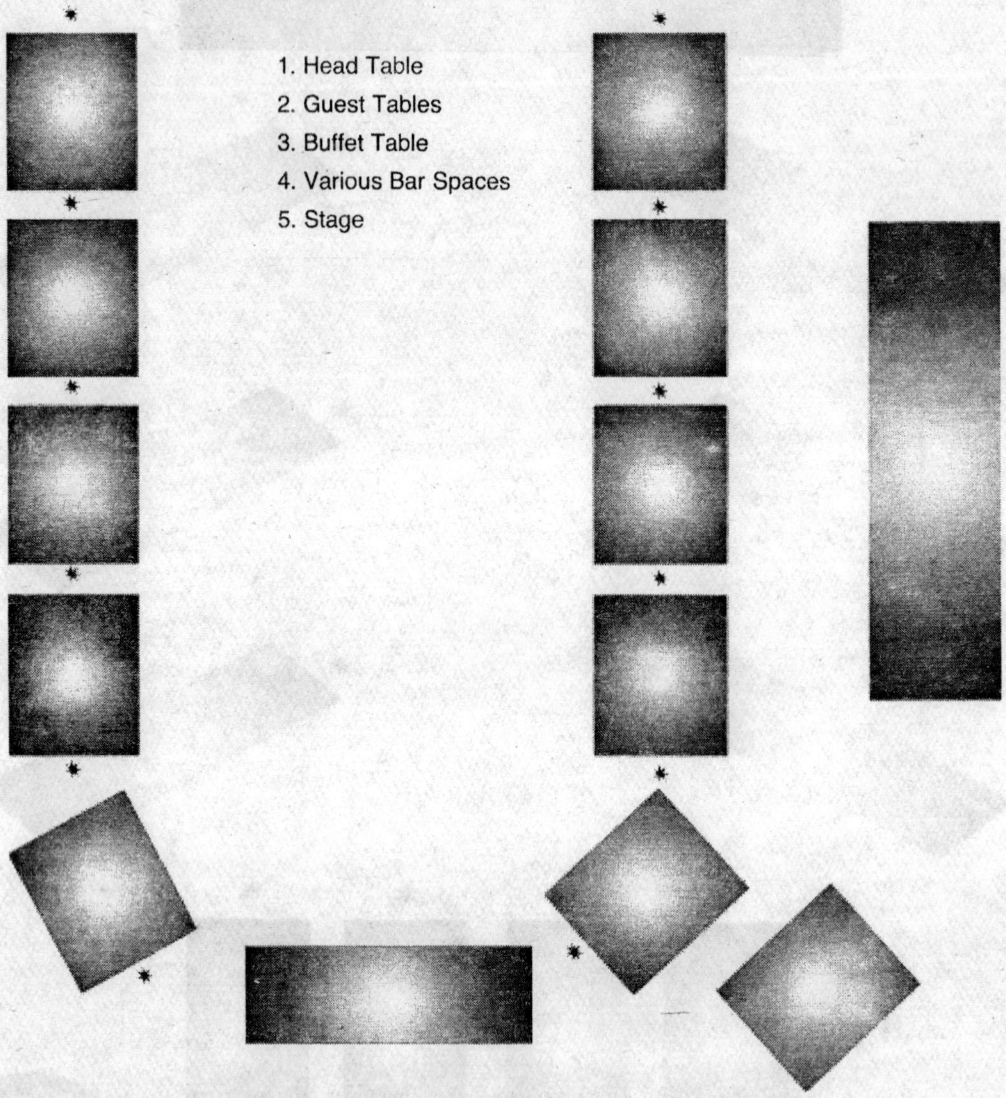

FIG. 5.5. A Typical 'U shapped Floor Plan. Buffet and Bar plus Room for Dancing or Fashion show For Serveral Meals, Buffet Table can be eliminated. Bar can be set up at indicated Optional places. No space-cutting where marked. *

Floor Plan IV : 'L' Shaped Floor Plan *(for smaller room)*

FIG. 5.6. A Typical 'L' shaped Floor Plan
Buffet and Bar can be in Room.
Space Allowed for Dancing.

FLOOR PLAN V: Heering Bone Floor Plan

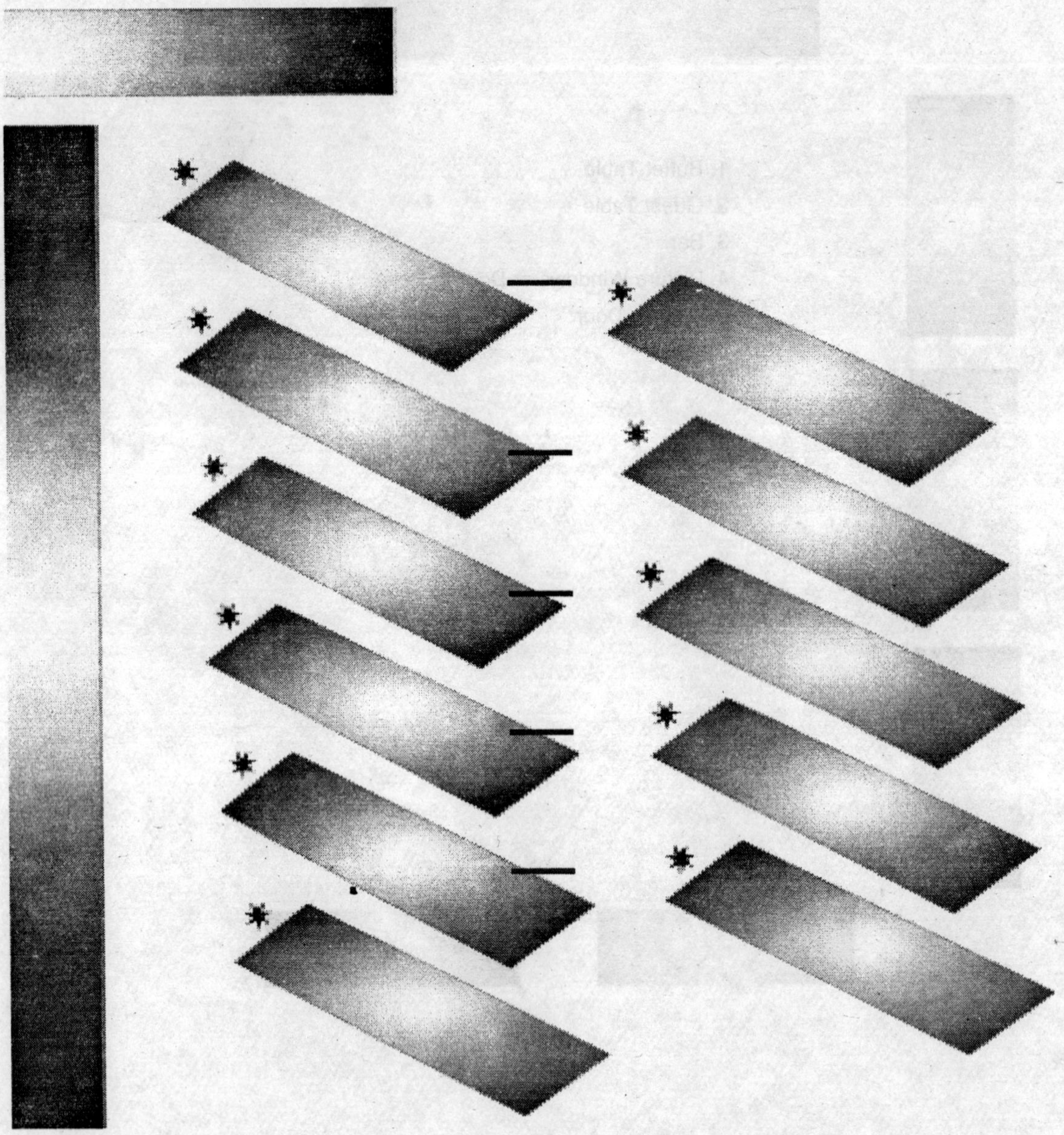

FIG. 5.7. A Typical Floor Plan — Excellent for Smaller Rooms
296 Seats (9 at side Tables, 8 at Central tables)
232 Sets (7 at side tables, 6 at central table)
No Seating where marked * So No Guest sits with his back to head table.

Banquet layout *(for 100 Guests)*

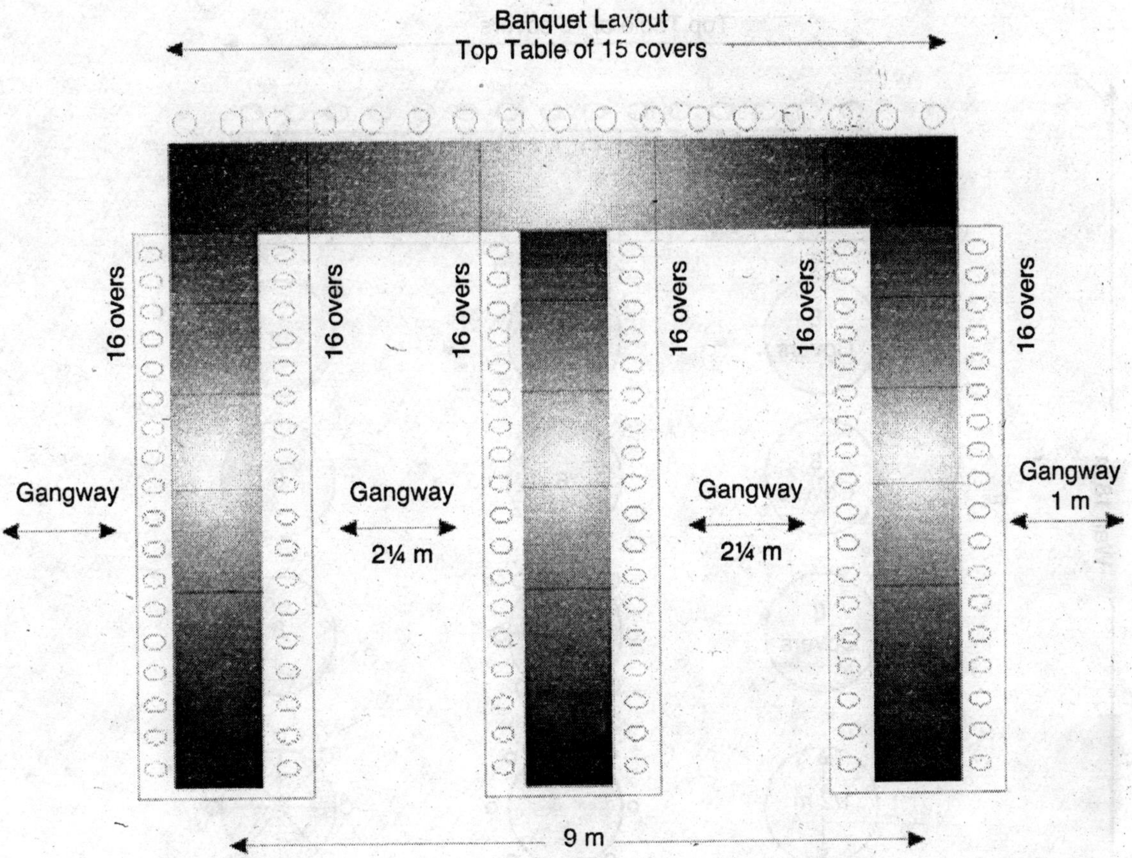

Guest = 110
Top Table = One (15 guests)
Springs = Three (32, 32, 31)
16 covers × 60 cm (2f) = 9.7 m (32 ft)
= 6 × 2 m (6 ft) Table

FIG. 5.8. A Typical banquet layour Plan
Top Table and Springs

Banquet Layout *(110 Guests)*

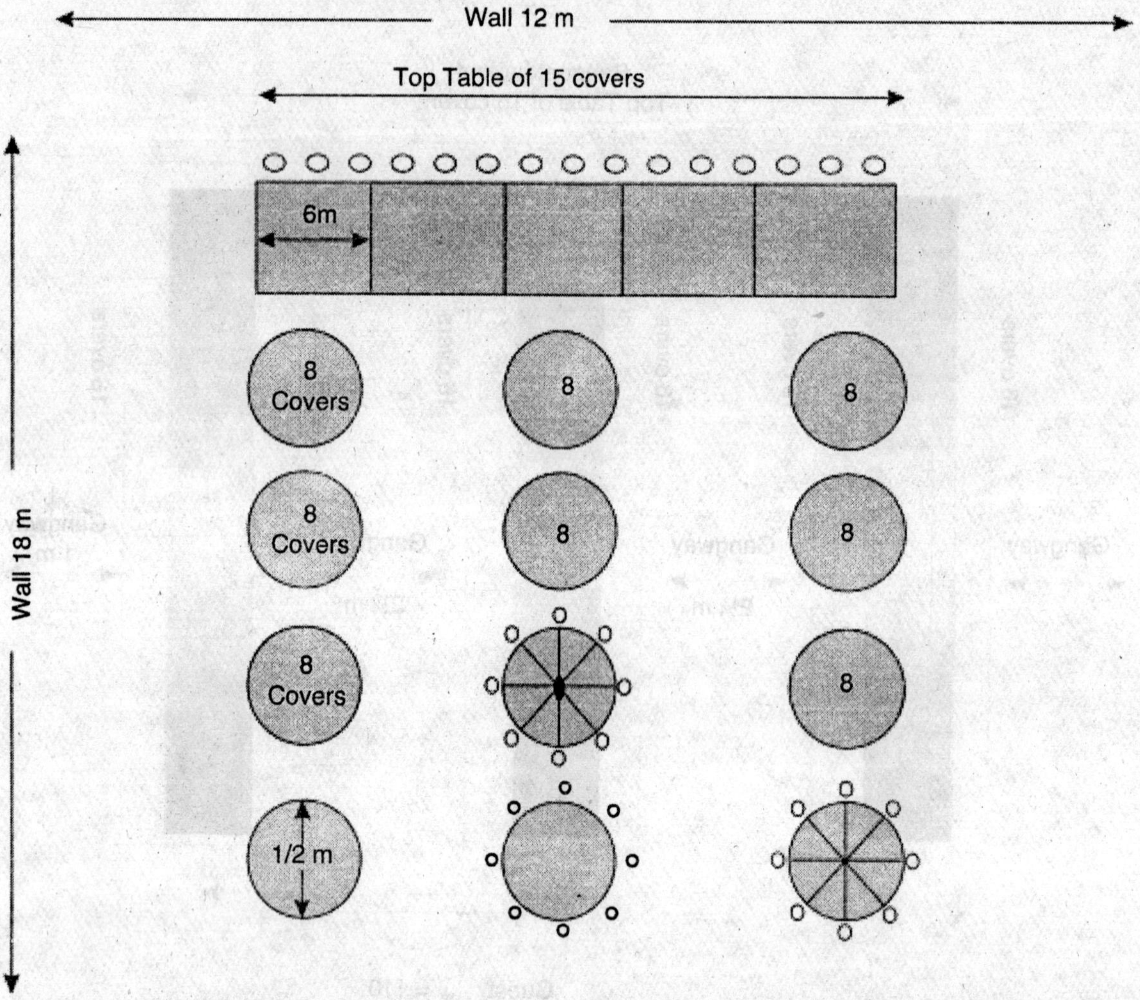

FIG. 5.9. A Model Banquet Layout : Top table and Round Table (For 110 Guests)

Banquet: Allotting Stations

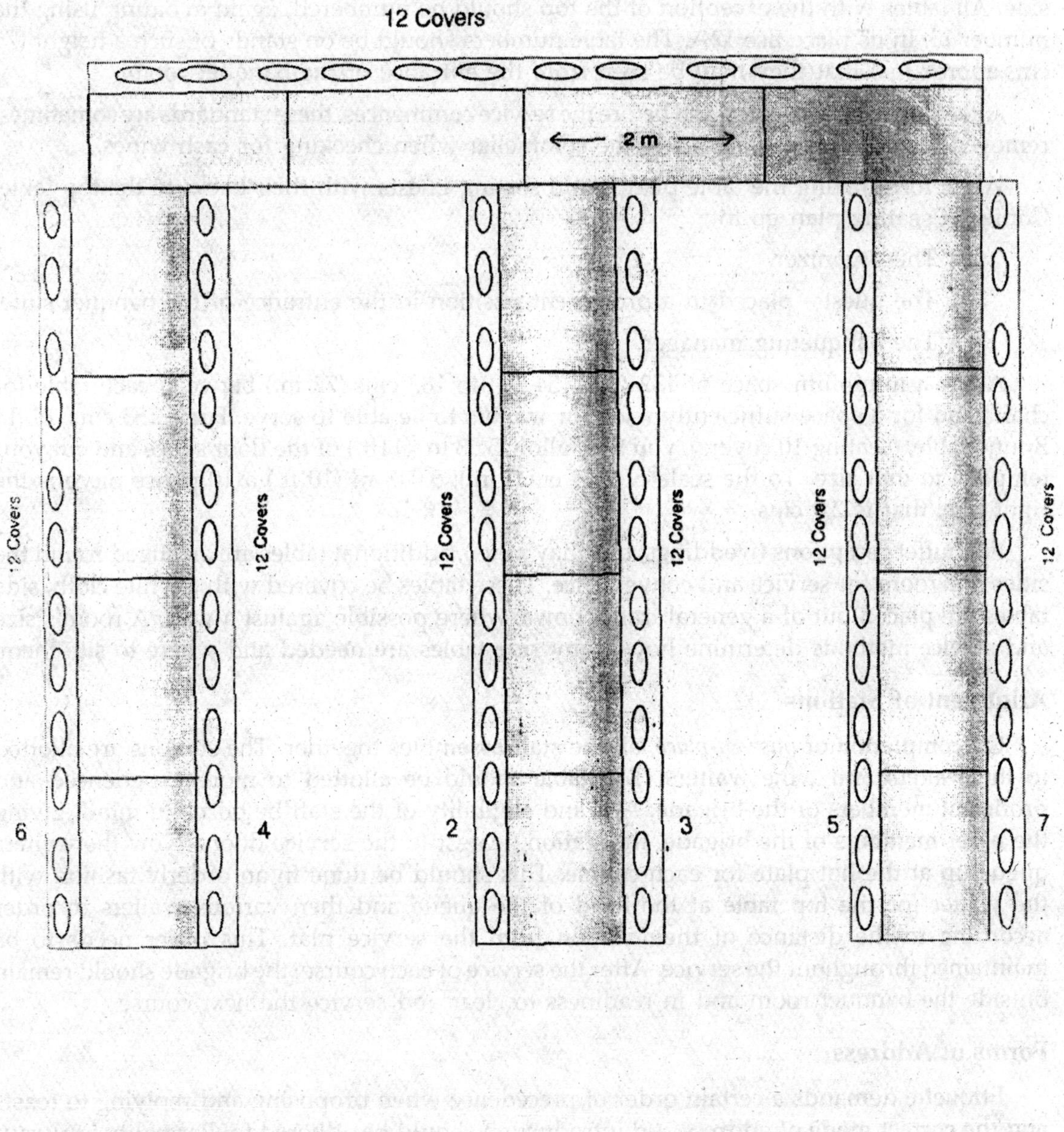

FIG. 5.10. A Typical Allotting Stations and the Order of the Hot Plate (84 Covers)

Seating Arrangements

Determine how many people will be seated on the top table and how many on springs, round or as long table; making up the file table plan. It must be known whether the numbers on the top table includes the ends and care should be taken to avoid seating thirteen on this side. All tables with the exception of the top should be numbered, again avoiding using the number 13. In its place use 12A. The table numbers should be on stands of such a height (75 cms.approx.) so that they may be seen from the entrance of the banquet room.

After the guests are seated and before the service commences, these standards are sometimes, removed or else they are an aid to the sommelier when checking for cash wines.

When formulating the table plan, avoid seating guests with their backs to the top table. Copies of seating plan go to :

1. The organizer.
2. The guests- placed in a prominent position in the entrance of the banquet suite.
3. The banqueting manager.

Allow a minimum space of 132 cms. (54 in.) to 183 cms.(72 in.) between each table for chairs and for a space sufficiently wide for waiters to be able to serve. For a 153 cms. (5 ft.) Round table, (seating 10 covers), you may allow 5.53 in. (11ft.) of the floor space and cut your template to that size. To the scale of 2.54 cm.(l in.): 3.048 m (10 ft.) a 10 pence piece is the right size: that is 2.8 cms.

For buffet receptions (weddings, birthday's etc.), additional tables are arranged round the sides of a room for service and convenience. These tables be covered with a white cloth, side tables are placed out of a general traffic flows; where possible against a wall. A room's size and service methods determine how many side tables are needed and where to site them.

Allotment of Stations

On completion of *mise-en-place,* all the staff assembles together. The stations are allotted to the waiters and wine waiters. Top table should be allotted to more experienced and proficient members of the brigade. Age and eligibility of the staff be borne in mind, giving the older members of the brigade, the station nearest to the service doors. Now the waiters queue up at the hot plate for each course. This should be done in an orderly fashion with the waiter for the top table at the head of the queue and then various waiters in order according to the distance of their station from the service plat. This order needs to be maintained throughout the service. After the service of each course, the brigade should remain outside the banquet room and in readiness to clear and service the next course.

Forms of Address

Etiquette demands a certain order of precedence when proposing and replying to toasts and the correct mode of address and introduction should be adhered to. Formality is always followed on occasions involving members of the Royal Family. The social forms of address are given for Peers, Baronets and Knights. The members of the Royal Family listed are shown in order of precedence in Table ....., Starting the correct modes of information, address and place correct for both formal and social seasions :

Formality is always followed on ocasions involving members of the Royal Family.

The social forms of address are given for Peers, Baronets and Knights. For details related to more formal events, *Debrett's Perage and Baronetage or Debrett's Correct Form* should be consulated.

The members of the Royal Family listed in Table 5.9 are shown in order of precedence.

TABLE 5.9.
Precedence and forms of address

Title	Introduction	Verbal address	Place cards
1. *The Royal Family* (a) *The Queen*	'Her Majesty the Queen	'You Majesty' and subsequently 'Ma''am'	
2. *The Duke of Edingburgh*	'His Royal Highness, Prince Philp, the Duke of Edinburgh'	Your Royal Highness' and subsequently 'Sir'	
3. *A Royal Prince*	'His Royal Highness, Prince Chrles, The Prince of Wales'	'You Royal Highness' and subsequently'Sir'	His Royal Highness, The Prince of Wales
	'His Royal Highness, Prince Andrew, The Duke of York'	"Yor Royal Highness' and subsequently 'Sir'	His Royal Highness, The Prince Edward
	'His Royal Highness, The Prince Edward' Duke of Yourk'	'Your Royal Highness' and subsequently 'Sir'	His Royal highness, The Prince Edward
	'His Royal Highness, The Prince Edward' subsequently 'Sir	'Your Royal Highness' and	His Royal Highness, The Prince Edward
4. *A Royal Princess*	'Her Royal Highness, The Princess Anne'	'Your Royal Highness' and subsequently 'Ma' am'	Her Royal Highness, The Princess Anne
5. *A Royal Duke*	'His Royal Highness, The Duke of Gloucester	'Your Royal Highness' and subsequently 'Sir'	His Royal Highness, The Duke of Gloucester
6. *A Royal Duchess*	'Her Royal Highness, The Duke of Gloucester'	'Your Royal Highness' and subsequently 'Ma' am'	Her Royal Highness, The Duchess of Gloucester
7. Peers, Baronets and Knights			
(a) *Duke*	'The Duke of Somerest	'Duke'	The Duke of Somerest
(b) *Duchess*	'The Duchess of Somerest	'Duchess'	The Duchess of Somerest
(c) *Earl*	'Lord Salisbury'	'Loard Salisbury'	Lord Salisbury

(d) *Countess*	'Lady Salisbury'	'Loard Salisbury'	Lady Salisbury
(e) *Viscount*	'Lord Wilton'	'Lord Wilton'	'Lord Wilton'
(f) *Viscountees*	'Lady Wilton'	'Lady Wilton'	Lady Wilton
8. *Government members*			
(a) *The Prime Minister*	By appointment or by name	By appointemnt or by name	The Prime Minister
(b) Chancellor of the *Exchequer*	By appointment or by name	'Chancellor' or by name	Chancellor of the Exchequer
(c) *Ministers*	'Mr. Salmon	'Minister' or 'Mr. Salmon	Mr. Roy Salmon
9. *The Clergy*			
(a) *Archbishops*	'The Archbishop of York'	'Archbishop' (socially)	His Grace, The Archbishop of Your
(b) *Bishop*	'The Bishop of Downton'	'Bishop'	The Loard Bishop of Downton
10. *Local Government*			
(a) *Loard/Lady Mayor*	By appointment or appointment and name	'My Loard/Lady Mayor' or 'Lord/Lady Mayor'	The Lord/Lady Mayor
(b) Mayor	By appointment or appointment and name	'Mr/Madam Mayor'	The Mayor of Woodfails
(c) Mayor's Consort	By appointment or appointment and name	'Mayoress'	The Mayoress of Woodfails

The Loyal Toast

An any formal function it is common for the Loyal Toast to be made. The toastmaster generally announces this toast as soon as the sweet course has been cleared, but before the coffee/tea is to be served. Staff should ensure before this time that all glasses have been 'charged' in readiness for the coming toasts.

The Loyal Toast should be announced by the toastmaster and is then normally proposed by the host for the evening, for example, the Chairman or President of an Association. The Loyal Toast is a toast to the reigning monarc: the Queen.

Traditionally at formal functions, no guest would smoke until after the Loyal Toast. Increasingly it has now become common for smoking not to be allowed at any time within a function room. If smoking is to be allowed, then the toastmaster indicates immediately after the Loyal Toast that the company present has the 'Chair's permission to smoke'. Staff should then ensure that ashtrays are placed on the tables.

The toastmaster generally announces the toast as soon as the sweet course has been 'cleared', but before the coffee is to be served. Staff should ensure at this time that all glasses have been charged in readiness for the coming toast. The toastmaster should announce the Loyal Toast and it is then normally proposed by the host for the evening- Chairman/President of an Association. The Loyal Toast is a toast to the reigning monarch. Immediately afterwards, the toastmaster indicates that the company present has the 'chair's permission to smoke'. Staff should ensure that at this time ashtrays have been placetfon the tables. No guest should smoke until after the Loyal Toast.

Example of an order of service for a formal function (table service)

1. The toastmaster announces the luncheon or dinner.
2. Guests proceed to their places in the room.
3. Grace is said.
4. Guests are seated. Chairs pulled out by waiters. The Waiters place napkins across the guests' laps.
5. Water and first wine is served.
6. If first course is not already on the table, proceed to hotplate to collect first course.
7. Line up according to the conventional system (see page 371), top table first.
8. Serve first course – top table waiter to commence service first.
9. All waiters (food) to leave room after each course is served.
10. Take in fish course plates.
11. Clear first course.
12. Second wine is served.
13. Lay fish plates.
14. Take out dirties and collect fish course.
15. Serve fish course. Leave room taking dirty silver.
16. Take in meat plates.
17. Third wine is served.
18. Clear fish coures.
19. Lay meat plates.
20. Take out dirties and collect potato and other vegetabe dishes.
21. Place on a hotplate on a sideboard or side table.
22. Return to hotplate and collect main meat dish.
23. Present on each table and serve together with sauces if appropriate.
24. Serve accompanying potatoes and vegetables.
25. Leave room taking dirty silver.
26. Continue with a similar process for the remaining courses of the meal through to the beverages.

Note: The headwaiter will control all the food waiters at the hotplate although variations on this service may be adopted according to the situation. The headwaiter also controls the exit from the hotplate into the banqueting room.

The order of service on the top table at functions, especially very formal occasions, is the one time when the host might be served first or at exactly the same time as the Guest of Honour, should they be seated on different stations.

At formal functions there may be speeches and toasts. These often take place at the end of a meal. However, it has become more common for these to take place at different times during the meal.

Formal Function : Order of Service

The headwaiter controls all the food waiters at the hot plate and also their exit from the hotplate into the banquet room.

The order of service on the top table at the formal functions is the onetime when the host is always served first or at exactly the same time as the guest of Honour should they be seated in different stations. A typical order of service for a formal function is given below :

1. Dinner announced by the toastmaster
2. Grace
3. Guest seated, chair pulled out by waiters, serviettes across laps
4. If first course is not ready on the table, proceed to hotplate to collect first course
5. Line up as previously mentioned, top table first
6. Service first course-top table waiter to commence service first
7. All waiters (food) to leave room after each course is served
8. Take in fish course plates
9. Clear first course and lay fresh plates
10. Take out dirties and collects fish course
11. Serve fish course. Leave room taking dirty'silver
12. Take in meat plates
13. Clear fish course and lay meat plates
14. Take out dirties and collects potato and other vegetable dishes
15. Deposit on sideboard or side table on a hotplate
16. Return to hot plate and collect main meat dish
17. Present on each table and serve
18. Serve accompanying potatoes and vegetables
19. Leave room taking dirty silver
20. Continue until end of the meal.

Reception and Wine Ordering Procedure

A bar may be set up in the reception area away from the main entrance. There should always he a good stock of drinks and keep one barman on duty at all times. Depending on the function, drinks may be served without cash or inclusive. A stock take should be made when the service is completed. Don't forget to have on hand the price lists, till, floats, notices regarding size of measures, occasional license (if required).

When the drinks are to be served on cash basis, there should be a wine waiter on duty near the table plan in the reception area together with commies. They should have a wine list, menu, check pads, wine waiter's names, stations and table plan. Get as many orders as possible for wine to accompany the meal prior to the meal service commencing. The order should be written in duplicate, one copy going to the cellar or dispense bar and duplicate to the correct wine waiter. The order should be prepared by the dispense barman or cellar man and when the wine waiter shows the duplicate, he should be given the required order. Never open the bottle until the guests arrive at the table-red wine at room temperature and white wine chilled. At a cash reception, the wine waiters may often actsas lounge waiters. They are always to hand to receive any orders in readiness for the service.

As for food services, the top table must always be served first with drink. The toasts every often commence immediately the coffee is served. By this stage the wine waiters should have taken all the liqueur orders, served them and collected all the cash outstanding in the case of cash drinks. Whilst the speeches are going on, all the food waiters should e out of room. The wine waiter may circulate, if necessary.

On completion of the function and when the food and wine waiters have cleared their stations and the later returned any floats, they should be paid off after returning service clothes, jackets and other equipment provided for service.

Banquet Planning

Fluctuations in economic situations, traditions, the prevailing political conditions, trends in social life, changing social customs, the manner in which competition operates, all these often require a last minute changes in arrangement of rooms, room set up and sometimes even the menu selection. Good planning is, therefore, essential in the banquet business.

The Function Book

Function space is controlled through the use of a diary or function book. This book has one double page for every day of the year, listing the day, date and all available function space. The space is normally divided into columns for morning, lunch, afternoon receptions and dinners. Only one person, the function clerk, is authorized to make entries in the function book or diary. There are two types of entries - definite and tentative. A definite entry is made when proper written confirmation has been received from the customer accepting the proposal of the house. It is entered in the diary in ink. A tentative booking is made when a prospect has expressed definite interest but a letter of confirmation has not been received. This entry should be made in the diary in pencil.

Forecasting Revenue

Forecasting for the banquet business is based on the "Diary. The figures entered in the

Diary are only estimated attendance figures given by the client. When the date of the function draws nearer, these figures can change considerably. Walk-in business can be estimated by knowing what is going on in the city, how the competition is doing, and having faith in the abilities of the sales staff. Revenue forecast of the banquet be made based on the above factors.

Banquet Meetings

In large banquet operations, it is very important to call formal banquet meetings between management, the banquet sales staff, the headwaiter, the chef and the head horseman to discuss pertinent problems. In small hotels, the banquet meetings can be friendly get together over a cup of coffee to evaluate past functions and discuss previous encounter. It is recommended that not more than five items be discussed at one meeting. Subjects to be included in these meetings are given below.

1. Weekly review of fills covered by each banquet sales person
2. Review of high food cost/menus
3. Lost business reports
4. Referral
5. Call reports
6. Year's sales goal for each banquet sales person
7. Review of progress report of business booked for each month
8. Evaluation of quality of food and service
9. Review of high labour costs
10. Review of banquet profit and loss reports
11. Late distribution of menus
12. Guarantees
13. Condition of banquet space
14. Engineering charges
15. Condition of 'big four'- china, silver, glasses and linen
16. Proforma Report of the banquet market plan.

Banquet Policy

All reservations and agreements are made upon and are subject to rules and regulations of the hotel and the following conditions: -

1. The quotation herein is subject to a proportionate increases to meet increased cost of foods, beverages and other costs of operation existing at the time of performance of the undertaking by reason of increases in present commodity prices, labour costs, taxes or currency values. Patron expressly grants the right to the hotel to

raise the prices herein quoted or to make reasonable substitutes on the prices herein quoted or to make reasonable substitutes on the menu and agrees to pay such increased prices and to accept such substitutes.

2. In arranging for private functions, the attendance must be definitely specified at least 48-hours in advance. This number will be considered a guarantee, not subject to reduction, and the charges will be made accordingly.
3. All federal state and municipal taxes which may be imposed or be applicable to this agreement and to the services rendered by the hotel, are in addition to the prices herein agreed upon and the Patron agrees to pay them separately.
4. No beverage will be permitted to be brought into the Hotel by the Patron or any of the Patron's guests or invitees from the outside.
5. Performance of this agreement is contingent upon the ability of the hotel management to complete the same and is subject to labour troubles, disputes of strikes, accidents, government (central, state or municipal) requisitions, restrictions upon travel, transportation, foods, beverages or supplies and other causes, whether enumerated herein or not, beyond the control of the management, preventing or interfering with the performance. In no event shall the hotel be liable for loss of profit or other similar or dissimilar collateral or consequential damages whether based on breach of contract, warranty or otherwise.
6. Patron agrees to be responsible for any damage done to the premises during the period of time they are under patron's control or the control of any independent character hired by patron.
7. The Hotel will not assume any responsibility for the damages or loss of any merchandise or articles left in the hotel prior to or following patron's party.
8. Payment shall be made in advance of function unless credit has been established in advance with the hotel.

Banquet File

When the contact is called to solicit business, a Banquet Call Report Form (see Fig.5.11), is made out. The Banquet Call report form goes in the banquet file and is the basis for future evaluation. In large and luxury hotels usually have a computerized banquet file and Banquet files contain historical data on local businesses that have active and continuous food functions. Banquet files contain sufficient information concerning the prospects, previous functions, with records of correspondence and suggestions for solicitation of future business. Thus a banquet file contains :

1. All banquet functions held in the hotel on a regular or repeat basis.
2. All other banquet functions held in the city on a regular or repeat basis.
3. Newspaper leads on new functions planned or considered.

4. Inquiries coming into operation-regarding possible future bookings.
5. Personal contacts established.

All files must be reviewed monthly at least eight months prior to the potential event to allow sufficient time for solicitation. Every time a solicitation is made, a call report form must be filled out and added to the file. If the solicitation efforts are not successful, a lost business report is made out; lost business report should be reviewed to find out:

1. Are the prices too high ?
2. Is the room too small ?
3. Is the equipment not up to date ?
4. Is the food not good enough ?
5. Is the service bad ?

.... Hotel

BANQUET CALL REPORT FORM

Group .... Date ....

Contact .... File No ....

Address .... Title ....

Telephone .... Best Time To Call ....

New Prospect? () Yes; () No. What Month or Year ....

Number of Persons .... What Month or Year ....

Comments ....

....

Date of Decision .... By Whom ....

Report Made By .... Trace Date ....

FIG. 5.11. Specimen Banquet Call Report Form

After considering the above-mentioned points, find out the reason and the solution. The format of the different types of forms used to maintain the records of the banquet hall is given in figure 5.11.

....................Hotel

BANQUET SOLICITATION RECORD

.... Hotel   Date ....

MONTHLY BOOKING REPORT

Definite Booking   BANQUET SOLICITATION PROGRAMME

Name of Organisation	File No.	New Business	Report Business	Date	Type	Size	Estimated Value	
Totals								

Number of Outside Calls ....

No ....

Number of 'C' Files

This Month ....

Number of 'C' Files titled

This Month ....

Computer Completed This year: Yes ....

Number of Newspaper Leads

Followed this Month..........................

Sales Person ....

Approved By ....

Manager/Dirctor (Banquet)

FIG. 5.12. Specimen Banquet Solicitation Record

Note : It is advisable to use a preprinted Banquet Inquiry Form (Figure 5.13)

.... Hotels

BANQUET INQUIRY FORM

Date................. Estimated Attendance .... Room ....

Type of Function ....

Organisation ....

Person Incharge ....

Address ....

....

....

Telephone ....

Tentative .... Definite............. Deposit Required ....

Menu And Arrangements :

Estimate of Costs ....

Pre Person ....

Reception ....

Smorgasbord ....

Menu ....

Cake...

Beverage.......................................

Check Room...................................

Misc.Expenses ....

Graqtities ....

Taxes ....

Total : Estimated Expanses ....

Flowers .... Pre Person ....

Music .... Salesman ....

Photography .... Date of Enquiry ....

FIG. 5.13. Specimen Banquet Inquiry Form

The banquet Booking Form (Figuare 5.14) Indicates a style of arrangement.

BANQUET BOOKING FORM

.... Hotel

To ensure that all arrangements for your function are up to your complete satisfaction, will you please complete the following details and return to us at least one month before the function.

We would be grateful for your written confirmation and Rs............................ deposit, as soon as possible. Deposits are not returnable if a function is cancelled within two months of the date it should take place.

Name of the Organisation:

Name of the organiser:

Date of Function:

Type of function:

Venue:

Time of Arrival:

Function Close:

Menu and Cost:

Bar From .... To .... Cash/Account .... Rs. .... Bar Hire

Flowers We can arrange at an additional cost Yes/No

Table Plan: Top table with springs/informal/Square/ horse shoe/herring-bone. (Please let us have your table plan seven days before your function).

Back Ground Music Required Duridng Reception: Yes/No

Meals:

Band or Disco: We can arrange at an additonal cost Yes/No

Accommodation: Please inform us if you require any accommodation. Yes/No

Deposit Paid .... Other comments ....

Singed ....

Date ....

The meal will be served promptly at the designated time. If the guests are late thereby causing a delay, we may have to proceed with functions in other venues before being able to continue your service.

FIG. 5.14. Specimen Banquet Booking From

Banquet or Function Prospects

A catering establishment's function prospects take care of many customers' need for detail and helps eliminate possible misunderstandings and queries. The Function Order Form (Fig. 11.5) records the customer's demands-the-praspectus details - what is to be provided; and Banquet or Function (Fig. 5.15).

BANQUET FUNCTION ORDER FORM

Organisation..

Address...

In Charge..

Telephone No...

GUARANTEE

Guarantee figure......................Guarantee means the number Ot meals to be served. We will be prepared to serve 10% More without delay. Should the number served be less than The guarantee the minimum charge will be for 95% of the Guarantee.

Menu :

....

Starter ....

Entree ....

Potato ....

Vegetable ....

Salad ....

Dessert ....

Coffee, tea, milk-rolls and butter included with All regularities.

Price Per Cover Rs............................

Plus Sales Tax and 15% service charges.

Coffee Breks

....

Tea/coffee Rols Biscuts

..............A.M.

..............P.M.

BAR REQUIREMENTS

....

Potable : Yes.......... No..........

Bill to ....

....

Function Date..

Day..

Starting Time...

Recetion...

Meal Time..

Vacated By...

BANQUET ROOM

Lobby Bulletin Board Positions

....

Tables and Seating

Top Table: Yes ....No.....................

Number of persons at the top table..............

Double set up ....

Separate tables for meeting and dinning ....

SPECIAL NEEDS

....

Movie Screen..

Pay System Rostrum.......................................

Black Boards.........................Stages................

Easels.........................Piona.........................

Others..

Please Sign...

(Authorized representative) Date:..................

Return To:..

Banquet manager...

Date...

FIG, 5.15. Specimen Banquet Function Order Form

The Function Form

The 'blue print' for a function is the function form, which lists only the services required for the function in question. It is a written summary of the details contained ,in the file and forms the basis of the direct organization of the function. This form is multi-duplicated for issue to the kitchen or dinning hall, etc. the function form must show all what is required in the simplest way in order to present an overall picture of the function. It is not a substitute for detailed instructions to the staff involved, but does show how each part of a function fits into the whole. It is also the basis for billing the function and for planning any repeat business. Figure - 5.16 shows a framework of a Function Form.

FUNCTION FORM

(DINNER-DANCE)

Organiser.. Date................

Covers..

Style..

Venue..

Time..

Price..

Cloaks..

Reception..

Menu..

Wine..

Liqueurs..

Toasts..

Speeches..

Tableplan..

Service..

Flowers..

Band..

Printing & Seating Plan.......................

Extensions..

Kitchen..

Dt. Room..

Bar..

Notes..

....

....

....

FIG. 5.16. Specimen Function Form

Banquet-Dinner Menu

For a dinner of approximately 25-50 guests, offer a choice of one appetizer from three. However, be sure that it will not duplicate or conflict with the main dish or salad. Have a relish tray on each table.

For the main dish, again offer three choices. If the vegetables are the same for all three dishes, list them separately on the menu, below the main dishes, together with the salad. Specify the salad dressing offered.

1. Main dish
2. Main dish
3. Main dish
4. Potato and green vegetable
5. Salad with dressing.

On the other hand, if each main dish calls for different vegetables, they should be listed together with the main dish. The salad is listed separately.

1. Main dish-boiled potato, green beans
2. Main dish, rice, tomato rice
3. Main dishes, broccoli, broiled tomato
4. Salad with dressing.

The type of bread offered should fit with the meal and should always be served with a plate of butter. For dessert, a choice should also be offered. It should wither be the occasion cake or fmit or gelatin etc. suggested beverage should be listed in general classifications such as wine, champagne, beer, coffee, tea, soft drinks or punch. The sample ideal menu is given in Figure 5.17

INDIAN BANQUET MENU (10-150 GUESTS)

Choice of One	POMEGRENATE JUICE CRANBERRY JUICE.
Main Course	Eight Boy Curry (Shrimp, Beef or Chicken curry with rice and eight condiments from which the guest makes his choice): 1. Hard cooked eggs, chopped. 2. Chutney. 3. Fresh grated coconut. 4. Green peppers diced. 5. Bacon, crisp, crumbled. 6. Current jelly. 7. Pickles chopped. 8. Salted peanuts, chopped. RICE, STEAMED MIXED VEGETABLE SALAD, WITH FRENCH DRESSING FRENCH BREAD AND BUTTER (OPTIONAL)
Dessert	Fruit Sherbet
Beverage	Iced Beer with Dinner Coffee, Tea.
Service	Fimily Style

FIG. 5.17. Sample Banquet Menu

Banquet Menu

Well-made menus should contain a harmony of flavours. Dishes should balance each other.

Structure of a Banquet Menu

1. Cold appetizer
2. Hot soup
3. Hot appetizer
4. Main course
5. Vegetables
6. Salad and cheese
7. Dessert
8. Coffee.

Banquet Stencil/Function Form

The original banquet menu with the attached instructibn sheet becomes a legal document. It is a contract between the operation and the client-as soon as it is signed. From the original banquet menu and instruction sheet, copies are made for distribution. These are known as Banquet Stencil.

The banquet stencil is a work order. All the notes scribbled down during meetings with the guest, all promises that were made and all information pertinent to the party are put on a paper in a clear language.

A typical banquet stencil varies according to the events ranging from a reception for 100 guests to a banquet of 1200.

The Function Checklist

Preparing of Function Checklist is a theoretical exercise, which has definite practical implications. It itemizes every possible aspect of any possible function the caterer may ever be called upon to provide. The functional checklist will vary from establishment to establishment but it is a challenge and its production is simply a matter of assessing the potential of the establishment. It is an aide-memoire and its purpose is to record whether a service is required of the caterer, is to be provided by someone else or is not required at all. The essential aspect of a function checklist is that no item is allowed to remain blank.

Figure 5.8 is a typical Functional List. Whenever an inquiry is received and the file opened, the functions check list is the second document in that file. The first document obviously is the original inquiry. It is most unlikely that very aspect of the function will be touched upon, let alone decided, without several letters or meetings between the caterer and the organizer; often spaced out for months. Each letter is filed and the salient point of every meeting or telephone conversation are also written down and filed and every decision reached are noted on the function check list, which must always be upto date.

List of Service Equipments for Banquet

1. Cutlery

(a) Soupspoons
(b) Ice bucketsFish knives and forks
(c) large knives and forks
(d) Dessertspoons
(e) Small fruit knives and forks
(f) Ladles
(g) Butter knife
(h) Desert knives and forks

2. Hollowware

(a) Soup tureens
(b) Individual soup bowls
(c) Trays
(d) Oval flat with lids
(e) Oval or round vegetables dishes with lids
(f) Oval or found under-dish for vegetables
(g) Souffle cases
(h) Oval or round entree dishes
(i) Oval or round dishes for entree
(j) Round flats with covers
(k) Water jug
(l) Cocktail juice container
(m) Salver for serving
(n) Salver for clearing
(o) Ice tongs
(p) Ice buckets
(q) Champagne bucket with stand'
(r) Coffee pots
(s) Hot milk (Creamer)
(t) Tea pots
(u) Hot water jugs
(v) Cream jugs (Creamer) :
(w) Toast racks
(x) Sugar pots
(y) Wine cooler
(z) Chaffing dishes (complete set)

3. Special Tableware

(a) Sugar tongs
(b) Finger bowls
(c) Set of cruets
(d) Ice cream scoops
(e) Sauce ladies
(f) Soup ladles

(g) Sundae spoon
(h) Ice cream spoon
(i) Pastry form-cum-knife
(j) Corn on cob holder
(k) Butter knife
(l) Cheese knife
(m) Grapefruit spoon/cup
(n) Nut cracker
(o) Gateaux slice

4. Chinaware

(a) Soup plate
(b) Entree plate
(c) Hors d'oeuvre/fish/entree courses/soup under plate
(d) Meat or fish plate — main course
(e) Sweet plate — often the plate is used for sweets/puddings
(f) Dessert or fruit plate
(g) Side plate
(h) Tea saucer

5. Cups

(a) Soups (two handles)
(b) Tea cups
(c) Coffee cups
(d) Demitasse cup
(e) French onion soup bowl

6. Special Food Service Equipments

(a) Ashtrays
(b) Bread boats
(c) Flower vases
(d) Fruit stands
(e) Tea strainers
(f) Candle stands
(g) Wine cradles
(h) Oil, Vinegar bottle
(i) Jam pot
(j) Toothpick stand
(k) Straw stand
(l) Chaffing dishes
(m) Burner for dishes
(n) Cooper pans
(o) Burners
(p) Shaker
(q) Stirring spoons and bowl
(r) Punch bowl and ladle
(s) Supreme bowl

FIG. 5.18. Function Equipment Checklist

Costing of a Function

Banquets and other functions contribute importantly to profits and must be carefully costed and priced. Food commodities required to give effect to the menu must be identified and charged to function together with staff costs, room costs and other overheads. A simple example of a Basic Function Cost Sheet is shown in figure 4.17 and indicates the scope of such costing.

For economic viability, the functions catering need to establish costs in advance and use the knowledge as a sound basis for estimates to potential customers. For accuracy in costing, the cost estimates may be divided into fixed and variable expenditure given in Figure 5.19

Classification of Banquet Cost Structure

Cost Expenditure

Fixed Expenditure	Variable Expenditure
1. Rates, ground rent, licenses	1. Food cost.
2. Interest on funds borrowed for any reason.	2. Wages for extra staff and/or overtime.
3. Insurance against fire, theft, public liability.	3. Extra fuel for heating, lighting, cooking.
4. Security and safety.	4. Laundering of linen.
5. Control, stationary booking and checking systems, accounting and auditing.	5. Flowers and other forms of room/ table
6. Wages of key staff.	6. Decorations.
7. Cleaning and maintenance by contract (Machinery, window cleaning, laundry service).	7. Transport.
8. Internal cleaning and maintenance expenditure (Cleaning materials and appliances, polishes deodorants, etc.)	8. Printing of menus and seating plans notice.
9. Contribution and fees to professional bodies and local charities of a regular nature.	9. Entertainment, music, cabaret, displays.
10. Advertising	10. Expenditure non-production facilities e.g.cloak-rooms, toilets, carpets, etc.
11. Fuel for heating and lighting.	11. Extra direct cleaning costs.
	12. Hire charges for crockery, linen, cutlery, flower vases, ashtrays, tables, chairs, tenting and other equipment and miscellaneous items.

FIG. 5.18. Classification of Banquet Cost Structure

Based on these estimates, experience and with forethought; assess the largest single area of expenditure, Based on thaese estimates, experience and with forethought; assess the largest single area of expenditure, which is usually, the food. The costing system should cope with the assessment of the future, price trends, forecasts of fluctuations, adjustment if necessary, accurate portion estimation an control at all stages, estimation of waste, cue of left over foods, consolidation of expenditure and presentation of count.

The compilation of a guide to quantities of food per portion he conveyed to all staff concerned and should form the basis of all menu planning. It should be flexible enough to compensate for variances of bulk and price in completed menus.

WEEDING FUNCTION

The initial steps for a wedding function are those similar to that of booking a function. Some additional points to bear in mind are regarding wedding cake, stand and knife, and whether a room should be available for the bride and bridegroom to change prior to leaving the function to go on their honeymoon. There may also be need to display wedding presents and the services of a photographer may also be required.

The type of menu offered will depend on the cost per head to be paid. For wedding, the menu is often printed in silver, together with the name of the couple and the date. If the wedding is a sit down affair then note the spacing of tables, covers, gangways and service. In this instance, the cake will be cut at the end of the meal, after the coffee and will be followed by only necessary toasts. A seating plan should be available for a wedding breakfast and the table plan may be either 'U' shaped, top table and springs or top and rounds.

For sit down function, the space required is 1.1 sq. m. (12.5 sq. ft.) per person and 0.9 - 1 sq. m. (10- 12 sq. ft.) per person for buffets.

The buffet should be clothed up correctly in that the buffet cloth reach to within 1.27 cm (½ in.) of the floor and both ends be boxed neatly. The buffet is split into three sections for ease of service of food, tea and coffee and wines and alcoholic and non-alcoholic beverages. The floral arrangements are an important aspect of the decoration and help show of fthe room to the best effect.

The wedding cake may be used as a separate focal point away from the buffet and should be placed upon its stand with a knife on a special table clothed up for the purpose. The bride's and bride-maid's bequest are often placed on the table around the base of the wedding cake, together with any telegrams of congratulations that are to be read out by the best man or toast master. Occasional tables and chairs should be placed at regular intervals around the room and clothed up in suitable manner. The photographer/video will probably take photographs/recording of the bride and bridegroom on arrival at the reception, together with a group of those in the receiving line, one of the bride and bridegroom cutting the cake and one or two of the buffets while it is complete. Fully attended cloakrooms must be available for all guests on arrival.

In a buffet type reception, the staff requirement could be as follows :

1. Head waiter/Banqueting headwaiter	–	1
2. Waiter for every 40-50 covers	–	1
3. Wine waiter to every 50 cove	–	1
4. Barman to every four wine waiters	–	1
5. Commies for fetching and carrying and clearing	–	2
6. Chef for every 40 – 50 guests for service	–	1
		7

Procedure

1. The casual staff should report one hour before hand to complete the necessary mise-en-place; to be allocated duties and to be briefed.
2. 30 minutes before the arrival of the bride and bridegroom, the toastmaster is to be on duty. He must liaise with the best man to discuss the timing of cutting of the cake, the toasts and who is to give them.
3. The bride and bridegroom should arrive first, followed by the parents of the bride and bridegroom and bridesmaid and/or pages. The people will generally make up the 'receiving line' to greet the guests as the toastmaster announces them.
4. All the guests should generally arrive together.
5. The toastmaster could 'count' guests entering room.
6. The wine waiters should be at strategic points.
7. After reception, the buffet should be open for service.
8. At the agreed time, the toastmaster should announce the cutting of the cake. Portions of the cake should then be passed around to all guests and the Champagne taken around by the wine waiter;

   thereafter .the toast should commence.
9. The bride and bridegroom should then change and food and champagne should be placed in the changing room.
10. When the bride and bridegroom have left the reception, the flowers should be placed up for the host to take away.

Guidelines for Buffet Service

The various types of buffet are knife and fork, fork and finger buffet. The basic principles to be followed in any buffet service are :

1. The buffet should be set up in a prominent position in the room.
2. There should be ample space on the buffet for display and presentation.
3. The buffet should be within easy access of the stillroom and wash up so that replenishment of the buffet and the clearing of the dirties may be carried out without disturbing type guests.

4. There must be ample space for customer circulation,
5. Provisions should be made for sufficient occasional tables and chairs.
6. The total presentation of the room be attractive and promote the right atmosphere.

The buffet should be covered with suitable clothes making sure that door of the cloth is within 1.25 cm (½ in) of the ground all the way around the front side of the buffet. If more than one cloth is used, the creases should also be lined up. Where the clothes overlap one another the overlap should be facing away from the entrance of the room. The end of the buffet should be 'box' pleated with the aid of stickpins, which must be used under the folds of the cloth so they do no show, thereby giving a better overall presentation of buffet.

Guidelines/or Counter Service

In this form of service the customers collect a tray from the beginning of the service counter. They move along the service counter sliding their meals, pay cash and then collect the appropriate cutlery and flatware for their meals.

The menu offered in this type of service would show a wide range of dishes from simple hot and cold snacks and beverages. All items are individually priced for limited 'table d 'hote' menu with the set prices of meal show against the main course dishes offered.

The menus are prominently displayed at the entrance of the establishment, so that customer may decide what they will purchase before arriving at the service points. The dishes are found in the order in which they appear on the menu e.g. the order could be as under :

1. Hors d'oeuvre
2. Pnat juices
3. frost cocktails
4. Cold meats and salads 5. Bread rolls
6. Butter
7. Soups
8. Hot fish dishes
9. Hot meat dishes
10. Hot Vegetables
11. Hot sweets
12. Cold Sweets
13. Ice cream Assorted Sandwiches
14. Cakes and pastries
15. Beverages and Cold drinks.

The meal is either pre-plated or the main meat/fish dish plated and the potatoes, vegetables, sauces and other accompaniments added according to the customer's choice.

The length of the counter will generally be determined by the size of the menu offered.

At the end of the counter, the cashier is seated who charges for the meals chosen by the customers before they pass on to the seating area. Cutlery and tableware stands should be placed after the cashier certain portion control equipment be used to ensure standardization of the size of portion served. Such equipment includes scoops, ladles, bowls, milk dispensers and cold beverage dispensers. Pre-portioned foods such as butter, sugar, joints, cream, cheeses and biscuits are used.

In case the customer turnover rate is high, a number of separate service points may be operated. The seating arrangements will depend on: -

1. The size and shape of the food service area.
2. The design of the tables and chairs used.
3. The allowance made for gangways and clearing trolleys.
4. The type of the establishment.

Outdoor/Outside Catering

Off premises catering or outdoor catering is a business, which continues throughout the year. At these functions, the organizer should aim to have a fully comprehensive sales service, covering not only meals and drinks but such things as confectionery, cigarettes, hot dog kiosks and so on. The organizer should aim to give a fully comprehensive sales service covering confectionery, cigarettes, hot dog kiosks etc. the organization should be planned to the last detail and an initial survey should be exact and thorough. The points to be included in the initial survey are :

1. Type of function
2. Date
3. Site and distance
4. Local transport
5. Local purchase
6. Staff recruitment
7. Layout of site
8. Number of people expected to attend
9. Availability of water, gas, electricity, drainage, refrigeration, etc.
10. Spending power of people attending
11. Kiosks and stand details
12. Time allowance for setting up catering units and dismantling
13. Type of license required
14. Mobile units adaptable to hot and cold food
15. Lines of communication to ensure control of staff and continues supplies

16. Photographers/video
17. Press
18. Change-rooms/toilets
19. Insurance against the weather/fire
20. First aid
21. Cost of overheads on a particular site
22. Type of service
    (i) Buffet style.
    (ii) Takeaway meal service in disposable containers.
    (iii) Supply of simple hot dishes - soup, fish and chips etc.
    (iv) Flexibility of drink service- hot or cold.
23. Washing up facilities
24. Containers supplied for litter and disposable items.

The majority of staff employed is casual; therefore, all administration formalities and legal aspects are to be observed. Each employee should receive engagement pack containing:

1. Casual worker registration form
2. Legal requisite form
3. Acceptance of offer signed by the employee.

High charges paid for outside catering reflect extra costs involved in, for example, transporting equipment, food and staff. These vary according to distance. Erecting a marquee or providing gas equipment can further add to costs.

All equipment must e checked out of store, checked at the function and again when returned to store, if stock is not to decrease. Packing equipment so that it can be safely transported without crockery and glass breakage, demands not only experience but also special boxes. Moreover, holding stocks of equipment to meet peak catering periods is also costly.

Several functions in one day can stretch equipment and staff to the maximum but on another day there may be no function at all or only one or two small ones. Active selling and planning is needed to keep turnover steady and to keep permanent staff and equipment employed. Some functions may be only marginally profitable but they help cover wages and are preferable to paying staff for no work or for tasks, which normally command a lower wage rate.

Details of menus, numbers, date of the event have to be obtained from the organizer, as for any function. Additionally, the caterer (or his representative) should visit the function site preferably with the organizer to ascertain what space, cooking equipment, facilities for washing-up, and furniture are available. He checks whether staff can have prior access to the premises for preparation, whether equipment must be removed immediately after and similar relevant details.

The day before a function, equipment needed is packed and checked against a list, which accompanies it for subsequent checking. Similarly food and quantities to be allocated are carefully listed. An item inadvertently omitted can cause chaos during service. Organizing causal-waiting staff often involves arranging transport either in the company's own vehicles or, if numbers and distance justifies, by hired bus.

Problems of recruiting casual staff or jobbing waitresses are often associated with family ties; what day's waitresses are able to work or accept work. Even prior agreements may be breached because the husband or the baby sitter may renege on arrangement. Many who apply for waitress work do not realize what is involved and need rapid training. Building a team of reliable part time waitresses is an important element in outside catering success.

Staff Space and Equipment

For outside catering in marquees, allow 100 sq. ft. (9.29 sq. m.) per eight persons (standard marquees are 40 ft. (12.19 m) wide or if butted 80 ft. (24.38 m) wide. Catered for 700 persons under canvas for a banquet, in traditional style, use about ninety waitresses for food service, thirty waitresses for wines and reach a total or 200 staff (including headwaiters, chefs, barman, cloakroom attendants, porters and so on).

For example, for 700 persons, the furniture includes :

1. 90 × 6-ft. (1.829 m) oval tables
2. 700 chairs
3. 6000 pieces of crockery
4. 6000 pieces of cutlery
5. 3500 glasses

Other items required are culinary and service equipment, linen and other requisites. Today's aids in preparation and reconstitution of foods (including frozen or chill techniques) enable economies of staff to be achieved but the foregoing indicates some of the logistical problems and the magnitude of the task of setting up temporary function facilities in tents and furnishing them.

Catering Equipment

Assemble equipment in units to meet the needs of fifty guests and using boxes and packs approximately sized. Crockery, silver and glass and linen requirements for restaurant use have been listed in previous chapters and can also help guide in function catering. For outside catering tasks, the following may additionally help.

CROCKERY

50 hors d'oeuvre plates

50 soup plates

50 fish plates

50 meat plates

50 sweet plates

50 side plates

50 dessert plates

50 teacups and saucers

50 ice plates

50 milk jugs

50 demitasse cups and saucers

6 sugar basins

8 tea pots, 8 dl (1½pt) each

8 hot water jugs 5 dl (1 pt) each

8 coffee pots, 5 dl (1 pt) each

CUTLERY

12 sauce boats

50 soup spoons

50 fish knives and forks

50 large knives and forks

50 dessert spoons and forks

50 side knives

50 teaspoons

50 sundae spoons

30 pairs table spoons and forks, as servers 6 sugar tongs

6 mustard spoons.

GLASS

50 cocktail glasses

50 sherry glasses

50 Paris goblets

50 Champagne glasses

50 small tumblers

50 port glasses

50 tumblers. 3 dl (½ pt.) size

50 grapefruit glasses

6 water jugs 8 dl (1½ pt.) each

12 bowls (for salad and/or fruit

6 decanters

6 each oil and vinegar bottles

6 salt, peppers and mustards.

SILVER

12 entree dishes or flats

12 vegetable dishes (or more if for self-help, family service)

6 flower vases

6 waiter's trays 6 sugar sifters

OTHER ITEMS

Tabling: trestles and/or round

Chairs

Table linen, both long and square clothes

1 cake stand, pillars and cake knife

1 set carvers and steel, and cutting board

Ashtrays

Tea and coffee urns (installed)

Ice cream scoops

Gas rings, tubing and adapters to possible butane gas

Water boilers and hose

Corkscrews and bottle openers

Wine and spirit measures

Wash-up tubs

Dishcloths and tea towels

Tool box (including drawing pins and string)

Water carriers

Cash till.

FIG. 5.19. Approximate Catering Equipment (For 50 Persons)

Transport

In loading a van with equipment, commodities etc. a checklist should accompany the load to ensure that all requirements are loaded and for subsequent checking for return after the function. Fig. 5.19 indicates the type of form which may be devised to check the outside catering van checklist.

A separate form may be used for teas and similar receptions as-can-be seen in Fig. 5.19

CONFERENCES AND CONVENTIONS

The success or failure of any conference or convention largely depends on the quality of the speakers; the amount of information and the degree of learning which participants receive. All these elements are out of the control of the hotelier. However, the hotel has some other aspects of responsibility, which directly affect the arrangements of conferences. More thought and care be given to arrangements for receiving and treating conference guests and to the efficiency an ease with which the conference area is set up. The more impressed organizers and the leaders of such meetings are likely to be with the fact that the hotel manager knows what he is doing. Confidence in the smooth running of these arrangements will undoubtedly lead to more business in the future.

You should prepare a checklist of the sort of information, which will be needed from the conference organizers in order that a systematic plan of campaign can be set up, The following list may serve as a basic guide, which may needed to be augmented by details that will vary with the domestic needs and arrangements of individual hotels.

CHECKLIST FOR CONFERENCES

1. Dates to be set :
   (a) Majority of group arrives.
   (b) Majority of group leaves.
   (c) Late arrivals
   (d) Release of reserve rooms not taken up.
2. Attendance to be ascertained
   (a) Total number of guests expected; plus wives or children, if any.
   (b) Total number of conference numbers.
   (c) Total number of wives.
   (d) Total number of children, if any.
   (e) Grand total of those attending the meetings to include members, organizers, receptionists, speakers or other conference visitors.
3. Sleeping accommodation to be ascertained :
   (a) Number of double rooms with bath.
   (b) Number of double rooms without bath.
   (c) Number of single rooms with bath.
   (d) Number of single rooms without bath.
   (e) Number of suites.
4. Meeting requirements and equipment:
   (a) Conference room(s).
   (b) Annexes(s).
   (c) Cloakrooms.
   (d) Number of tables.
   (e) Number of chairs.

(f) Notice/flag/banners.
(g) Changing rooms.
(h) Flowers/plants.
(i) Microphones.
(j) Projector or other visual aids.
(k) Ashtrays.
(l) Paper, pencils, notepads, etc.
(m) Lectern.
(n) Platform.
(o) Carpet.

5. Organization of meals and other breaks :

(a) Menu selection.
(b) Members per table.
(c) Shape of the tables.
(d) Bar facilities.
(e) Appetizers with drinks.
(f) Tea/coffee facilities.
(g) Starting and finishing times of meals and breaks.
(h) Place of meals and breaks.

6. Basic costs :

(a) Double room with bath.
(b) Double room without bath.
(c) Single room with bath.
(d) Single room without bath.
(e) Suites.
(f) Children rates.
(g) Conference room(s).
(h) Additional rooms i.e. changing rooms' etc.
(i) Garaging.
(j) Drinks ("by the drink" or "by the bottle).
(k) Main meals.
(l) Coffee/tea.

7. Other services to be costed

(a) Permission of special equipment i.e. projector, typewriters, microphone etc.
(b) Provision'of personnel serving of above.
c) Provision of flowers.
(d) Complimentary meals and/or accommodation.
(e) Signs/place cards.
(f) Cigarettes.'.if required.
(g) Gratuities

FIG. 5.20. An specimen checklist for control

List of Facilities

The manager should be prepared to make suggestions and arrangements for the entertainment of wives and possibly children, if and when they attend conferences with their husbands. In this connection, it would be helpful to have a list of facilities, which are available in the area to hand to the conference organizer. The sort of information to be listed would be :

1. Shops and stores of special interest nearby
2. Restaurant facilities
3. Theatre and cinema programmes
4. Any special exhibition or event in the area
5. Bus or other transportation facilities available
6. Taxi firms
7. Special tours
8. Baby sitting facilities, where necessary
9. Availability of guides.

On occasions, it may be possible to arrange a special event, such as fashion show, within the hotel. Opportunities for promotions of this nature should never be overlooked, as they can be a means of increasing income from the conferences.

1. Is the name board distinct & well appeared ?
2. Are all the directional signs at right place ?
3. Is the entrance clean ?
4. Is the door wel polished ?
5. Is the pre-function area cleaned ?
6. Are the chairs in good condition ?
7. Checking of Mis-en-Scene.
8. Are the banquet tables in good condition ?
9. Is the air-conditioning working properly ?
10. Are there adequate points for electricity ?
11. Is athe function room lights working ?
12. Is the store net and clean ?
13. Is the store well lit ?
14. Are the passages well-ventiated ?
15. Are the toilet clean ?
16. Is Audio-Video set up done.
17. Is Buffet prepared and all set for operation.

FIG. 5.21. Checklist for Convention

The Conference Room

The organization of conference room facilities means that the hotel has to consider the needs of a special sort of guest- a guest who is on the premises in the role of the student, to study, listen and absorb information.

A good conference room will never of itself results in learning something more quickly. However, there is little doubt that physical surroundings do have a marked effect on the responses of students, whatever their age.

The intention should, therefore, be to select and equip-room which will ensure a comfortable, awake audience, not distracted by outside disturbances, undue extremes of temperature or inconvenient tables and uncomfortable chairs. The room should be pleasing to the eye, comfortable to be in, and above all, flexible. Symbols and clues, which could remind the adult student of school days, should be kept to a minimum. Obviously, the size of the room selected will depend on the maximum number of participants at the conference. However, a room which at first sight may appear to be too large should not be rejected out of hand for although small group could feel comfortable in a large room-as uncomfortable in fact as a group that is over crowded in a small room-conditions can always be improved by the use of screens or curtains to partition off to the right size. There is nothing, which can be done with the room that is too small, other than reduce the number of residents, students/guests.

Services

The ideal conference room would probably be windowless, artificially lighted and air-conditioned and the following points will indicate why this should be so. Broadly speaking, it amounts to the fact that the speaker or instructor can then control all these factors.

Windows

It is likely that the attention of participants at any lecture or meeting will tend to move to the light service-the window. Particularly will attention be diverted when there is something else to look at outside those windows ? Other activities causing movement and noise will be a most disturbing influence, so it is for this reason that curtains or blinds should be pulled over existing windows to allow for greater concentration.

Lighting

It would e advisable to have a professional lighting specialist to advise on the type and placement of light fittings. The minimum requirement in this respect is an adequate number of electric points in convenient places. Extension cards are not only nuisance and unsightly-they are also dangerous. People can trip over them and valuable equipment toppled and broken. All light switches should be located for the conference organizer, labelled and checked, just before the meeting.

It is important to check on doors to see that when people come in or go out during film or slide presentation, light from the open door does not fall directly on the picture. A screen or curtain would be sufficient to overcome any difficulty in this respect.

Light fittings should be kept as simple as possible. Fussy design or an attempt to be too clever in the grouping of light fitting is likely to cause distraction. As the eye is always drawn to either the heighest luminaries point or the one on which has the highest colour intensity, it is important that the speaker should be illuminated and seen against a very simple background, which is preferably darker than the rest of the room. Beware of concentration of light, however, which can cause fare, forcing the speaker to step aside to avoid the painful experience or give his talk in some discomfort. It is a simple matter to shield or cover the light source.

Heating

The success of any central heating plan or any other form of heating is not to know what is operating. The noise of a bad air-conditioning or heating system in operation can be very disturbing even though people may initially react favourably to a sound, which indicates that something is happening to ensure their comfort.

There should be some air-conditioning to control the 'climate' of the room and to give consistency to the temperature, especially bearing in mind the fact that there will be occasions when what windows there areas, are either covered to cut outside goings-on or backed out for the projection of the film. An audience will be more responsive mentally if they are seated in a slightly lower than normal temperature and in this connection the temperature of the air plus five degrees ferenheit is considered suitable. There should be an awareness of a flow of air across the room or at least a movement of air and although it is difficult to achieve a 'warm day in spring' perfectly exemplifies the conditions, which should exist.

Temperature should be constantly checked by the Deputy manager especially after lunch when return from a meal or a drinking spree at the bar would ten to raise body temperatures so that a cooler room would be more comfortable whilst after a tea break at the end of the day, a few degrees warmer would be comforting.

Noise Control

Although there are no means of measuring the degree of annoyance caused by sound, it is obvious that in order to help concentration, it is important that distraction such as typewriters, lift operations, constant door openings and closing, and people walking about or talking are cut down to a minimum.

Colour

The effect of colour on human beings has been and is the subject of much study. Generally speaking, however, it can safely be presumed that ever individual has a very personal attitude towards it and therefore, a wise policy would be to 'play safe' by choosing pastel shades and plain fabrics for curtains and coverings. Patternedmaterials can be very disturbing and distorting.

Equipment

It is unlikely that in normal hotel operation there will be much equipment, such as chairs and tables, which are completely suited for use in the conference room. This sort of equipment needs careful selection.

Chairs

These should be comfortable with semi-padded seating but without a hard front edge.

They should not be so comfortable, however, that they induce sleepiness ? There is a case for special chair for the lecturer, which should be covered in a brighter coloured fabric to keep him the important target in the audience's field of vision.

Some consideration should be given to chairs of the stacking kind so that the room may become easily cleared when it is necessary to set up display equipment, accommodate some of the larger visual aids used in training or even as occasions have a session which calls for some audience participation.

Tables

Flat topped tables of uniform size are better than one or two large ones as they can be arranged in a greater variety of ways: Check that the tables are of light weight material; again possibly of folding kind; that there are obstructions for the knees and that ideally they have a rod underneath for the feet to rest on.

The professional looking student desk is comfortable and practical. The combination of relaxed seating and note taking at the slightly angled top of some of the desktops is combined with a lightweight, sturdy and efficient piece of equipment.

Display Material

Make as much pin-up space as possible around the walls of the room. Play backed felt squares and ordinary pegboards are ideal surfaces on which to pin and hang display material.

Platform

It is well to have a revise speaker's platform available. Apart from the advantage of being able to see a lecture, some of the problems governing sound direction are overcome. Sound travels across a room but decreases towards the back and as the ceiling acts as a conductor of sound it is obvious that the nearer the speaker is to the ceiling, the better will the audience at the back of the room be able to hear.

General

Obviously the layout of the room in which the meetings are to be" held should be discussed and planned beforehand. It is not always appropriate to have a theatre style arrangement as the delegates may be expected to split into working groups around separate tables or partake in more general discussions around a conference table.

A series of diagrams of seating arrangements should be drawn up and checked with the conference leader before each meeting. Further points for checking are: -

1. Seating arrangement:
   - (i) School style with tables
   - (ii) U-shaped conference table
   - (iii) Theatre style
   - (iv) Top-table and for how many persons.

2 Size of conference room:
   - (i) Length

(ii) Width

(iii) Height.

3. Is there space in conference room for coffee and tea break or will it be served in an outside area or room?
4. When may al necessary equipment (microphone, screen, projector etc.) be set up; the night before, the morning or the afternoon of the conference? This may depend on the event, which immediately precedes the actual conference meeting.

---

1. The seating is arranged as planned.
2. The location of an additional chairs and tables.
3. The room temperature.
4. Water pitcher, glasses at lecture table and conference table.
5. Ashtrays, pencils, notepads, nameplates, where provided.
6. Signs directing members to the conference room.
7. Acoustics; to be checked for echoes or dead spots.
8. All plug-in equipment is working.
9. Microphone cords long enough.
10. Where film screen provided-it is level and steady?
11. Spare fuses or standby circuits ready?
12. Sufficient extension cords and adapters.
13. If the room is dark enough for projection?
14. All heating, air conditioning and fan control system working.
15. That every one can see platform.
16. That '*in the event of fire*' notice is prominently displayed.

FIG. 5.22. Checklist Before Meeting

At the end of each meeting check :

1. For lost or forgotten property.
2. The removal of organizer's property for safekeeping.
3. The return of any hired equipment.
4. The removal of promotional material relating to the last session.

Unless the hotel staff is of sufficient size to accommodate a conference without inconvenience to other guests, it is of vital importance that their comfort is ensured. Nothing is more irritating and disturbing from the regular visitor's point of view than to find a hotel's activities geared to the needs of the conference. It is courteous and very necessary that guests should be warned of the conference and of the times the delegates will be taking their meals and separate arrangements made for the comfort of all other guests staying at the same time.

Exibitions

Apart from seminars and conferences, hoteliers are increasingly being asked for exhibition facilities. The advantages from the exhibition organizer's point of view are obvious-under one roof an air of luxury is added to the attraction of bars, dinning rooms and sleeping accommodations. The hotel should, therefore, study and give thought to its available accommodation recognizing that exhibition facilities should be source of additional income, particularly during its off peak periods.

Many of the precautions already mentioned under conference section apply to the planning of an exhibition. Stridently patterned carpets can instantly destroy the quality of display. Air conditioning must not only be adequate but constantly checked as the extra lighting needed generates considerable heat and people-Milo more heat than is generated during a dance function. For this reason plus the fact that hotel accommodation is small in exhibition terms and if well attended could result in very cramped conditions it is important to provide some over flow area which people can escape. Public rooms, usually adjacent to the area in case should be made available for this purpose to raise the level of pleasure and efficiency for both exhibitors and attendees.

Further though should be given to storage space, for every exhibition, however small, will carry with its crates, packing materials and articles which for one reason or another, will not be put on display. Because of this factor, extra portage can be useful. Exhibitions bring bulky things with them and although contractors and exhibitors may have their own staff, if space is not to be cleared and set up in short time, thy need hotel staff standing by for help.

The role of local fire officer must not be overlooked in these arrangements. His advice is of vital importance, especially as the chances are that the exhibition organizers may try and force stands into the area than are safe from a fire and escape angle.

Lighting can be a great problem if the hotel has not made adequate arrangements before offering its accommodation for use as exhibition areas. Lighting must be flexible with points ideally in the middle of the room, either at the door or ceiling level. Extra points laid at the last minute can be pricey and the organizers are unlikely to look very favourably on the hotel ho has provided the accommodation but has to ask the organizer to pay for extra points to be installed and then finds that the wiring is insufficient to carry the extra load.

A simple paging system should be arranged to avoid the use of tanny relayed into the exhibition room causing disturbances to everyone in the exhibition.

Similarly, care should be taken over the sign pasting system. Information, which is well-designed, prominent, flexible and clear, can save a great deal if irritation to members of staff and to all those involved in the exhibition. The statement on board, badly placed that the 'Himalayan Tourism & Recreation in Mountain's Exhibition' is being held in the Mahargaon suite is hopeless. The Mahargaon suite is obviously well known to the staff but not to the visitor.

Finally, the hotel should be well advised not to use bedrooms for exhibition purpose. Apart from the particularly cramped conditions, visitors are likely to ;feel trapped' one inside the door, with little hope of escaping unobserved. Freedom of movement is essential to the creation of overall sense of luxury.

QUESTIONS AND ASSIGNMENTS

Objective Type

Q 1. Single the odd word out (give reasons for each):

(a) Herring bone shape/Comb shape/Class room shape of eating arrangement

(b) Moet et chandon/Perrier Jouet/Marquis de pompadsour

(c) Function Prospectus/Function Enquiry Sheet/Letter of Confirmation

(d) Pastry Trolley/Hors d'oeuvre Trolley/Flambe Trolley

(e) Bar Spoon/Tea Spoon/Measuring Spoon. [BHM]

Q 2. Fill in the blanks:

(a) Size of a 4-cover square table is ....

(b) Name five banquet tools (1).........(2)............(3)...............(4) ....(5)...........

(c) Banquet Memorandum means______(Function sheet / Banquet Diary / Function Prospect us)

(d) Capacity of margarita (a stemware) is ______. (5 oz / 5¼ oz / 5½ oz /6 oz).

(e) Air space at top of a wine barrel due to evaporation or leakage is called ____.

(a) In a formal banquet toasting is done at the beginning of dinner or at the middle with rest course or at the end of dinner, (choose the appropriate one).

(b) Henry Charpentier accidentally invented flambe dish in the year ______.

(c) For a buffet service of 300 pax total space required would be ______ sq. ft. [BHM]

Essay Type

Q. 3. As a Banquet manager of a five star you have been approached to make arrangements for the annual dinner of Indian Hotelier and Caterers Association to be served in the month of December 2000. You are required to make arrangements for cocktail reception followed by a sit down dinner for 250-persons. Hon'ble Minister of Tourism is the chief guest :

(a) Submit a suitable seating plan assuming the banquet to be formal and 21-guests is to be seated at the top table.

(b) Submit a menu consisting of five courses

(c) Name the drinks and savouries you will serve in the Cocktail Reception.

(d) You are charging Rs. 400 per person; mention how much you will spend towards food cost.

(e) Estimate the requirement of furniture and service staff. [BHM]

Q. 4. Writes notes on any three in about 100 words each :

(a) Banquet

(b) Buffet

(c) K.O.T

(d) Menu Planning Considerations.

Q. 5. As a banquet manager plan the staff required in the Banquet department of a 5-star hotel operating 6-banquet halls with a maximum capacity of 2000-pax in all. [BHM]

Q. 6. In the form of a report to your Managing Director, draft proposals for marketing and selling banquet and conference business in either a hotel or a residential centre. In your report draw up procedures for handling individual booking arrangements.

Q. 7. Illustrate with a flow chart the sequence of cocktail dinner order for two persons served through room service, specifying the items and quantities involved. [BHM]

Q. 8. Prepare a Function Prospectus of a wedding party of 350-pax. booked for 10th February, 2004, from 5 pm to 11 pm, you are required to serve evening tea snacks and dinner. Make your own assumptions where every necessary.

Q. 9. Calculate the length of the top and spring table for a format sit down banquet of 250-packs with 11-person on the top table. Illustrate with the help of a neat diagram.

Q. 10. Prepare a job description of a Banquet Captain. [BHM]

Q. 11. Draw up a carefully designed function prospectus format.

Q. 12. The various forms of buffet service can be asset to the F & B service department. However there are certain drawbacks, with this kind of service. Give your opinion on the advantages and disadvantages of buffet service in about 20-lines. [BHM]

Q. 13. Design and explain function prospectus form required for the banquet department of a five star hotel. [BHM]

Q. 14. Prepare a simple Banquet Menu file for evening snacks function, with necessary instructions for organizers to choose the dishes.

Q. 15. For an efficient service, breakfast buffet is a necessity in hotels. Plan a breakfast buffet menu for Rs. 150/- and also explain the layout of the buffet table in right sequence. [BHM]

Q. 16. What are the different table-layouts used for formal Banquet Function What are the major factors taken into consideration to identify by the suitable layout. Your Banquet Department has booked a party for 100-covers (120-expected) lunch buffet-Indian menu 60% veg. and 40% non-veg. [BHM]

Q. 17. Prepare a function sheet with other assumed information and explain the use of function .sheet for effective functioning of a Banquet Department.

Q. 18. You are required to cater for a wedding buffet for 250-300 pax at Rs.120/- per head (inclusive). Plan an Indian menu; give the recipe for any one non-vegetarian dish.

Q. 19. Draw an organizational chart of the Banquet Department of a 5-star hotel having 6 variable banquet halls with a total capacity of three thousand guests. Also give a 3-lines description of the function of each of these staff.

Q. 20. Indicate the operational aspect of catering at a banquet function, which a big industrialist is holding in your hotel. [PGDT & BM]

Q. 21. What are the qualities that an outdoor caterer must possess in order to be successful?

Q. 22. Draw the format of various checklists that are necessary for the smooth functioning of an outdoor catering unit.

Q. 23. The quality of food produced by a mass-catering unit depends to a large extent on the available equipment:

(a) Classify with examples different types of equipment required for a mass catering unit

(b) What factors would be kept in mind while selecting equipment for an institutional catering unit

(c) List five reputed Indian manufacturers of kitchen equipment, [BHM]

Q. 24. Explain 'banqueting'. How is the banquet set up prior to seating of guest

Q. 25. Explain the term buffets, salad bars, oyster beers, dessert tables and smorgasbords. How do they differ from one another?

Q. 26. Prepare a job description of a Banquet Captain.

Q. 27. Draw up a carefully designed "Function Prospectus'format;

Q. 28. A buffet service has more advantages than disadvantages - explain in details.

Q. 29. Stepwise mention the protocol to be maintained in a formal state banquet.

Q. 30. Explain the following:

(a) Finger Buffet;

(b) Fork Buffet;

(c) Sit-down Buffet.

Q. 31. Write notes on:

(a) Menu Planning

(b) Buffet caterings

(c) Interior decoration

(d) Guest weekly Bill

(e) Hotel Health and Hygiene. [PGT& BM]

Q. 32. Define the term 'banqueting'. Explain in detail the full procedure of banqueting activities in a medium sized hotel. [PGT& BM]

Q. 33. Differentiate between 'Fork Buffer' and 'Finger Buffet'.

Q. 34. List the protocol regulations to be kept in mind while making the seating plan for formal Banquets. [BMS]

Q. 35. What are the different layouts used for formal banquet function? What are the major factors taken into consideration to identify the suitable layout^

Q.36. In the form of a report to your managing director, draft proposals for marketing and selling banquet and conference business in either a hotel or a residential centre. In your report draw up procedures for handling individual booking arrangements. [HCIMA (London)]

Q. 37. Write in brief on any two of the following:

Glossary

A

A la : In the style of, for example: a l'Anglaise (English style); a la Francaise (French style); a la Maison (style of the house)

a la broche : Cooked on a spit

abats offal, the internal organs of meat and poultry e.g., heart, kidneys, liver

accompaniment : Condiment or seasoning offered to a customer to add to and improve the flavour of a dish

Advocaat : Lqueur made up of brandy, egg yolks, caster sugar and vanilla flavouring; Dutch in origin.

agneau : Denotes lamb on the menu

agrodolce : Sweet and sour

aiguillettes : Long, thin, vertically cut strips of meat or poultry

ail Garlic.

ajo blanco Puree sauce of garlic and almonds (Spanish).

al dente Cooked until firm and crunchy (pasta/ vegetables)

ale : General term covering all forms of brewed beer.

allumette : Cut into matchstick shapes

amaretti macaroons (Italian), almond flavoured

amontillado Medium dry sherry, classified as a fortified (or liqueur) wine

amuse-bouche Small savoury snacks served pre-hors d'oeuvres

anchoide Provencalpaste-sauce of garlic, anchovy and olive oil

Angostura Bitters Proprietary brand of aromatic bitters used as a flavouring in drinks, *e.g.* pink gin

anguille Eeel

antipasti Starters other than pasta and rice dishes (Italian)

aperitif drink served prior to a meal in order to stimulate the appetite

arborio rice Short, fat-grained Italian rice used for risotto

Armagnac Quality brandy made in the Armagnac district of France

aroma Indicating smell, scent or fragrance and often alluding to wine

arrosto Roast (Italian)

arugula salad leaf similar to rocket with a sharp peppery flavour (Italian)

aspic Clear savoury jelly used in the decorating of joints of cold meat

assiette Platter or dish

assiette anglaise Plate of cooked meats

au bleu A method of cooking trout. When applied to grilled steaks it indicates 'very underdone

au four Baked in the oven

au gratir topped with breadcrumbs and grated cheese and browned under the grill

au just With cooking liquors or gravy

au nature uncooked or in its natural state

au sec until dry

auslese German wine label term indicating specially selected bunches of late picked grapes, high in sugar content, that make a sweet dessert wine

B

baba yeast sponge or bun that may be soaked in flavoured syrup to moisten, e.g. Baba au rhum

babaganoush aubergine puree (Middle Eastern meze dish)

Bacardi proprietary brand of white rum originating from Cuba

back of house work areas not seen or used by customers, e.g. stillroom, linen room, floor pantry

bage ring shaped roll with a tough, chewy texture

baguette long stick shaped loaf of French bread

bain-marie hot water bath or well in which smaller containers may be set in order to cook food items slowly or to keep them warm/hot in readiness for service

baklava Turkish and Greek sweet made from filo pastry, chopped nuts and honey

ballotine meat, fish or poultry, boned, stuffed and rolled

balsamic vinegar the finest is made in Modena in Northern Italy; Italian sweet wine vinegar used to make dressings for salads or a sauce for fish such as poached sea bass

balthazar Equivalent of 16 standard size 75cl bottles of sparkling wine

barqette boat-shaped tartlette case

basil flavouring herb; goes well with tomatoes

basmati rice aromatic, long-grained rice used in Indian cuisine, e.g. Biryani

baste to spoon over liquid during cooking, e.g. hot fat over a joint

baton stick-shape cut of root vegetables

bavarois Bavarian cream – a sweet custard made with eggs, cream and gelatine and served cold

bayleaf used fresh or dried to flavour various dishes such as casseroles; also found in a 'bouquet garni'

bearnaise hot sauce offered with fish and grilled meats, made from beaten egg yolks and reduced wine vinegar and flavoured with tarragon

Beaujolais fruity and light French red wine from the Beaujolais region of France

bechamel basic white sauce that is made from a white roux and seasoned hot milk. May be used as a thickening agent in cream soups or extended into other derivative sauces, *e.g.* mornay, moutarde, persil and anchois

beer term broadly covering lagers, ales and stouts. An alcoholic beverage made from fermented malted barley or other cereals and flavoured with hops

beignets deep-fried fritters (assorted fruits cooked in batter) or doughnuts

bercy a white wine-based sauce for fish

beurre blanc light emulsion sauce of white wine, vinegar, shallots and butter

beurre fondu melted butter with lemon juice and chopped parsley added; used to garnish some fish and grilled meat dishes

beurre manie butter and flour kneaded together and used to thicken soups and sauces

beurre noisette golden brown butter that may have a little lemon juice added to take away the greasiness and add bite

bhaji vegetable deep fried in gram flour batter (Indian)

bianco medium sweet type of white/golden vermouth

bien cuit degree of cooking of a grilled steak-well done

billfold style of wallet used for presenting the bill to the host and returning the receipted bill and any change

bind (lier) to thicken soups and sauces with eggs, cream etc. To mix pasta, chopped meat, vegetables, with sauce

biryani long grained rice, spiced and coloured yellow with saffron. An over baked rice to accompany meats (Indian)

bisque thickened shellfish-based puree soup, usually with tomato and cognac, e.g. Bisqe d'homad (lobster)

bistro small informal restaurant, bar or nightclub

bitters alcoholic spirits, flavoured and of different strengths, *e.g.* Angostura Bitters, Campari, Fernet Branca and Underberg

blanc water to which flour has been added and used to keep vegetables white when cooking, *e.g.* celery

blanch (blanchir) placing briefly in boiling water or hot fat/oil and then draining. Also allows part cooking without colouring

blanquette thickened white stew of lamb, veal, rabbit or white fish thickened with egg yolks and cream

blini small, thick, buckwheat flour savoury pancake. Accompaniment to caviar (Russian)

boeuf French menu term for beef

boeuf Strogonoff thin strips of beet in a thick creamy sauce with mushrooms, tomato, onion, seasonings and flavoured with dry white wine, lemon juice and tarragon.

boeuf bourguignonne braised, marinaded beef casserole made from braising steak, flavoured with red wine and garnished with button onions and mushrooms, lardons of bacon and heart- shaped croutons

bollito misto mixture of boiled meats

Bolognaise savoury meat sauce made from lean minced beef, demi-glace (a half glaze basic brown sauce), red wine, onion, tomato and seasonings including garlic and described generally as a meat and tomato sauce

bombe an ice cream dessert made by using two different types of ice cream mixtures

bonito flaked dried tuna used to make Japanese broths and essential for 'dashi', a Japanese soup stock

bonne femme mushroom garnish for fish, with onions and bacon for chicken

bonne-bouche small savoury bite, often in a vol-au-vent case

bordelaise rich brown sauce flavoured with red wine

borlotti dry speckled haricot bean used in dips and salads

Bortsch rich duck flavoured consomme of East European origin

Bouchees small sweet or savoury puff pastry bites, being a minature version of a vol-au-vent

boudin French versio of the British black or white pudding with the black containing pigs' blood while the white may have chicken, veal or pork.

bouillabaise Mediterranean fish soup made by the stewing method with the most popular version coming from Marseilles. Fennel, garlic and saffron are among the many seasonings used

bouillon unclarified meat or vegetable stock

bouillon, court made up liquor for cooking (poaching) fish. Seasonings may include sliced root vegetables, peppercorns, bayleaf, rosemary and condiments

bouquet aroma or small, e.g. of an improving wine

bouquet garni parcel of herbs such as parsley, thyme, bay leaf and peppercorns used to flavour stews, casseroles, stocks and sauces

bourbons American whiskey made from a fermented cereal (maize) base

bourride garlic flavoured fish stew from the provence region of Fance

braise French menu/cookery term denoting 'braising' of a joint or portion of meat

braising pan (bisiere) covered cooking dish

brandy spirit distilled from wine using the 'pot still' method

brasserie small restaurant and bar where food and drinks are served. French in origin

breadcrumb (paner) to cover a piece of fish, meat, poultry etc. with breadcrumbs after first dipping it in seasoned flour, then in beaten egg or melted butter

breathe to allow a wine to come into contact with the air upon removal of the cork, which then enhances the bouquet

brioche soft, light textured roll or bun mde from eggs, butter, flour and yeast

brochette, en indicates grilling on a skewer, e.g. Kebab, which is Turkish in origin and often served on a bed of braised rice

brodo Italian term for stock, a base ingredient in soups, sauces and casseroles

broyer to crush or grind finely

brunch late morning meal that often replaces both breakfast and lunch

brunoise a name used to describe vegetables, ham or chicken cut into tiny dice

bruschetta toasted or baked slices of bread, oiled and sprinkled with herbs and served as an appetiser

brut Champagne/sparkling wine label term indicating very dry

Burgundy wine producing region of France, also a smooth, soft, dry red wine from that same region.

busboy/girl American term indicating a person who carries out clearing duties in a food and beverage service area and also used as a general term meaning waiter or server

butter (beurrer) to coat or brush the inside of a mould or dish with butter

C

caffeine bitter white alkaloid found in tea, cocoa and coffee and used as a stimulant

canapes small pieces of bread, usually toasted and of varying shapes, or dry cracke/water biscuits, covered with a variety of savoury items and then served as appetisers

cannellini beans creamy white kidney beans, having a slightly fluffy texture and mainly used in Hallan cooking

cannelloni type of pasta shaped in large rolls, normally stuffed with cheese, meat and minced vegetables, covered with a cheese sauce and then baked in the oven (Italian)

cannoli Sicilian pastry tubes filled with ricotta cheese, chocolate and candied peel

canteen style of restaurant found in a school, hospital or industrial catering where the style of service is usually self-service.

This term may also indicate a temporary or mobile eating place set up in an emergency

Cantonese from of cuisine usually found in westernised restaurants and is one of the five main styles of Chinese cuisine

capsicum Peppers, either sweet or hot, available in many colours and sizes

carafe form of glass bottle or jug used for the service of wine or water at the table. May also be defined as a decanter

caramel burnt sugar, also known as 'Black Jack'

caramelise (carameliser) to line a mould thinly with caramel sugar, or to coat fruit with, or dip it in, cracked sugar. Also to slowly brown sugar or foods such as onions and carrots over heat

carbonara spaghetti sauce of egg, bacon and parmesan

carbonnade beef braised in beer and brown stock and seasoned with garlic

carciofo globe artichoke

carpaccio originally thin slices of raw red meat, now also applied to fish

carpet bag steak fillet steak, filled with oysters, then sealed and grilled

carre French menu term indicating the 'best end' of lamb which is made up of all the lamb cutlets

carte du jour card/menu of the day. Lists the various dishes available on a particular day and the styles of menu available in the eating area

carte, a la menu where all dishes are individually priced and often cooked or finished to order

cassata ice cream dessert made up of layers of different flavoured ice creams, usually three, and mixed with glace fruits flavoured with liqueur

casserole, a style of stew cooked in a casserole dish

casserole, dish fireproof earthenware dish, round or oval in shape, with a lid

Cava term used to indicate Spanish sparkling wines made by the traditional method

caviar roe of the female sturgeon and named after the species of sturgeon that provides it, *e.g.* Sevruga or Beluga

celestine strips of savoury pancake and is a garnish found in consomme

chafing dish style of frying pan used on a flare lamp for cooking at the table or to maintain the warmth of food

champignons French menu term for mushrooms

chantilly whipped cream with sugar and vanilla

chapatti thin flat cake of coarse unleavened br4ad, Indian in origin. Accompanies various curries

char grill cooking food on a grill which has coke or coals over an artificial electric or gas heat source

charcuterie cold, cooked and cured meat products, especially pork, such as pates, hams, sausages and bacon

chard spinach-like leaves with thick, white edible ribs

chariotte moulded dessert of pastry cream, custard, mousse or pureed fruit

charsiu Chinese glazed pork fillet

chartreuse herb-flavoured, brandy-based liqueur

chartreuse, en feathered game served with cabbag

Chateaubriand double fillet steak cut from the head of the fillet of beef

chadfroid sauce for cold buffet work, a jellied brown or white sauce used as an aspic to decorate and garnish cold meats and fish

chemiser to lin a mould

chermoula Moroccan fish marinade

chervil green leafed herb used in seasoning, especially in French cuisine, with a flavour similar to anise (aniseed)

chevre goat's milk cheese

chiffonade salad leaves (lettuce) or vegetables, cut in fine shreds, used in prawn cocktail or as a vegetable dish, e.g., chou (cabbage)

chilli con carne stew of minced meat, normally beef, chillies and purple kidney beans. Mexican in origin

Chinese green teas most familiar as the teas served in Chinese restaurants. These teas are all mild with a fruit flavour. The tea leaves are unfermented and produce a very pale drink with a light favour

chine backbone of beef, lamp, pork or venison with meat attached

Chingkiang dark rice wine vinegar of Chinese origin and similar to Balsamic

chioca yams

choisum Chinese greens with yellow flowers

chop suey Chinese-style dish consisting of small pieces of chicken or meat cooked with bean sprouts and other vegetables and served with a savoury rice

Chorizo spicy pork meat and fat sausage. flavoured with garlic, paprika and pimento and of Spanise origin

choucroute see sauerkraut – pickled cabbage

choux pastry for sweet fillings, e.g. as used for eclairs and profiteroles

chow mein Chinese dish made up of varying combinations of stewed meat and vegetables and served with fried noodles

chowder creamy thick soup or stew made from shellfish, especially clams, and vegetables, e.g. Clam Chowder

cilantro see coriander

citron French menu term for lemon

civet garne stew, usually related to hare

clafouti baked batter tart usually filled with cherries

claret traditionally a red wine from Bordeaux, the wine producing region in France

clarified impurities removed from butter, stock, soup or jelly

cloud ears form of dried Chinese mushroom with uses in soups, fish and chicken dishes

coat (napper) to cover a dish or sweet entirely with a sauce, a jelly or a cream. To mask, to dip

cocotte small, round, fireproof, earthenware dish for cooking an egg, e.g. oeuf en cocotte. Also used to describe a larger oval casserole with a lid for slow cooking chicken, ragout (brown stew) etc.

Cognac quality brandy from the Cognac region of south west France

compote fruit poached in a sugar/fruit syrup and recognised as stewed fruit

concasse roughly chopped (tomato), having many uses in French cuisine, *e.g.* sauces, stews, salads, garnishes

conde cold sweet made up of poached fruit (pears) on a creamed rice base

condiment seasoning offered to a customer to give added flavour/contrast to a dish served, e.g. salt and pepper, apple sauce, horseradish sauce

confit virtually boneless meat (game, duck, goose or pork) cooked slowly in their own juices and fat

confitre French menu term for jam

consomme clear soup made from beef or chicken stock and may be served hot or cold, with various garnishes added

coque, a la soft boiled in its shell, *e.g.* eggs

coquilles Saint-Jacques scallops

coral roe or eggs of some shellfish

corbeille denotes a 'basket', usually of fresh fruit and nuts and offered as an alternative to the sweet course

cordial fruit-based, sweet, non-alcoholic drink. Also term for concentrated fruit squash, such as lime cordial

cordial fruit-based, sweet, non-alcoholic drink. Also term for concentrated fruit squash, such as lime cordial

coriander sometimes known as Chinese parsley, this herb has a fresh taste, similar to orange and is an important ingredient in curry

corkage charge made for opening and serving bottles of wine brought into a restaurant by customers

Corked spoilt wine due to a fauly or mouldy cork, or becase of bad storage

cos sometimes called Romaine lettuce, this has long, slender, crisp but coarse leaves and is mainly used in salads and for garnishing

cotechino Italian origin, this is a sausage made with lean and fat pork, white wine and species and is often served hot with beans

coulis puree of fruit or vegetable, used to garnish and decorate

courgette British term for a 'baby' or miniature marrow. Called 'zucchini' in America and often termed 'Italian squash' in ltaly

court bouillon seasoned poaching liquid, usually for fish

couvert a cover. Number of guests at a function. A place setting for a guest for a set meal. A place setting for a specific dish ordered.

cover charge an additional charge added to the customer's bill

creme Anglaise rich custard sauce, of pouring consistency, to accompany a sweet

creme brulee thick, smooth and rich custard with a covering of caramelised sugar

creme fraiche thick cream that has had a 'culture' aded to it. Available either plain or in varying fruit flavours

creme patissiere custard or pastry cream, thickened with flour or other starch

crepe thin pancake with sweet or savoury filling

crevettes French menu term for shrimp

croissant crescent-shaped roll, made from a yeast-based Danish pastry dough

croquettes minced fowl, game, meat, fish or vegetables bound with a sauce, seasoned and shaped like a cork, then flour, eff and bread crumbed and deep fried

cross-contamination transfer of bacteria to food from another food, equipment or work surface

crostini bread canapes, see 'canapes'

croustades deep, scalloped, tartlet cases with either sweet or savoury fillings

croute bread or pastry crust

croutons fried as a garnish, cut into small cubes for soups and other dishes in a variety of fancy shapes, e.g. heart-shaped croutons

crudies served as an appetiser and made up of small pieces (batons) of vegetable, such as carrot and courgette, with an accompanying savoury dip

crumb down to brush debris (crumbs) from the tablecloth between courses

D

Daikon large, white radish, sometimes called the Japanese pickled radish and often eaten with fish. May be greated and used as a garnish

darne thick slice from a round fish, including the central bone

dashi Japanese soup stock made from bonito flakes and konbu seaweed and combined with 'miso' to produce miso soup

daube, en method of cooking meat (stews of beef or mutton) very slowly in the oven, in a hermetically saled dish (daubiere) to preserve its full flavour

dauphinoise sliced potatoes baked in cream (or milk and cheese), seasoned with nutmeg and garlic

decant to pour a wine or other liquor, slowly, off the sediment in its container with the aid of muslin or filter papers

deglaze dissolve caramelised sediment in a roasting pan by adding wine or stock

degorger to soak fish or sometimes vegetables to remove impurities

delice French menu term denoting a trimmed and folded fillet of fish, e.g. Delice de sole

demi-glace refined Espagnole (basic brown sauce). Smooth glossy sauce of pouring consistency used as base for other sauces, soups and stews.

demi-tasse half-cup (espresso coffee cup)

depouiller to remove skin or scum formed on top of liquid

dessert fresh fruit and nuts served from the fruit basket, but now-adays it also means the choice of sweets available from the menu

dessert wine style of sweet wine, e.g. Sauternes, Muscat, Auslese, often offered with the dessert (sweet) course

dhal thick puree of lentils offered as an accompanying dish with curry

digestif any alcoholic liquor served as an after dinner drink, e.g., liquers, brandy, port

dim sum Chinese meal consisting of a variety of hot snacks

donburi Japanese dish of a bowl of rice topped with leftovers

dorer egg wash pastry or bread goods with yolk of egg beaten with water. Some bread goods may be brushed with milk

du jour A French menu term literally translated as meaning 'of the day', e.g., carte du jour, which lists an establishment's daily menus

Dubarry garnished with or containing cauliflower

dum Indian method of steaming, especially for pilau rice

dumb waiter indicates either the sideboard found in a food service area or the small lift that sends food from the kitchen to the dining room or to hotel floors

duxelles finely chopped mushrooms and shallots, sweated in butter and used as a stuffing or flavouring in sauces or as a garnish

E

earthenware type of strengthened china much used in the hospitality industry

elver young eel

embrocherio-place on a spit for spit roasting or on skewers for grilling or frying

en cocotte cooked in a round, earthenware dish. May be egg (oeuf en cocotte) or meat (pot-roasted)

en papillote freach menu term indicating fish or meat baked in a greaseproof bag in the oven

endive vegetable with a slightly sharp taste used in salads or braised, known in Britain as chicory and endive in France and America

entrecote steak of beef coming from the boned out sirloin (contrefilet de boeuf)

entree meat dish served with a sauce and made up of small cuts of butcher's meat or poultry, frequently served as a main course, e.g. garnished cutlets, sweetbreads

entremets sweet course on the every day menu and includes a selection of mainly cold sweets and a limited number of hot dishes

escalopes thin slices of flattened and boneless veal, beef or pork. Veal escalopes come from the fillet or cushion of veal, pork from the fillet or boned out pork loin and beef from the boned out sirloin

etuver method of simmering food very in butter, or very little liquid, in a closed casserole, *e.g.* Chou etuvee

Evian brand of spring water from France

F

falafel rissoles made from dried broad beans, shallow fried and served with a piquant sauce

faraona Italian term for guinea fowl with a slight tanginess of game, reminiscent of pheasant. May be roasted, braised or casseroled

farce cuisine term for a savoury stuffing

fennel bulbous leafstalk which can be used raw with salads or braised whole and served as a vegetable, sometimes with a cheese sauce. The fresh or dried, aniseed tasting leaves are traditionally used with fisl dishes whilst the aromatic dried seeds of the fennel plant are used with fish dishes, curries and apple pie

fenugreek seepls of this plant are ground and used as a spice in curries and chutneys. Associated mainly with Indian cuisine

fettuccine thin ribbons of pasta similar to tagliateile, available in a green and white version, the green being mixed with a spinach puree

feuillantine puff pastry strips brushed with egg, sprinkled with sugar and baked

feuilletage puff pastry used to produce savoury and sweet dishes, e.g. vol-au-ven bouchees, tranche, cream horns and man; others

feuillete triangle-shaped puff pastry case

feves board beans, often served bound in cream sace

filet comes from the fillet of lamb and is also used to indicate a small round fillet steak cut from the whole beef fillet

filo pastry thin and crisp paper-like pastry, used in the making of sweet dishes, mince pies, fruit filled filo pastry cases etc.

fine champagne one of the best styles of Cognac and indicative of quality

flageolet small, pale-green kidney bean

flageolet to cook or finish cooking a dish at the table and then 'flaming' it by pouring a spirit or liqueur over, *e.g.* brandy, rum

fleurons crescents and other fancy shapes of baked puff pastry used to garnish a variety of dishes such as entrees, poached fish and shellfish dishes

float sum of money of varying denominations placed in a till prior to service commencing

flute stemmed glass with a tall but narrow bowl and used in the service of sparkling wines. The shape assists in retaining the sparkle (effervescence) of the wine

focaccia flat, round, flavoured Italian bread

foie de veau French menu term denoting calves liver and may be served with onions (Lyonnaise) or with bacon (au lard)

foie gras liver of specially fattened geese either served as a piece or used to make a pate

forestiere garnished with mushrooms

fortified wine wine whose alcoholic strength is increased by the addition of alcohol, usually brandy, e.g. sherry and port. Called liqueur wine in the EU

four, au baked in an oven

frappe Chilled, e.g. melon frappe, or over crushed ice, e.g. creme de menthe frappe

friandises another name for petits fours and offered at the end of the meal with coffee. See also petits fours and sweetmeats

fricassee, white stew in which poultry, pork, veal or rabbit is cooked in a thickened sauce throughout the cooking period

frittata fiat unfolded omelette

froid cold, Applies to any item of food or liquor *served* cold or chilled

fromages, assortis Fench menu term meaning assortment of cheeses

frost to decorate a glass by dipping its rim in lemon juice and then caster sugar that may be coloured. Applicable to certain cocktails

fruits de mer fruits of the sea. French menu term indicating an assortment of sea foods

fume denotes smoked when used on the menu, e.g. Truite fume

fumet stock from fish, meat, game or poultry and the basis for sauces, stews, soups etc.

funghi Italian term for wild mushrooms, the cep being the most well known and is a quality tasting mushroom eaten widely in Europe

fusil sharpening steel

G

gailan Chinese spring greens

galangal root spice related to the ginger family, used in Thai cuisine and has a faint flavour of camphor. Available in root or powder form and is used in the Far East in curries and in Malay dishes

galantine cold dish of poultry or meat, boned, stuffed, braised in concentrated stock and then coated with aspic and garnished

galette flat, round, sweet or savoury cake or biscuit

ganache cake filling or topping made from couverture and whipping cream and may also be used for warm piping or cold modelling

garnish any ingredient which decorates, accompanies or completes a dish. Many dishes are identified by the name of their garnish, *e.g.* chicken Maryland (corn fritters, sautee banana, grilled bacon rolls and tomatoes), horseradish sauce would be offered separately

gastrique caramelised sugar and vinegar mixture used to flavour sauces

gateaut usually a rich sponge cake that may be decorated and flavoured in a wide variety of ways, *e.g.* Gateau Moka (coffee gateau) or Gateau Foret Noir (Black Forest gateau (chocolate)). Certain gateaux do not have sponge bases, *e.g.* Gateau MacMahon (shortbread base) or Gateau St Honore (puff pastry and choux pastry base)

gazpacho cold soup of pureed tomato, cucumber, onion, red pepper and garlic. Sometimes garnished with croutons

gelato soft whipped icecream (Italian), available in a variety of flavours

genoise very rich and light sponge cake made from equal quantities of egg, caster sugar and soft white flour, plus a small quantity of melted butter

gentlemen's Relish proprietary brand of anchovy paste, butter/herbs and spices. Used mainly as a spread, often on canapes

ghee Indian term denoting clarified butter and is the yellow liquid left when the sediment has been removed

gibier game, e.g. pheasant, partridge, grouse

glace French menu term for ice cream

glaze (glacer) to dust a cake or sweet with icing sugar and brown under a grill; to simmer vegetables, cut into fancy shapes, in butter until they have a glossy coating; to give meat a glossy appearance by frequent basting; to give cold dishes, cakes and sweets a shiny appearance by coating with aspic or jelly that is on the point of setting

gluhwein spicy mulled wine served hot, the main ingredients being red wine, caster sugar, lemon, orange, nutmeg, cinnamon and vanilla sticks

gluten protein substance found in cereal grains, **plainly** wheat, and used as a ffour substitute

gnocchi farinaceous (pasta) type dish, from a starch base that may be flour, semolina, potatoes or maize flour. Italian in origin

gomme syrup white sugar syrup used as a flavouring ingredient in certain cocktails, e.g. whisky sour, and in fruit cups

gosht Indian term indicating meat

gougere ring of choux pastry with savoury filling, often cheese

goujons French menu term denoting thin strips of fillet of fish, e.g. goujons de sole, prepared by dipping in seasoned flour, beaten egg and bread crumbs (pane), then deep fried

goulache casserole of stewing meat, either beef, veal, lamb, pork or mutton and onions, flavoured with paprika and tomato

grana grating cheese

gratin, au a dish that has been sprinkled with grated cheese, possibly mixed with breadcrumbs and a little butter, and then browned under a grill or in a hot oven. May also simply mean a sweet or savoury dish that is browned under a grill

gravadlax/ gravlax faw salmon cured in sugar, salt, pepper and dill

gremoiata combination of lemon zest, parsley, garlic, tomato concasse and seasoning used to garnish osso buco (knuckle of veal casserole)

griottines Morello cherries, usually preserved in alcohol

grissini long, thin and crisp bread sticks offered as alternatives to rolls (Italian)

gros sel coarse or rock salt, this is a less refined salt than table salt

guacamole spicy avocado sauce with tomato, onion; hot green chilli, cilantro (the fresh leaves of the coriander plant), lemon juice and cream added to the mashed flesh of the avocado

gueridon (trolley or service side table on which food is served or prepared and cooked at the customer's table

gumbo/spicy casserole of seafood and vegetables, including okra (thickening agent). In the USA this term applies to any dish incorporating okra as one of its ingredients

gurnard small round salt water fish known as the 'sea robin, e.g. Red gurnard and Ray gurnard, and may be braised or baked

H

HACCP Hazard Analysis Critical Control Point, a food safety self-inspection system

hacher French term meaning to mince or finely chop meat such as stewing beef, e.g. hachis de boeuf (savoury beef mince)

haggis (traditional Scottish dish made of oatmeal, chopped offal of either a sheep or calf and seasonings and boiled in the stomach lining of the animal

hala meat killed and prepared according to Muslim law

Haldi Indian term for turmeric. See turmeric holloumi goats milk cheese

hang to keep freshly killed meat or game in a cool place and exposed to the air. for a period of time, until it becomes more tender and improves in flavour

harissa red chilli paste of medium strength that has-been seasoned with cloves of garlic, coriander, cumin, caraway seeds and dried mint, used in the North African dish of couscous and also in Moroccan cuisine

harusame transparent, rice-flour noodles

hash browns dish of American origin made up of pureed potato and onion, bound with egg, shaped and fried

haute cuisine originally a French term meaning highest standard of cooking and service

Hawthorn strainer essential piece of equipment in the cocktail bar and used in conjunction **with** the Boston shaker and bar mixing glass when making cocktails

hock English name for German wines produced the vineyards along the banks of the river Rhine

hoisin sauce made from soy, flour, vinegar, garlic, sesame, salt and pepper

Hollandaise egg yolk and butter-based sauce. This or one of its derivatives may be offered with grilled steaks e.g. sauce bearnaise

Hollands Dutch style of gin made from malted barley and rye and double distilled in a pot still. Often sold in stone bottles

homard lobster

homardine white wine sauce finished with lobster butter and garnished with diced iobster

hors d'oeuvre an or starter, may be hot or cold

house wine red, while or rose wine recotnmendea by the establishment as being accepiabie to **the** average paiate and sold at a modest price. May be served by the glass, half bottle or bottle and sometimes by the carafe

I

infuse to soak ingredients, e.g. herbs, tea leaves, in liquid to impart flavour

insalata indicates salad, either served as a dish in its own right or used as a garnish to decorate a particular dish (Italian)

Irish coffee liquer coffee made using Irish whiskey, sugar and floating double cream over the surface

J

jaggery unrefined sugar latticed pastry strips

jambonette ham and pork sausage-like dish jambonneau small leg - applied to poultry

jardiniere matchstick-shape cut of spring vegetables, used as a garnish or as a vegetable dish

Jasmine tea Chinese green tea scented with jasmine flowers

Jeroboam large bottle holding the equivalent of four standard size (75 cl) bottles

joue beef or pork cheek

jugged hare traditional hare dish made with red wine marinated hare cooked in a casserole with its own blood being added at intervals to flavour and thicken the cooking sauce. A little red wine, vegetables and seasoning are also added to this sauce

julienne foods, especially vegetables, cut into fine, even strips

jus Juice, e.g. fruit juice or juice extracted from roasted meats

jus lie thickened gravy

K

Kebab Turkish term equivalent to the French en brochette meaning grilling on skewers. Requires small, evenly cut pieces of meat, such as chicken livers, lamb or veal kidneys and liver and bacon or fish, with vegetables and seasonings. Marinaded prior to use

kedgeree savoury dish of cooked rice mixed with hard boiled egg, smoked fish (usually haddock) and may be flavoured with either turmeric or saffron

ketjap manis/thick and sweetened derivative of soy sauce and the main condiment in the Far East and China, used in place of salt

khao niao (glutinous rice from Thailand which, when boned, becomes sweet and sticky and is used mainly in confectionery and baking

khoresh meat stew with

khoresh meat stew with fruit and'nu

khoshaf macerated dried frun-salad. containing apricots, raisins and alm

kilojoule (kj) the metric measure of 'energy' contained in food

knead (fraiser) towork dough on a p board or marble slab with the ball of hand

kohlrabi Curnip/cabbage style vegetab is either purple or green in colour anc swollen, edible stem with a delicate flavour. Boiled *or* grated and used in :

konafa Turkish pastry which resemble shredde wheat

korma mild spicy, meat casserole that cooked in a rich coconut sauce and originates from northern India

Kosher meat killed, and food prepared served according to Jewish dietary law

kuiebyaka Russian salmon and rice pie

kulfi Indian ice cream made from reduce milk

kway teow Malaysian flat noodles

L

lady's fingers originating from Africa and indicates Okra or Gumbo. Used to thicke soups and stews and also eaten as a vegetable

lager bottom fermented beer laifen type of Chinese tubular noodles lait, au denotes 'with milk' as in cafe au lait

laksa nooele and seafood soup from Malaysia

langouste denotes a crawfish and is almost the size of a lobster but clawless. Preparec and cooked like lobster and classified as a crustacean

langoustine scampi, classified as a crustacean. See 'scampi'

lard (larder – piquer) to draw strips of larding bacon through the middle of a piece of meat by means of a larding tube (larder). To lard the surface by means of a larding needle (piquer)

lardoan strip of bacon or pork fat that may be used to enhance the flavour of raw meat during its cooking process and also used as a garnish in both salads and with vegetables

lasagne large flat pieces of ribbon pasta made with whole wheat dough or with the addition of pureed spinach (lasagne verdi)

legume Vegetable with seeds in a pod, such as peas, board beans, mange tout and lentils

lentil type of bean, rich in protein and the basic ingredient of dhal which is a side dish to curry. Also produces a thick soup

levin starterdough made from live yeast and flour

linguini pasta cut into long and very thin, flat strands

liqueur Sweetened and flavoured spirit, sometimes termed a digestif

loin joint of meat, either lamb, pork *or* veal, that maybe boned, seasoned, rolled and tied and stuffed if required. Ail regarded as first class roasting joints

lumpfish roe eggs of the lumpfish and often referred to (incorrectly) as caviar, available in both orange and black. Usually from Iceland

lyonnaise saucejsauce of chopped onions sauteed in butter wfth wine vinegar and demi glace

lyonnaise, a la denotes a garnish or sauce of onions, e.g. pomrties lyonnaise or foie de veau saute, sauce lyonnaise

M

macaroon chewy almond flavoured biscuits made with caster sugar, egg whites and ground almonds and sometimes coconut

machiato strong espresso coffee served with a dash of cold milk

mace outer covering of nutmeg

macedoine small, evenly cut dice of vegetables or fruit, e.g. macedoine de legumes

macerate to pickle briefly, to steep, to soak or to souse. A term that is generally applied to fruit, usually diced, and then sprinkled with caster sugar and liqueurs in order to improve the flavour and soften the fruit

magret-boneless breast of the mallard duck

maitre d'hotel butterierb butter containing parsley and lemon juice and served with grilled meats.

malt cereal grain, the best is barley, soaked in water to germinate and then dried by hot air. The duration and intensity of this drying process (kilning) produces different coloured malts, from pale malt to black malt. The degree of kilning determines the type of beer to be produced, *e.g.* pale malt makes pale ale

mancha powdered green tea

mandolin manual vegetable slicer

mange tout thin, fiat, green pea that is eaten whole after topping, tailing and cooking

mantecato the action of beating butter and Parmesan into risotto (Italian)

marbling fat deposited within muscle tissue

marinade Reasoned liquid used for flavouring and tenderising raw fish, meat, poultry and game

marinate to soak fish, meat, poultry and game for a short while to improve flavour and make more tender, in a marinade

marjoram perennial, seasoning herb with a very delicate flavour and very similar to oregano. Appears in many French and Italian dishes, especially tomato-based sauces

marmite, petite beef and chicken flavoured clear soup (consomme) and also the name given to the container in which the soup is served

marron chestnuts that may be eaten raw, roasted, boiled *or* preserved in sugar and then glazed in syrup, e.g. Marron glace

Marsala fortified (or liqueur) wine from Sicily, classified as a dessert wine and used mainly in cooking

Martini brand of Vermouth, which is an

aromatised wine that has been fortified. May be red, white or rose and dry or sweet (Bianco) given (o the container in which the soup is served

matron chestnuts that may be eaten raw, roasted, boiled or preserved in sugar and then glazed in syrup, e.g. Marron glace

Marsala fortified (or liqueur) wine from Sicily, classified as a dessert wine and used mainly in cooking

Martini brand of Vermouth, which is an aromatised wine that has been fortified. May be red, white or rose and dry or sweet (Bianco)

masalas aromatic spice blend originating from India and known as masalas, it may be mild or strong. Ingredients of the blend may include pepper, ginger, turmeric, coriander, cumin, clove and chillies, e.g. garam masala

matelote-French freshwater fish stew made with red or white wine

meat glaze (glace de viande) boiled down bone broth of marrow bones etc., and reduced to the thickness of jelly. Used for glazing cooked meats and improving their appearance and flavour

medaillon small round cut of meat that may also be termed a 'rosette' and is cut from the boned out, rolled and tied loin of lamb. Often sauteed

melba toast very thin, curled toast, made either by splitting toasted bread, after removing the crusts and toasting the untoasted sides or from toasting very thin sliced bread

methode Champenoise process by which French Champagne is made

meuniere menu term that denotes shallow fried e.g. filet de plie meuniere

mignonette coarsely crushed peppercorns

miolle-feuille gateau ouff pastry cake filled with jam and whipped cream and decorated on the surface with fondant

millet ggrain native to Africa and Asia

mineral water (water containing various minerals and said to promote health. May be still or sparkling, e.g. Perrier, Evian, Buxton, Vichy

minestronet-soup containing a wide variety of assorted vegetables, vermicelli and herbs in a meat *or* vegetable broth (Italian)

minute steak they, tender steak, often cut from the sirloin and sometimes termed an entrecote minute. May be fried or grilled, but very quickly (for a minute) to seal the outsides without overcooking the interior

Mirepoix: garnish of diced, browned onions, carrots, celery and bacon, with various herbs and used to flavour stocks, soups, sauces and stews

mirin sweet Japanese rice wine, used in sukiyaki and Japanese sauces

mise-en-place (French term meaning 'to put in place'. Refers to preparation beforehand, this includes all the tasks that have to be completed to get a food service area or kitchen ready for service

miso halted and fermented soy bean paste available in red or yellow, enhances the taste of many dishes.

mitsuba (Japanese green leaf used as a herb mizuna^saJad leaf with a peppery flavour

mocha Arabica type of coffee bean. Produces a very strongly flavoured coffee. Originally from the old port of Mocha in Yemen

moelle beef; marrow

monte (to-enrich by incorporating butter, egg yolks, cream

morilles edible fungus with a delicate flavour and sometimes termed the sponge mushroom, picked fresh during spring and early summer

mornay Cheese sauce, normally made with milk and^vith dried mustard added to improve flavouring, *e.g.* Choufleur mornay

mortadella large Italian sausage that has been lightly smoked. The ingredients may Consist of pork, garlic and seasonings

Moselle lively and crisp-tasting white wine produced in the vineyards lying along the banks of the river Mosel in Germany

moule French menu term denoting a mussel that may be steamed open and served in the half shell. Classified as a mollusc. Best known for its use in the classic dish moules mariniere

moussaka dish of Greek origin, made of minced lamb or mutton, aubergine, tomato, onion, garlic and seasonings with a topping of cheese sauce and baked

mousse light and fluffy mixture, which is usually sweet to the palate, and served cold, *e.g.* mousse aux frais (strawberry mousse)

mousseline ligfit fish or meat puree strained extra fine and mixed with cream. Sauce mousseline is a derivative of sauce Hollandaise, having whipped cream added to the basic sauce, and is served with poached fish or vegetables

muddle cocktail-making term that indicates a number of ingredients being crushed together in the bottom of the bar mixing glass using the flat end (muddler) of the bar mixing spoon, *e.g.* mint and caster sugar

mulled winered wine siowly heated, with sugar, citrus frtiits and spices added to the liquor. Served hot

murgh, Indian term for chicken

muselet wire muzzle used to damp the cork of a bottle Bf sparkling wine securely in place

mushimono dapanese cuisine term for steaming a food item

N

naan fflatjbut puffy and light leavened bread that may accompany curry

nage, a la pooked in a court bouillon

nam pla Thai chilli sauce

nantua crayfish sauce

nappe to mask or coat evenly with a sauce or jelly, *e.g.* aspic used in cold buffet work

naturei, au in its natural state, e.g. plain boiled without additional flavouring, ingredients or garnish

navarin brown lamb or mutton stew with vegetables and potatoes

neat *isrifJ* relating to liquor and meaning undiluted, e.g. neat rum

nicoise French salad dish that traditionally includes green beans, tomatoes, potato, tuna, anchovies, olives and garlic

nimono Japanese cuisine term indicating a simmering technique

nip gmall measure, legally recognised, and usually of spirits, e.g. nip of whisky (25 ml or 50 ml)

noisette smail cut of meat from the rib, usuaiiy lamb

nori thin, black seaweed sheets used in wrapping sushi, a Japanese sweetened vinegar rice

nose combination of the aroma and the bouquet of a wine when wine tasting

nouvelle cuisine form of French cooking that promotes lighter alternatives to replace the very rich dishes of the traditional classic French cuisine

O

oeuf en cocotte egg baked in its own dish (cocotte) in a bain marie in the oven

oeuf molletf soft boiled and shelled egg, the boiling timebeihg five minutes

offal the organs of animals, e.g. heart, liver, brains} kidneys, tongue, tail, tripe and sweetbreads

on-the-rocks poured over a quantity of cubed ice, e.g. scotch on-the-rocks

oregano perennial seasoning herb similar to marjoram that Wends well with oil and vinegar salad dressings, French, Italian and Greek dishes and tomato-based sauces

osso buco knuckle of veal casserole stewed in a dry white wine, tomato and vegetable sauce flavoured with garlic, chopped parsley, basil and thyme and traditionally served with rice

ouzo aniseed-flavoured spirit of Greek origin and similar to Pernod, coming under the heading of pastis (aniseed or liquorice flavoured spirits)

oyster shellfish usually eaten raw, the best coming from Colchester and Whitstable, and may be served either hot or cold. Classified as mollusc

oyster cruet group of accompaniments offered with oysters and comprises of cayenne pepper, peppermill, Tabasco sauce and chilli vinegar

oyster sauce brown sauce used in Chinese cuisine for flavouring various dishes

P

paella rice dish flavoured and coloured with saffron, containing chicken, shellfish, various vegetables including peas, pimento, garlic sausage, chopped garlic and seasonings. Cooked in chicken stock

pak choi'Chipese white cabbage - classified as a brassica, this plant does not form a 'heart' and appears-very similar to leaf spinach. Eaten raw in salads, but may also be stir-fried with rice and is used mainly in Chinese cuisine

pakora Indian term indicating **a** deep fried vegetable fritter

panada dough used to bind forcemeat that is made from flour, milk or water, eggs and butter

pancetta streaky bacon (Italian)

panee food item dipped in seasoned flour, egg and breadcrumbs, then either shallow or deep fried

paneer fresh milk curds used in Indian cookery

panna cotta cooked, rich, cream Italian dessert, similar to bavarois, the consistency of which is similar to a sauce sabayon

papillote paper wrapping to contain aroma and flavour when cooking meat or fish

pappardelle-long, flat egg noodles with a crimped edge

paprika powdered red spice produced from dried and ground sweet peppers, giving an appealing flavour to food as well as a deep red colour, e.g. Hungarian goulash

parboil to partially cook in boiling liquid

parfait enriched ice cream made from a caster sugar, egg yolk and double cream base

Parma ham delicate tasting, cured Italian ham, served with salads or as a starter dish, *e.g.* melon and Parma ham

Parmesan very hard dry cheese *of* Italian origin, eaten as a cheese and used in Italian cooking and as an accompaniment

passato pureed and sieved or strained

pasta pastes made from Durum wheat semolina hour, in a variety of shapes and dried, *e.g.* macaroni, spaghetti, vermicelli, noodles, lasagne and ravioli

pastilla (traditional Moroccan dish of pigeon pie in egg; lemon and onion sauce sweetened with almonds in pastry layers covered with cinnamon and sugar

pastis anseed or liquorice-flavoured alcoholic beverage such as ouzo and Pernod

pate de foie gras made by blending together a fine paste of fattened goose livers and decorating/garnishing with truffles. See foie gras

pate-maison pate particular to the establishment (house) and made according to the chef's recipe

paupiettes thin slices of meat or fish filled with forcemeat (sausage meat stuffing) then rolled up, tied and braised in the oven. Usually of beef, veal or sole, e.g. paupiettes de boeuf braises

pave a special cut of rump steak that is gleaner and less sinewy than a traditional rump cut

Pavlova meringue cake filled with whipped cream and topped with fruit and may be served with a fruit coulis, e.g. raspberry

paysanne/vegetables cut into small, very thin slices the size of a 1 p piece and used as a garnish e.g. Consomme paysanne

Peach Melba sweet dish of peaches, vanilla ice cream and a raspberry sauce (coulis). Decorated with whipped cream

pecorino ewes milk cheese peperonata 5epper and vegetable stew (Italian)

pepperoni dry Italian sausage that is made up of coarsely chopped pork and beef and strongly seasoned with ground red pepper and other spices. Commonly used on pizzas

persillade chopped parsley spiked with crushed garlic

petits fours wide variety of tiny, fancy, oven-cooked cakes or biscuits, but now used to also mean fruits dipped in chocolate or sugar syrups or other sweetmeats made up of such things as marzipan, ice cream, stuffed dates and fruits, shortbreads etc. Offered with coffee and sometimes termed friandises

piatto plate or dish (Italian)

piccata Italian term denoting an escalope

pieds de mouton sheeps' trotters

pilaff/dish of spiced rice braised in the oven and garnished with prawns, chicken livers, ham, mushroom or chicken. Literally translated pilaff means braised savoury rice

pilau Ineian version of pilaff and usually includes cnicken. mutton or goats meat or a mixture of these and is well seasoned

pimento large, sweet red pepper

pimenton. Spanish spice similar to paprika and made from the Spanish pepper which, in its fresh form, is more well known as the red stuffing inside green Spanish cocktail olives

pipe to force a soft mixture or dough through a forcing bag containing a plain or fancy nozzle. In liquor terms it also relates to a cask holding 523 litres (115 gallons) of port

piquant denotes spicy, sharp, appetising, a sharp flavour, a bite to the sauce or dish, *e.g.* sauce piquante {a combination of shallots, capers, gherkins, wine vinegar and fines heroes added to demi-glace)

piquer food studded with fat, garlic, truffle, cloves, etc

pirozhk small savoury pastries

pitta bread of Greek origin, sometimes called 'pocket bread as it can be split open and filled. It is a double-layered bread that is flat and round or oval in shape

plancha a la grilled on a griddle

poach (pocher) to simmer dishes in a mould in a bain marie until done or to cook food in water that is kept just on boiling point (simmering), without actually letting it boil, e.g. Oeuf poche

poeler to casserole in butter, in a covered dish, with the absolute minimum of liquid added together with diced root vegetables and is sometimes known as a pot roast. Used only for the better cuts of meat and poultry

point, a denotes medium degree of cooking of a grilled steak

polenta (maize flour which is ground from Indian corn and can be eaten either as a type of porridge or used to garnish fish and meat dishes

pomme de terre potato

pastry filled With frangipane cream and macaroons. **Pommes** pont neuf are large, thick, deep fried, chipped potatoes

poppadum very fine, **thin** and crisp wafer-like pancake, made from lentil flour, deep fried or grilled and served with curry

pot roast joint of meat baked in the oven with stock and vegetables, in a covered pan or **casserole dish. See peeler**

pot still traditional still used to distil cognacs, armagnacs, dark rums, tequila, calvados and malt whisky. Here the spirit is distilled in batches

pot-au-feu french dish of meat and vegetables cooked in stock - the broth is eaten first followed by the meat and vegetables as a main course

poulet French menu term for chicken, e.g. pouiet roti a 'Anglaise

poussir baby or young (spring) chicken weighing from 450 - 900 g (i - 2 Ib), that may be roasted, grilled, sauteed or baked. It is usual to serve one to a portion

praline almonds, sometimes with hazelnuts added, caramelised in sugar, then crushed and added to a variety of sweet dishes

preserves assorted jams that may be offered at either breakfast or afternoon tea, e.g. strawberry, raspberry, cherry, plum, marmalades

profiterole (bold sweet dish of small choux pastry buns filled with whipped cream and coated with chocolate, either fondant or couverture

prosciutto Parma ham originating from Italy. A raw, delicate tasting, cured ham that is sliced very thinly. See also Parma ham

Prosecco term now used to indicate Italian sparkling wines

Provencal sauce of tomatoes, onions and garlic sauteed in olive oii

Provencale, a la provincial or regional way or style and generally accepted as meaning cooked with garlic, onions and tomatoes pumpernickel dark brown or black rye bread that may be used as a base for canapes

ounch alcoholic beverage made from a wine base with spirits, liqueurs, fruit juices, lemonade, tisanes and fruit syrups added to enhance the taste. Can also be flavoured with spices, such as cloves, cinnamon and nutmeg and citrus fruits. Sometimes served hot

punt hollow found in the base of some wine bottles which strengthens the bottle, especially if a secondary fermentation takes place in the bottle itself, e.g. Champagne

puree to finely mash or pass food through a sieve or a thickened variety of soup, namely a puree

Q

quail small game bird that may be roasted, grilled or sauteed. Often serve two birds per portion

quenelle Oval shaped. Also indicates light ovai-shaped dumplings, made from various types of fine forcemeat, such as veal, chicken, game and fish, that are poached.

quiche flan case filled with a savoury egg custard plus other added ingredients, such as vegetables, mushrooms and bacon

quince/hard, yellow and acid tasting Asiatic fruit, with a delicate scent, which when cooked turns pink and is mainly used in preserves

R

rable French menu term indicating the saddle, and usually of hare

rack (of lamb) term indicating a joint made up of the lamb cutlets - a best end (the ribs) - usually roasted, *e.g.* carre d'agneau roti

ragout thick and rich brown stew/casserole meat, usually beef or lamb and cooked with root vegetables, e.g. ragout de boeuf

ragu basic meat sauce for pasta raita yoghurt-based side dish of Indian origin

remekin small earthenware, individual, circular baking dish holding one portion

rang french term indicating the team or brigade of food service staff and their level **of** authority within that team, e.g. commis de rang

rapini member of the broccoli family with a bitter, assertive flavour

rare degree of cooking of a grilled steak meaning underdone

Ras-el-hanout Moroccan spice mix used to flavour rice, couscous, and 'tajines', the slowly cooked stews common to Morocco

ratatouille Provencal vegetable stew of diced aubergine, tomato, courgettes, red and green peppers, onions and garlic, cooked in olive oil

ravioli small meat or vegetable filled pasta squares (Italian)

rechaud Spirit lamp used for cooking at the table and *to* keep food warm

rechauffe reheated dish made with previously cooked ingredients

reduce to add wine or other liquid to the pan residue and simmer down to a desired consistency to concentrate flavours

remoulade cold mayonnaise-based sauce containing capers, gherkins, anchovy essence, parsley and fines herb for flavouring

rrillettes shredded belly of pork cooked in its own fat, mixed until smooth and potted. Sometimes has goose or rabbit added. French in origin

ripieno Italian stuffing

ris de veau calves sweetbreads that are pale in appearance and delicate in taste, coming from the thymus glands found in the neck and heart of young animals and are braised, fried or sauteed.

risotto savoury rice containing vegetables, such as finely chopped onions, and a bouquet garni for flavouring, cooked in chicken stock

roast (rotir) roast meat, poultry or game and vegetables, *e.g.* potato, parsnips

roe fish eggs, the soft herring roe having a creamy, smooth texture and is served as a savoury dish or garnish. Smoked cod's roe is used for taramasalata which is of Greek origin

romesco Catalonian sauce of tomato, almond, sherry, garlic and paprika

rosti (grated and fried potatoes

rotic of Indian origin and denoting bread. Usually a circular, flat unleavened bread similar to chapati

roti French menu term indicating a roasted item, e.g. cote de pore roti

roulade stuffed roll of food that may be sweet or savoury, e.g. thin slice of meat stuffed and rolled - paupiette de boeuf, or a thin, flat sponge spread with jam and whipped cream and rolled swiss roll style

roux rnix of flour and butter cooked together slowly uhtil white, blonde or brown in colour and used to thicken soups and sauces

royale, a la Franch menu term denoting a garnish for a soup, e.g. consomme royale (diced savoury egg custard)

rye, cereal used in the making of bread and also used in its fermented form in the making of American whiskey

S

sabayoni French term meaning a dessert sauce and used to thicken, enrich and improve the appearance; of various dishes. Together with Marsala and caster sugar produces the Italian sweet Zabaglione

sable French shortbread

sachertorte rich chocolate cake, coated in ganache with apricot jam

saffron spice used for flavouring, produced from the stigmas of the crocus. Colours food bright yellow and is a key ingredient in paella, bouillabaisse and the liqueur Chartreuse

sake originating from Japan, this is a slightly "* sweet, colourless rice beer, usually served warm but may also be served chilled

salamander grill with top heat and used for browninc and cooking

salami strongly seasoned sausage of Italian origin and served cold. Made from beef, pork and pork fat and seasoned with garlic and pepper, often used for antipasto and in hors d'oeuvre

salmis game birds and ducks, skinned and boned after roasting, placed in a rich, brown, red wine flavoured sauce and served as a game stew

salpicon mixture of foods cut into a small dice, bound with a sauce and used as a filling, *e.g.* Salpicon de volaille (Salpicon of chicken)

salsa (Mexican in origin but nowadays means an uncooked tomato-based relish flavoured in varying degrees by onion, cilantro and chillies

salsify white root vegetable with oyster-like flavour

sambal sharp, spicy and vinegary sauce or chutney of raw vegetables or fruit, used as a relish or in cookery. Comparable to chutneys in Indian cuisine

samosa small, pastry coated food item with a spicy meat or vegetable filling and deep . fried

sansho prickly ash powder sprinkled on grilled meat

sashimi Japanese origin, this term indicates sliced fish eaten raw

satay cubes of fish *ox* meat on a skewer and grilled over a charcoal grill, served with a thick peanut flavoured sauce

sauce gribice cold sauce, mayonnaise based and mixea with capers, gherkins, hard boiled egg whites and seasonings

sauerkraut (choucroute) pickled, finely shredded white cabbage served hot with bacon and sausages. National dish of Germany and Alsace in France

sautefshallow fry in butter, with a little oil added, to a golden brown colour

sauter quick cooking process, to brown quickly in a saute or frying pan, or toss in fat anything that requires quick cooking at considerable heat

sauteuse shallow pan with sloping sides ane a lid, in which food may first be fried and then braised

savarin circular yeast sponge cake, often soaked in a rum-flavoured syrup and filled with fresh fruit salad, e.g. savarin au fruits

scampi ecognised in Britain as the Dublin bay prawn,' in America as the saltwater crayfish and occasionally known as langoustine

schnitzel thin slice of veal or chicken. A breaded veal cutlet, e.g. wiener schnitzel

scorel parallel cuts made on the surface of food items

sec degree of sweetness of Champagnes and sparkling wines or the amount of suga they contain; here it means medium sweet

sekt quality German sparkling wine produced by the Charmat method (secondary fermentation in a sealed tank)

sepi a cuttlefish, prepared like calamari (squid), either sauteed whole in oil *or* stuff< and poached while the legs are blanched and stewed

service cloth cloth approximately the size < a table napkin?used by food service staff a protection against heat and to assist in handling equipment and in the service of food

shaoxing an amber-coloured rice wine

Sherry Fortified (or liqueur) wine, having a grape spirit (brandy) added to improve the alcoholic content, and is made from white grapes

shiitake dark brown Japanese mushroom that has a distinctive earthy flavour and is used for garnishing and flavouring

shish kebab term of Turkish origin indicating small pieces of meat, usually fillet of lamb, interspersed with button mushrooms and grilled on a skewer. May be accompanied by a Madeira sauce

shooter-layyered cocktail consisting of alcoholic liquors of varying densities, the heaviest lying at the base of the glass and the lightest on the top. Also known as the rainbow cocktail or pousse cafe and served in an Elgin shape liqueur glass

short (of pastry) having a high fat content

shred (emincer) ta-cut meat or vegetables into thin slices or strips

sichuan peppercorns fragrant Chinese seasoning from a plant unrelated to pepper

skim (to remove impurities and fat from the top of soups and broths by using a skimming ladle

skorthalia garlic sauce of Greek origin

smorgasbord teerm of Scandinavian origin which indicated a self-service buffet. In Scandinavia this may take the form of quite a substantial meal of several courses, offering a varied number of dishes such as salads, cheeses, pates, cold meats and almost always includes dishes of herrings

smorrebrod open or Scandinavian sandwich. Various breads, wholemeal, rye, pumpernickel, bread rolls and white and brown sandwich bread, are used for these sandwiches, onto which selected food items (meats, soused fish, meat and fish pastes, salami and salad) are placed

sobanoodles, Japanese in origin, made of white wheat or golden buckwheat and accompanied by nori (Seaweed) and horseradish

soffritto a sauce/stew base of fried diced vegetables and sometimes pancetta (streaky bacon)

sorbet soft fruit-flavoured water ice, sometimes flavoured with liqueur or wine and served as a sweet dish or between courses to cleanse the palate

soubiset smooth onion pulp served with a variety of meat entrees

souffle sweet or savoury baked pudding made with whipped egg whites

soy bean round bean, rich in protein and used to make tofu (unfermented bean paste), it can be cooked fresh or dried in stews

soy sauce key ingredient of east Asian cuisine, and in particular Chinese and Japanese cuisine, enhancing many dishes, *e.g.* soups, stews and sauces. Made from the soy beans, the Japanese equivalent is shoyu

spaetzele (spaetzeli) Swiss and Austrian paste speciality made by pressing an egg noodle dough through a colander and simmering it in salt water

spare ribs rip bones of beef or pork, marinated and then baked or grilled

spatchcock young game bird or chicken that is split open down the backbone and flattened and then fried or grilled (English style). The French style is termed crapaudine (the shape being toadlike), e.g. Poulet en Spatchcock or Poulet en Crapaudine/**

spirits, overall term for all distilled alcoholic liquors, the most common of which are whisky, brandy, gin, vodka and rum

spring roll pancakeftype roll of Chinese origin, filled with minced meat and vegetables and deep fried

spumantectfalian wine label term denoting sparkling

station/refers to the sideboard (or workstation) from which the food service team work together with the group of tables they are responsible for serving

still equipment used to produce spirits, either the pot still or the continuous still, e.g. brandy distilled from wine in copper pot stills

stillroom area in the back of house that provides those items, both food and beverages, not provided by the key sections of the kitchen or bars

stillse tiraditional commercial installation consisting of a water boiler and bulk storage containers for coffee and hot milk. The latter is steam heated and a steam injector will also be attached

stir fry the East Asian process of preparing food by cooking over a very fast and high heat

stockfish idried salt cod, braised, stewed, fried

and eaten raw in salads. Also pounded to make a savoury paste or butter used in pates

stout strong dark beer with a smooth, malty flavour and creamy consistency and brewed from a very dark roasted malt

strudel fruit dessert made of either a puff pastry or filo pastry case filled with various mixtures of fruit and served hot or cold

sugar syrup, sweet liquor of sugar and water boiled together and when used as an ingredient for cocktails it is termed Gomme syrup

sumac middle eastern spice, the berries being deep, brick red when dried. Used whole or ground and may be sprinkled on fish, added to salads and used to season kebabs

supreme denotes cuts from the wing or breast of poultry and feathered game. Also indicates a cut of fish on the slant and free from bone

sushi dapanese sweetened vinegar rice and toasted nori sheets (a tissue-thin Japanese seaweed used as a wrapping) are key ingredients in sushi. Other fillings may be spinach, mushrooms or pickled ginger

sweetmeat sugar-coated confection, e.g. small fancy cake, and may also take the form of crystallised fruits. Also see petits fours

syllabub rich dessert dish of sweetened cream and lemon juice, flavoured with sweet white wine and brandy, served well chilled in a glass

T

Tabasco pungent Indian pepper sauce, two key ingredients of which are vinegar and red peppers. Used largely in Creole cooking. Also a very hot sauce

tabbouleh salad of bulgur wheat mixed with tomatoes, onion, lemon juice, mint and parsley

tagliolini thin noodles. Italian in origin

tahina crushed sesame seed paste, widely used as a flavouring in Middle Eastern and Latin American cuisine

tamarind fruit pods of an African tree that may also be found in India. Pods contain a very sour juice used in some Indian curries. Fruit of the tamarind tree is dried and ground and used in flavouring curries

tandoop open topped clay oven originating in Northern India

tandoori food that has been cooked in a charcoal fired tandoor, e.g. tandoori chicken

tannin obtained from the pips and stalks of grapes during the wine making process and acts as a preservative, especially in red wines. Is also the brown colouring of tea

tapenade paste of capers, black olives, anchovies, garlic and often tuna

taramasalata week in origin, a dish made from dried, salted and pressed roe of mullet *or cod*, seasoned with garlic, lemon juice olive oil to form a pink, creamy paste

tarka Indian method of tempering spices in hot oil

tarragon flavouring herb with long, narrow, green leaves and found in fines heroes, sauce bearnaise, poached fish and chicken dishes. Used either fresh or dried

tartare cold mayonnaise-based sauce with

finely chopped capers, gherkins and fines

herbes added. Served with deep fried fish

tartare, steak minced raw fillet of beef mixed with parsley, capers, gherkins, finely chopped onion, raw egg yolk and seasonings and served cold

tarte tatin French apple tart baked upside-down

tartufo Italian term for truffle, an edible fungus, see truffle

T-bone steak (porterhouse) steak on a T-shaped bone that is cut from the fillet end of a sirloin of beef. Includes both the fillet and the sirloin of beef

tempura seafood and vegetables dipped in batter and deep-fried

tequila Mexican spirit distiiled from the fermented juice (pulque) of the agave plant

teriyaki fish or meat marinated in teriyaki which is a mixture of mirin (sweet Japanese rice wine), Japanese soy sauce and chicken stock

terrine mixture of meat, fish or vegetables and seasonings in a lined dish that is cooked, cooled and served cold in a terrine -an oblong, straight-sided cooking utensil with a close fitting lid

tian shallow gratip of chopped, layered vegetables.

tikka marinated pieces of fish, meat or poultry. Indian in origin, e.g. tikka masala (aromatic spice blend). Also see masalas

timbaled half conical tin mould. The dish is cooked and served in this single portion mould. Usually fish, meat, rice or vegetables in a sauce, or fruit with Chantilly

tisane all torms of herbal teas containing no caffeine or tannin and consumed either cold or hot, *e.g.* mint, rosehip and lemon

tofu a highly nutritious unfermented bean paste made from soy beans, Japanese in origin

tokay ungarian sweet white wine, available in three styles, the most well known of which is probably tokay aszu

torte (Gerrnan for a round, rich, layer cake or flan, decorated and divided into portions. Contains nuts, cream and fruit or jam

tortilla Mexican round, flat, unleavened pancake made from cornmeal, filled with beans or meat and a sauce. Served hot

tostada Spanish for toast

tournedos fillet steak cut in round, neatly trimmed portions from the heart of the fillet of beef

toxin poisonous substance, secreted by certain organisms

tranche length of puff pastry, with a puff pastry wall either side and often with a fruit filling. Served hot or cold, *e.g.* tranche aux pommes (apple)

trenette long flat pasta; another name for linguini

trifolato method for sauteing vegetables in oil, garlic and parsley

tripe lining from the first and second stomach of oxen. The classic dish is stewed tripe and onions

tronc collection of tips received by food service staff

troncon protion of flat fish cut across the body, on the bone, *e.g.* troncon de turbot

truffle edible fungus found underground near the roots of oak or beech trees. The Perigord black from France and the Piedmontese white from Italy are noted for their taste and scent. The black truffle is used as a decorative garnish in pate and aspic dishes; the white truffle is grated raw on salads, risotto, pasta and egg dishes. The word is also used to indicate a round chocolate

truss to bind or truss poultry or game birds for cooking, giving them a better shape

tuile crisp biscuit, traditionally flavoured with almond

tureen deep, covered dish from which soup is served when working from the gueridon. The tureen may be large enough for one portion only or for a number of portions

Turkish coffee Traditionally made in a long handled container called an ibrik. A dark, very strong but sweet coffee served in small cups

turmeric mild peppery spice, bright yellow in colour and used in many curry mixtures. Called hatdi in India and obtained from the root stems of a plant belonging to the ginger family. The stems are dried and then ground producing the powder called turmeric

tutti frutt (confection, especially ice cream, mixed with a variety of diced candied fruits and Italian in origin

U

udon very narrow, ribbon-like, Japanese white wheat noodles served in hot soups and mixed meat and vegetable dishes

Underberg proprietary brand of German herb-flavoured bitter with a brandy base

underliner an underplate. Plate or flat with a napkin, doily or dish paper on it placed underneath another dish or accompaniment

univalve mollusc with a shell consisting of one valve, e.g. snails, clams

V

vacherin (sweet (dish made up of meringue, fresh soft fruit such as raspberries or strawberries, whipped cream and a fruit coulis

veal meat of a calf, the French menu term being veau, e.g. escalope de veau. Also see escalopes

vegan strict vegetarian and one who consumes no animal products at all

vegetarian person who does not eat either fish or meat, but may eat eggs and dairy products

veloute (rich, smooth, white sauce made from white stock, a white (blond) roux and seasonings. The style of veloute relates to the variety of stock used: fish, veal, mutton or chicken, e.g. Veloute de volaille. Also used to indicate a soup made in the same way

verjuice sour grape or crab apple juice used in place of vinegar

vermicelli very thin pasta style noodles, Italian in origin and often used to garnish soups. Capellini is the finest ribbon pasta

vermouth fortified and flavoured wine. Three main types are bianco, rosso (Italian) and white dry (French)

vichyssoise thick potato and leek soup, garnished with chives and usually served cold

viennoiserie (yeast dough bakery products

vierge whipped butter or olive oil, seasoned with salt, pepper and lemon juice and served with vegetables

vindaloo overy hot, sour curry sauce from southern/India and spiced and flavoured with vinegar, e.g. chicken vindaloo

voiture term for a trolley used in the food service area, for the purpose of hors d'oeuvre, sweets, cheeses, liqueurs, carving and the like

Vol-au-vent round or oval, open baked, puff pastry cae being a large edition of a bouchee and filled with savoury items such as chicken, mushroom or asparagus, each bound with a thick, creamy sauce

yellow bean sauce made from fermented and pureed yellow soy beans that are highly nutritious

yum neau Yum is a form of cooking unique to Thailand, involving searing the sirloin steak in a steak and spice combination to produce a hot and sour flavour and then tossed with a salad of cucumber, tomato, onion, coriander and fresh chillies

yuzu Japanese citrus fruit

Z

zabaglione light and creamy sweet dish made by whipping together egg yolk, caster sugar and Marsala (a dark, sweet, fortified wine from Sicily). Accompanied by sponge finger biscuits

zahtar Lebanese seasoning of thyme, salt and sometimes sumac

zest outer skin of citrus peel, without the oils it produces and the pith and obtained by rubbing on a fine grater. Used as a flavouring in a variety of desserts, confectionery and in salads

zucchinic American term, known in Britain as courgette. A baby or miniature marrow. May be sliced and eaten raw with dips, steamed, baked, used in soups and stews, or battered and deep fried

Bibliography

1. Developing Hospitality Properties an Facilities by Josef Ransley
2. Resort Development Handbook (Community Building) by Urban Land Institute
3. Ultimate Hotel Design by Aurora Cuito
4. Building Type Basics for Hospitality Facilities by McDonough
5. Designing the World's Best Resorts by Wimbery Allison Tong
6. Tourism and Recreation Handbook of Planning by Manuel Baud -Bovy
7. Hotel Design, Planning and Development by Walter A. Rutes
8. Hotel Management and Operation by Denney G. Rutheford
9. Resort Management and Operation by Robert Christie Mill
10. Exotic Retreats: Eco Resort Design by Julia Faiers
11. Building Type Basics for Recreational Facilities by Richard J. Diedrich
12. New Hotel Design by Otto Riewoldt
13. Luxury Hotels: Beach Resorts (Luxury) by Martin Nicholas Kunz
14. Design Hotels Yearbook 2007 by Design Hotels
15. Check In; Check Out: Managing Hotel Operations by Jevona J. Vallen
16. Luxury Hotels: Spa & Wellness Resorts by Martin Nicholas Kunz
17. Congress, Conventions and Exhibition Facilities by Fred Lawson
18. Developing Retail Entertainment Destinations by Michael D. Bevard
19. Hotel Revolution: 21st Century Hotel Design by Howard Watson
20. Hotel Investments: Issues and Perspectives by Lori E. Releigh
21. Spa and Wellness Hotels (Design Pockets) by Cristina Moutes
22. Spa and Club Design by Encarna Castillo
23. Managing Hotel Effectively: Lessons from Outstanding General Managers by Eddvstone C. Nebel
24. The Design Hotel Yearbook 2005 by Design Hotels
25. Luxury Hotels: Golf Resorts (Luxury Hotels) by Angelika Lerche
26. Mixed-use Development Handbook by Dean Schwanke
27. Building Type Basics for Retail and Mixed - Use Facilities (Building Type Basics) by The Jevde Partnership
28. 21st Century Hotels by Graham Vickers

29. Financial Decisions for Hospitality Decision Makers (Hospitality, Leisure and Tourism) by Chris Guilding
30. Best design Wellness Hotels: north and South America, Caribbean, Mexico/Novd-Und sdumerika, Karibik, Mexico by Martin Nicholas Kunz
31. Hotel Operations Management by David K. Hayes
32. Shopping Environment: Evolution, Planning and Design by Peter Coleman
33. Restaurants Clubs and Bars by Fred Lawson
34. Accounts and Financial Analysis in the Hospitality Industry by Jonathan A. Hales
35. Heads in Beds: Hospitality and Tourism Marketing by Ivo Raza
36. Hotel Front Office Management by James A. Bardi
37. Hotel Assessment: Principles and Practices by Paul Beals
38. Hospitality and Restaurant Design Vol.3 by Roger Yee
39. Spas (Archi Design) by Katya Pellegrino
40. Cool Hotels (Tools) by Aurora Cuito
41. Saloons and Spas: The Architecture of Beauty by Julie Sinclair Eakin
42. Hotels and Resorts: Planning and Design by Fred Lawson
43. Successful Restaurant Design by Regina S. Barban and Joseph F. Derocher
44. New Restaurant Design by Bethan Ryder
45. Restaurant by Design by John Riodan
46. Asian Bar and Restaurant Design by Kim Iglis and Masano Kawana
47. Design and Equipment for Restaurants and Food Service - A Management view i. by Costas Katsigris Thomas
48. Ultimate Restaurant Design by Paco Asensio
49. Food Service Professional Guide to Restaurant Design: Design, Construction and Renovating Food
50. Service Establishment (The Food Service Professional Guide 1. by Sharon L. Fullen
51. Design and Layout of Food Sendee Facilities by John C. Birchfield and John, Jr. Birchfield
52. Bon Appetite - Restaurant Design by A.Bokern, S, Martin Pearson, S. Moreno, and E. Vanonna
53. Restaurant Planning Design and Constructing: A survival Manual for Owners, Operators and Developers by Jeff B. Hatz
54. Restaurant Design by Bethan Ryder
55. Cafe and Restaurant Design by Martin Nicholas Kunz
56. Design for Restaurants and Bars Inspirations for 100s International Hotels by Tina Skinner
57. Hotel, Restaurant, Bar, Club Design by Studio GAIA
58. 1000 Restaurant Bar Cafe and Graphics: From Signage to Logos and Every Thing in Between a by Luke Herriot
59. Restaurants, Cafes and Bars by Carles Broto
60. Restaurant Graphics by Grant Gibson
61. Hotel and Restaurant Design No. 2 by Roger Yee
62. New Perspectives: Cafes, Bars and Restaurants by Arian Mostaedi
63. Dinning by Design: Interior Design Handbook of Dinning and restaurant Facilities a. by Edie Lee Cohen and Sherman R. Emery

Index

C

G

H

S